THE DESCHU

THE OREGON TRUNK RAILWAY
THE DES CHUTES RAILROAD

– 1911 –

PRINEVILLE
City of Prineville Railway
Trout Creek Bridge
Trout Creek Tunnel
GATEWAY
PAXTON
MADRAS
MADRAS
Willow Creek Bridge
Warm Springs Tunnel
Mecca
MECCA
VANORA
PELTON
AGENCY
METOLIUS
CULVER
OPAL CITY
Crooked River
Crooked River Bridge
TERREBONNE
PRINEVILLE JCN
REDMOND
DESCHUTES
BEND
Deschutes River
Metolius River
Shitike Creek

THE DESCHUTES RIVER RAILROAD WAR

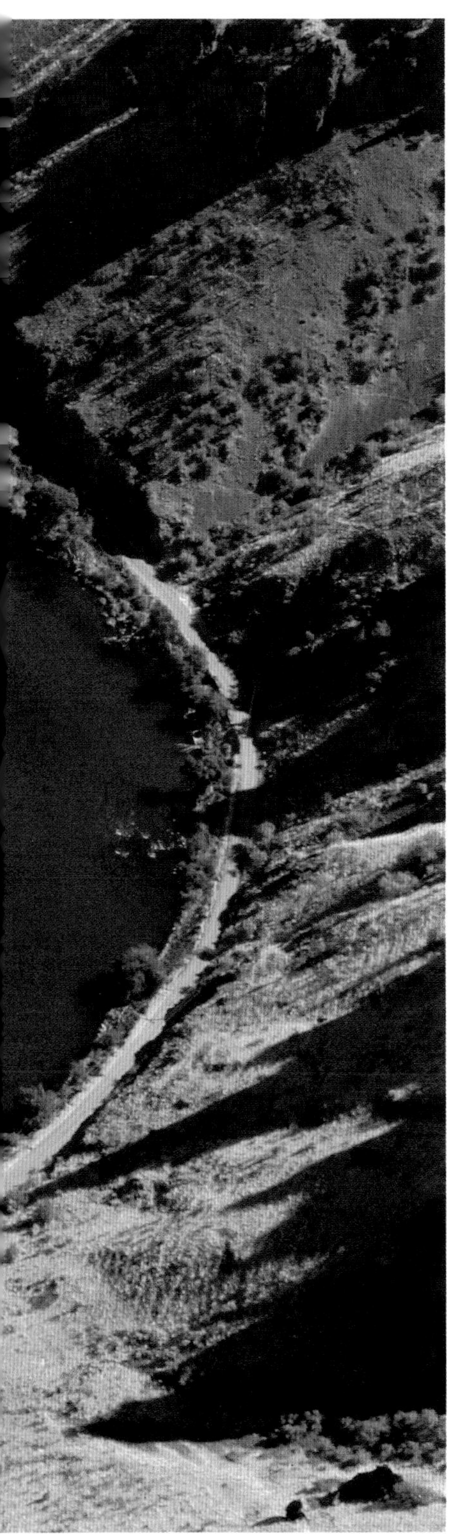
North Junction Bridge

THE DESCHUTES RIVER RAILROAD WAR

LEON SPEROFF, M.D.

Professor of Obstetrics and Gynecology
Oregon Health & Science University
Portland, Oregon

3739 SE Eighth Ave, Suite 1
Portland, OR 97202
arnicacreative.com

Library of Congress Cataloging-in-Publication Data

Speroff, Leon, 1935-
The Deschutes River railroad war / Leon Speroff.
p. cm.
Includes bibliographical references and index.
ISBN-13: 978-0-9745686-6-9 (hardcover : alk. paper)
1. Railroads--Oregon--Deschutes River Valley--History. 2. Railroads--Oregon--Deschutes River Valley--Design and construction--History. 3. Des Chutes Railroad--History. 4. Oregon Trunk Railway--History. I. Title.

HE2771.O7S64 2006
385.3'120979562--dc22

2006005224

Cover design by Aimee Genter
Text design by Becky Slemmons

3739 SE Eighth Ave, Suite 1
Portland, OR 97202

Phone: (503) 225-9900
Fax: (503) 225-9901

www.arnicacreative.com

DEDICATION

Leaving Portland on a cool, cloudy, rainy morning and crossing over Mount Hood to the other side of the mountain, we notice that the clouds disappear, the sunshine is warm, and the air is mountain-clear. This is the magic of eastern Oregon—sunshine despite rain in the western portion of the state. We encounter this magic in June when we make our annual fishing trip down the Deschutes River from Warm Springs to Maupin. When we were younger and could eat more, we stopped at Government Camp for breakfast at the Huckleberry Inn. I usually ordered a short stack of huckleberry pancakes, but we stopped going there when the waitress said, "Real men don't eat short stacks."

The Deschutes River has become special for us, as it must have for countless fishermen throughout the years. The first day on the river is like being with an old friend once again. We have our favorite fishing spots, preferred campsites, and at nightfall after fishing the evening hatch, we stargaze and, fighting to stay awake, tell old stories and lies. We have had our share of adventures, especially in Whitehorse Rapids, getting turned around in our McKenzie boats, having a raft blown by the wind into a *never-used* channel, losing or breaking an oar (we have done both), and our hearts racing when we see someone else's boat underwater or smashed and pinned against a rock by the current. The river teaches us that vigilance and caution must be our constant companions.

The railroad repeatedly makes an impact on your consciousness while traveling down the Deschutes River. Sleeping in a tent on the east bank of the Deschutes River on a summer night, the noise of the passing Burlington Northern train is so loud that you awaken, feeling that both ends of the tent should be opened to allow the entry and exit of the train.

I learned to fly fish on the Deschutes River, beginning on my first trip with the legendary guide, Oscar Lange. At dusk, when I returned to our camp at Whitehorse Rapids, having walked upstream on the railroad tracks, Lange said, "I forgot to tell you; at night, the rattlesnakes like to lay on those warm tracks."

Our river trips made us familiar with the story of the Deschutes Railroad War. We would spy a cave and wonder if it was a black powder storage site. We used the abandoned railroad roadbed as roads and trails. The current tracks are used by fishermen to hike from one fishing hole to the next. Engineers in passing trains like to wave to the fishermen standing in the water casting a line, and the fishermen enjoy this recognition.

Experiencing the Deschutes River provided me with the curiosity and motivation to research the Deschutes railroad story. For their friendship and camaraderie, with great affection, I dedicate this book to "the boys," my fly-fishing buddies on the Deschutes River:

Mark Delong

Mike Fredd

Lee Hickok

David Lee

Phil Patton

Peter Staples

Don Wolf

Table of Contents

Maps and Diagrams

PREFACE

Building along the east bank of the Deschutes River, there was the Des Chutes Railroad ("Des Chutes," spelled according to the original incorporation documents), part of E.H. Harriman's Union Pacific empire. On the west bank, there was the Oregon Trunk Railway, owned by the Great Northern and Northern Pacific railroads, headed by another magnate, James J. Hill. By this time, near the end of the first decade of the twentieth century, Hill and Harriman had already established a long history of competition between them: for railroad business, for financial backers, in the courts, and on the stock exchange. And here they were to compete once more, continuing their battle in the rugged canyon of the Deschutes River in central Oregon.

What in the world were these two railroads doing, each blasting their own path up the same river canyon? The goal was the small town of Bend (a population of 500 in 1910) in central Oregon. Interstate and transcontinental railroads depended on feeder lines for business, relatively short extensions that would bring settlers to the land and return freight to the markets. When the trees in the East and South of the United States had been largely consumed, attention turned to the vast forests of the West. Central Oregon provided access to billions of board feet of lumber. In addition, farmers and ranchers were raising grain and producing wool. The emerging system of irrigation promised a growth of agriculture that would require settlers and transportation. Building a railroad is *all* about business.

The competition along the Deschutes River was to be the last confrontation between the two railroad giants, Hill and Harriman, ending only with Harriman's death in 1909. Hill's lieutenant in the field was a rugged individual of the first order, John F. Stevens. Harriman's chief engineer was George W. Boschke, an equally tough man of national reputation. Both sides had accomplished and respected leaders, small armies of working men, enormous financial resources, and attitudes that had little tolerance for defeat. The stage was set for the Deschutes River Railroad War.

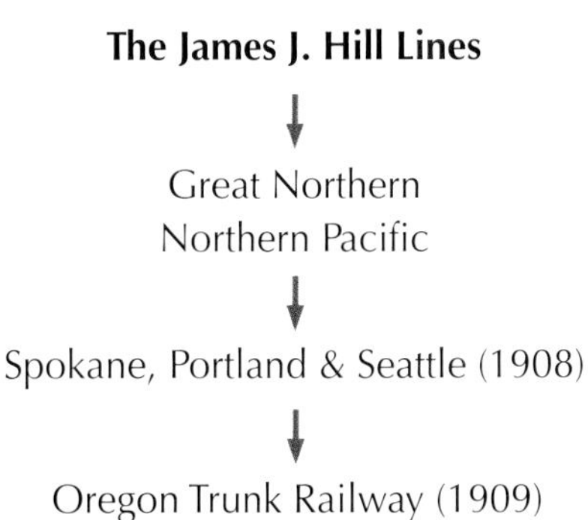

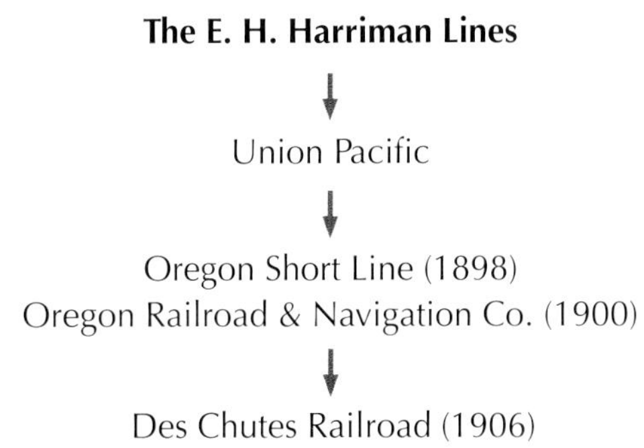

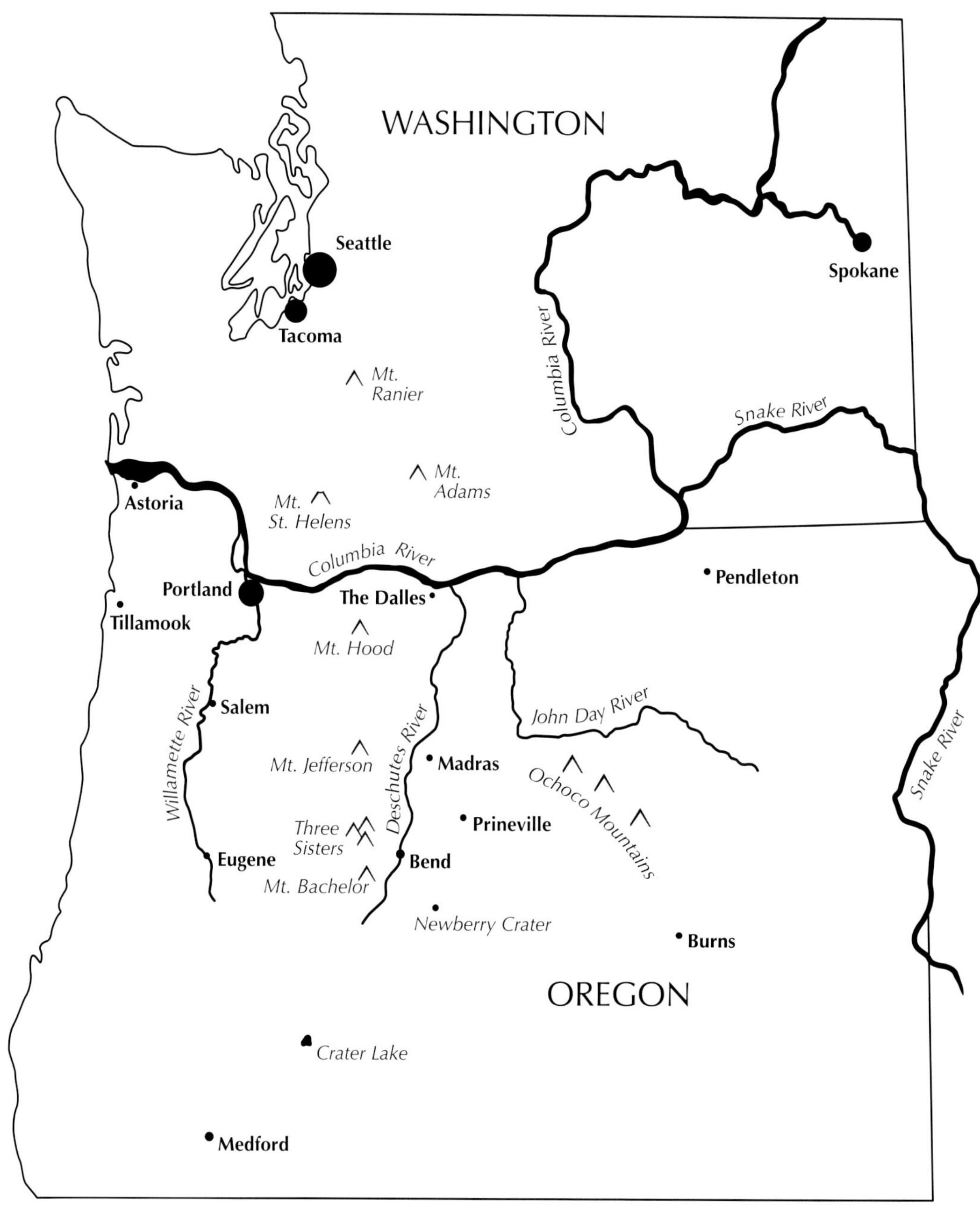
WASHINGTON
Seattle
Tacoma
Spokane
Mt. Ranier
Columbia River
Snake River
Mt. Adams
Mt. St. Helens
Astoria
Columbia River
Portland
The Dalles
Pendleton
Tillamook
Mt. Hood
Salem
Willamette River
Deschutes River
John Day River
Mt. Jefferson
Madras
Ochoco Mountains
Snake River
Three Sisters
Prineville
Eugene
Bend
Mt. Bachelor
Newberry Crater
Burns
OREGON
Crater Lake
Medford

Timeline

January/February **1905**	Oregon Trunk Surveys.
February 2, **1906**	Des Chutes Railroad incorporates in Oregon.
February 24, **1906**	Oregon Trunk Line incorporates in Nevada.
March 27, **1906**	Des Chutes files maps for first 20 miles.
April 16, **1906**	Oregon Trunk files maps for 100 miles, to Madras.
May 17, **1906**	Des Chutes files maps for second 20 miles, to Sherar's Bridge.
Summer **1906**	Oregon Trunk grades near mouth of river.
August 29, **1906**	Both companies' maps returned, requesting high line for dams.
April **1907**	Both surveys approved.
February **1908**	Spokane, Portland & Seattle completed.
June 18, **1908**	Central Oregon Railroad files maps from Madras to Bend.
July 21, **1908**	Oregon Trunk to Bend filed.
August 29, **1908** and October 9, **1908**	Des Chutes to Bend filed.
June **1909**	Both surveys approved.
July 27, **1909**	Construction begins; Horseshoe Bend confrontation.
August 15, **1909**	Stevens buys Oregon Trunk Line and Central Oregon Railroad.
August 16, **1909**	Hill's involvement announced.
August 24, **1909**	Judge Bean rules for Oregon Trunk.
November 3, **1909**	Oregon Trunk Railway incorporated in Washington.
May 17, **1910**	Des Chutes, Oregon Trunk agreement; tracks shared for 10.41 miles from North Junction to South Junction, and 42.7 miles from Metolius to Bend.
September 17, **1911**	First train over Crooked River Bridge.
October 5, **1911**	Oregon Trunk Golden Spike in Bend.
November 1, **1911**	First passenger train arrives in Bend.
January 5, **1912**	Oregon Trunk Columbia River Bridge at Celilo completed.
July 10, **1923**	Oregon Trunk abandons 30 miles of track, uses Des Chutes track between South Junction and Metolius.
March 28, **1935**	Des Chutes tracks abandoned, 72 miles from Ainsworth to North Junction; one line remains, owned by Oregon Trunk, shared with Union Pacific.

- CHAPTER ONE -

Every Rock Has a History

The Deschutes Canyon Is Millions of Years Old

The Deschutes River Railroad War was the result of a direct competition between the leading railroad barons, James J. Hill and Edward H. Harriman. But the nature of the competition and the sites of conflict were determined by the geological characteristics of the Deschutes River Canyon. The two work forces had to contend not only with each other but with the challenges and problems provided by the rocky canyon.

The Deschutes River flows through a harsh landscape. Understanding the peculiar characteristics of the Deschutes River and the difficulty in building a railroad in its canyon requires an appreciation for the geologic history of this part of the Earth.

The entire lifespan of the Earth is measured in geological time. Most people think about geology only when a meteorological or geological event occurs that threatens lives and lifestyle. We see and encounter rocks every day but we don't stop to consider the historical record trapped within. The geological beauty of a rock is that it has experienced far more than a human being ever can. Every rock is the result of a long history, and geologists are historians who decipher the events of the past by studying rocks. If we learn about ancient civilizations by studying shards of broken pottery, we surely learn the story of Earth by understanding the evidence in rocks and soil. It is a tribute to the mental abilities of human beings that the past can be so skillfully (although never completely) reconstructed from the present. But to understand and appreciate the geological history of the Earth, the human mind must adjust to unfamiliar dimensions. A "crust" becomes miles thick; creation and change take place at the rate of inches per year; events occur over thousands and millions of years. And the millions of years have their own calendar.

Radiometric dating of the asteroids and the oldest rocks on Earth indicate that our solar system formed about 4.5 billion years ago from the gas and dust of the explosion of an old star in the 11- to 13-billion-year-old Milky Way Galaxy. The Earth was molten in the beginning, changing from liquid to solid in the first 800 million years of its life. Earth as we know it today is the result of changes that required many more millions of years.

Learning about rocks gives one a new perspective on history. Changes must be viewed within a scale of at least a thousand years, usually more. If the Earth's lifetime were compressed into a single twenty-four-hour day, humans would have appeared only thirty seconds ago. A lifetime is the whole experience for an individual, but it is pitifully short in the timeline of geological history.

Precambrian Time: 4.5 billion to 543 million years ago
88 percent of Earth's lifetime

Paleozoic Era: 543 to 248 million years ago
First fish: 500 million years ago
First amphibians: 350 million years ago

Mesozoic Era: 248 to 65 million years ago
First mammals: 210 million years ago
Dinosaur extinction: 65 million years ago

Cenozoic Era: 65 million years ago to the present
Ice Age begins and first humans:
1.5 million years ago

The Geology of the Deschutes River Canyon

The oldest rocks on Earth are almost as old as the planet, about 4 billion years. At first, there was only one continent, known as Pangaea, and one ocean. Beginning about 200 million years ago, the familiar contours of today's continents began to separate, and the new Atlantic Ocean began to form. As the Atlantic Ocean grew (and it is still growing), the continent of North America began to move west. Eventually North America collided with the floor of the Pacific Ocean, beginning about 160 million years ago.

The old, original continent, Pangaea, was established 700 to 800 million years ago, with its western coastline located along today's western border of Idaho. This coastline existed for about 600 million years, and thus it had plenty of time to accumulate sediment that was crumpled up against the old continent by North America's collision with the ocean floor. The sediment was eventually covered by younger volcanic rock. Further inland, large parts of North America east of Idaho were covered by a shallow sea.

The collision of the Northwest coastline and the Pacific Ocean floor follows an established geological sequence of events. Where the eastern edge of a Pacific floor plate buckles, it begins to dive into the interior of the Earth. Ocean crust slides down this path, extending below the western edge of the continent, eventually reaching the hottest parts deep in the planet. The rock moving into the interior of the Earth absorbs heat until it reaches a depth of 100 to 200 miles and is changed into hot, soft rock (magma). The line where the ocean floor bends and begins to move downward is called an ocean trench, the site where several inches of ocean floor per year are engulfed. The margin of ocean floor being consumed is called a subinduction zone.

Pangaea

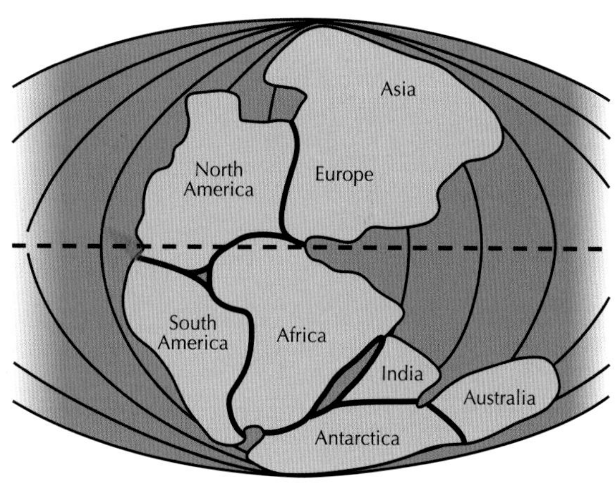

Tectonic Plate Movement

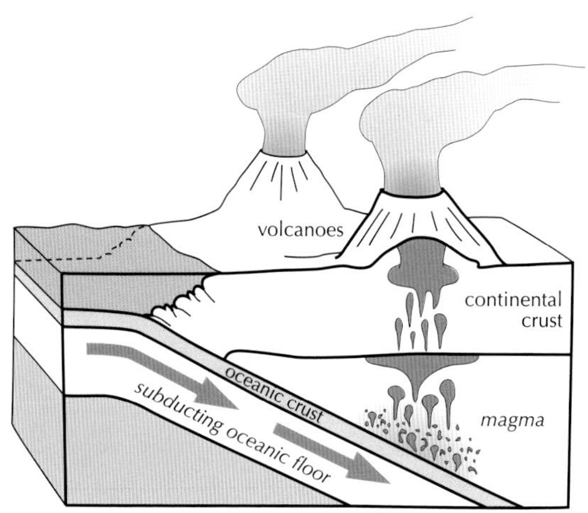

Volcanoes originate as a consequence of subinduction. The descending ocean crust is accompanied by water. Deep under the Earth, heat releases the water as steam. The steam lowers the melting point for rock and creates an enormous pressure to force the magma upward. Magma that reaches the surface is now called lava. This eruption can reach the surface as much as 100 miles inland from the coastline. Once the steam is dissipated, an eruption is followed by a relatively quiet lava flow.

Plate tectonics simply means that continents shift, but not always in an orderly fashion, resulting in separation, rotation, and re-connections. Geologists call ancient rock moved from one location to another distant location by plate tectonics, *terranes*. Volcanic islands such as Japan and the Philippines are the products of plate tectonics. Shifting plates drag the seafloor below the Earth's crust in the subinduction zone (marked by the ocean trench), scrambling and changing rocks in the intense pressure and heat of the Earth's magma before eruption, throwing the old seafloor to the surface.

Adding Terrane Land to the Continent

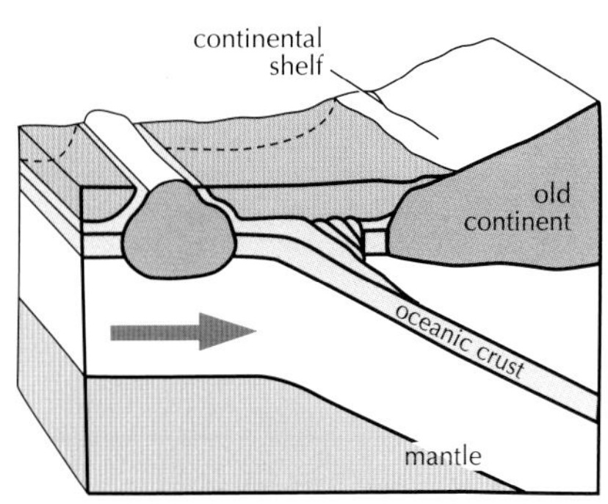

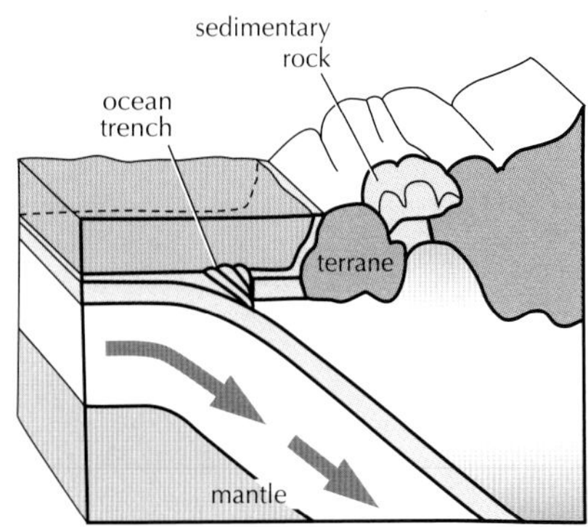

Millions of years ago, the North American continent moved westward, riding over the Pacific Ocean floor, which, in turn, was sliding deep into Earth's interior. The current geology of the Pacific Northwest is the result of the acquisition of land originating in the Pacific Ocean as a result of volcanic eruptions. As the Pacific trench allowed the ocean floor to be swallowed, the Pacific volcanic islands moved a few inches a year (about thirty miles every million years and over 900 miles in 30 million years) toward the continent, and the continent moved at the same pace toward the islands. The migration of these islands and the old continent over millions of years permitted the patching of this island land (terranes) onto the western edge of the continent.

As much as 100 million years later, a new trench appeared farther out in the ocean, producing a new wave of volcanic activity that produced Oregon's Ochoco Mountains. Today a Pacific trench extending the San Andreas Fault northward continues to swallow the ocean floor. Many years from now the ocean crust being swallowed will be thrust upwards to form a new coastal mountain range, west of the current one.

The Blue Mountains and the Wallowa Mountains are terranes made of complex volcanic rock affixed to the old western coastline of the continent by the trench process. Fossils of ocean fauna and flora are found in these rocks that formed about 250 million years ago and became attached to the continent about 100 million years ago. Earlier, in southern Oregon and northern California, a large terrane known as the Klamath Mountains also became fused to the continent.

The arrival of early "Oregon" followed the tectonic movement that separated North America from Europe and northern Africa. The oldest bedrock in Oregon (about 400 million years old), found in the northeast Blue Mountains and the southwest Klamath Mountains, was once ocean bottom. These rocks were part of volcanic islands in the sea and contain fossils of corals and marine invertebrates. Tectonic movement was not understood or appreciated until after the 1970s when technologic advances began mapping ocean floors and measuring magnetic fields. Acceptance of tectonic movement finally explained how old rocks were thrown into surprising locations juxtaposed with newer rocks and how sediments were folded and thrust in new directions.

Plate movement finally brought the rocks that are now in the Blue Mountains and the Klamath Mountains into contact with North America about 90 to 150 million years ago. The Klamath rocks formed the first new Oregon land about 144 million years ago, and the Blue Mountains were in place about 100 million years ago. Eighty million years ago, the sea level rose to 1,000 feet higher than where it is today, and the sea came close to reaching the new mountains in eastern Oregon and Idaho.

The terrane rocks in the Blue Mountains and the Klamath Mountains were formed by eruptions

The Old Continental Margin and Trench

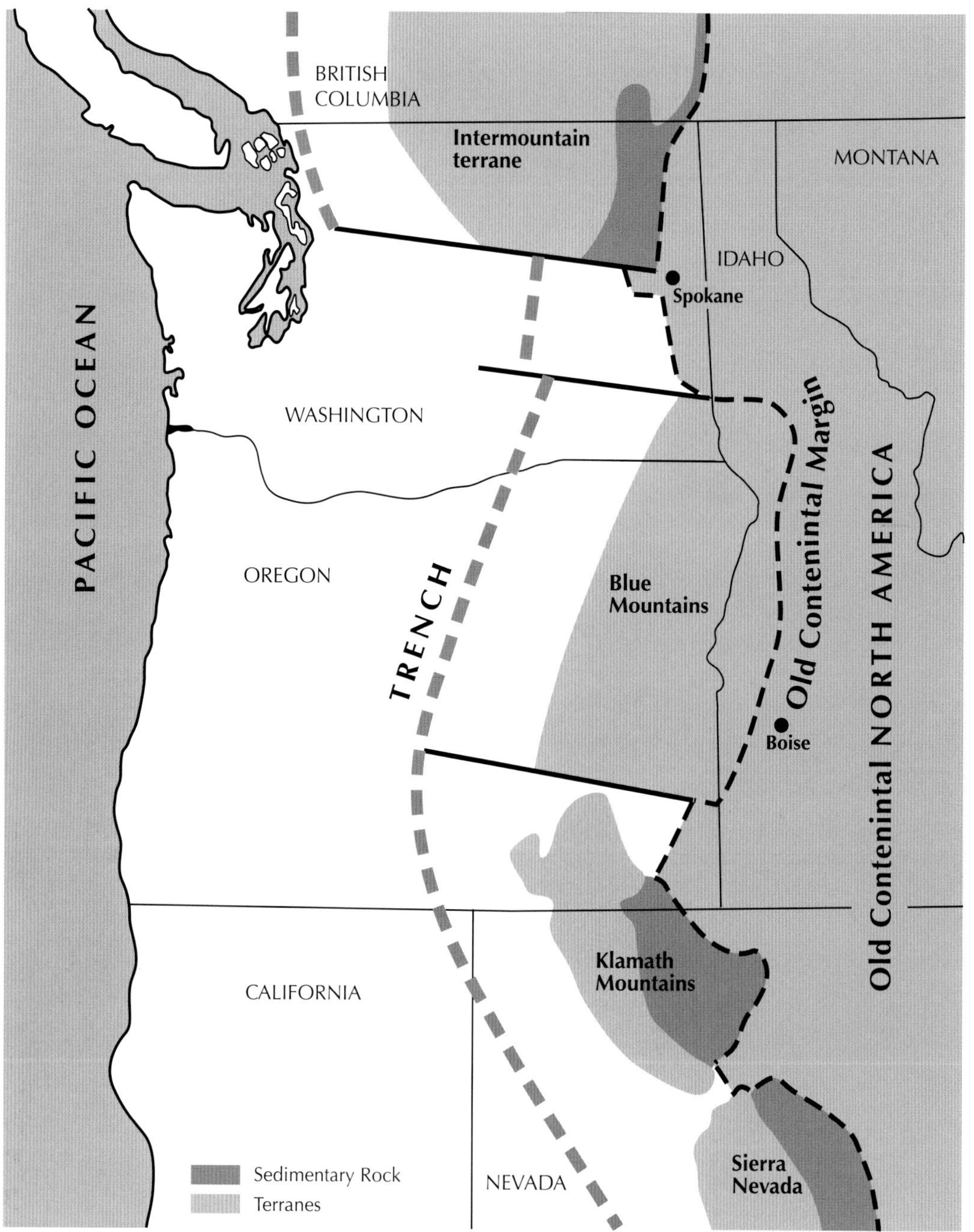

in the Pacific Ocean that covered a span of about 150 million years. The Cascade Range, however, was formed by volcanic eruptions on continental land beginning about 45 million years. Mount Hood and Mount Rainier were formed by more recent eruptions that began about a million years ago.

ABOUT 245 MILLION YEARS ago, perhaps because of enormous volcanic eruptions centered in western Siberia, approximately 90 percent of the world's animals were extinguished.[1] Sixty-five million years ago, another catastrophic event eliminated about 65 percent of animal life (including the dinosaurs that dominated the planet for about 165 million years). Geological evidence (for example the layer of clay discovered all over the world containing a rare element, iridium, found only in meteorites) indicates that this catastrophe was caused by the impact of a massive meteor. Such an impact would produce a shock wave of enormous pressure and heat, followed by a drop in temperature caused by the world-wide spread of dust, and ending with a destructive acid rain. The site of the impact is believed to be in western India. The Earth recovered gradually from this last catastrophe over a period of nine million years.

Fifty-six million years ago, Oregon's coastline ran from just west of Pendleton to Medford. Volcanic activity in the next 22 million years pushed the coastline westward to the Willamette Valley, which sits on a deep layer of sedimentary rocks deposited over about 25 million years. Deposits from the ancestral Columbia River draining the Blue Mountain land are found today forming the foothills just east of the coastal range. The rest of the coastal range, extending southward, sits on a foundation of deposits from the ancient Klamath Mountains.

About 40 to 50 million years ago, a new Pacific trench spawned the Ochoco Mountains, the volcanic rocks forming what is known as the Clarno Formation. Continued sinking of the ocean floor generated a new line of volcanoes about 35 to 40 million years ago, west of the current Cascade Range. These new volcanoes, called the Western Cascades, erupted for about 20 million years until about 17 million years ago, and today erosion has left only the foothills just east of the coastal range. East of these mountains, the land was covered with what is called the John Day Formation, sedimentary deposits of volcanic ash and flows of mud, sand, and gravel. The location of this formation, which is over 100 miles from the western line of volcanoes, is testimony to the strength of the eruptions that formed it.

The North American continent continued to move westward to collide with submarine volcanoes off the coast of early Oregon. This collision, about 34 million years ago, would account for the most recent large acquisition of land, a chain of seamounts offshore that were uplifted to form the present-day coastal range. The rock from these seamounts is found from Portland to Tillamook, an oceanside town eighty miles to the west of Portland. The origin of this rock is deduced from the marine sediment found between basaltic flows and in the round pillows of basalt formed by the action of cold seawater on hot lava.

About 34 million years ago, the Earth's climate began to cool and polar ice caps began to form for the first time. This climate change is attributed to the continuing shifting of plates, a change in ocean currents, and perhaps, another dust-creating meteoric impact.

TWENTY-FOUR MILLION YEARS ago, Oregon was mostly a plain of grass and trees. The Clarno volcanic peaks that erupted 20 million years earlier had since been diminished by erosion into hills. The Western Cascade Range was still present, twenty miles west of the present Cascade Range, but had been quiet since the westward movement of the continent overran its Pacific trench 25 to 50 million years ago. Almost half of this land became flooded by massive flows of basalt lava. One thought was that these flows were caused by a meteoric impact, but there is no evidence to support that idea. A better hypothesis traces the origin to the hotspot that today fuels Old Faithful in Yellowstone National Park, a hotspot that was once under eastern Oregon.[2] The movement of the hotspot to its current location is explained by the continued western migration of the continent.

Basalt, the principal rock of the Deschutes River Canyon, is uniform and compact, dark igneous (volcanic) rock containing augite (lime, magnesium, and manganese silicates), feldspar, and iron. A basalt flow, with its vertical columns, is easily recognized. Its distinctive shape is formed by shrinkage of the lava as it cools, solidifying from the top and the bottom and cracking into five- and six-sided polygons. The lava cools from both ends, meeting to form a zone called an *entablature,* which is closer to the bottom than the top. Where significant bodies of water were encountered, the lava was heaped into spherical or ellipsoidal shapes called "pillows," in contrast to the columns that formed over dry land.

Section Through a Basalt Lava Flow

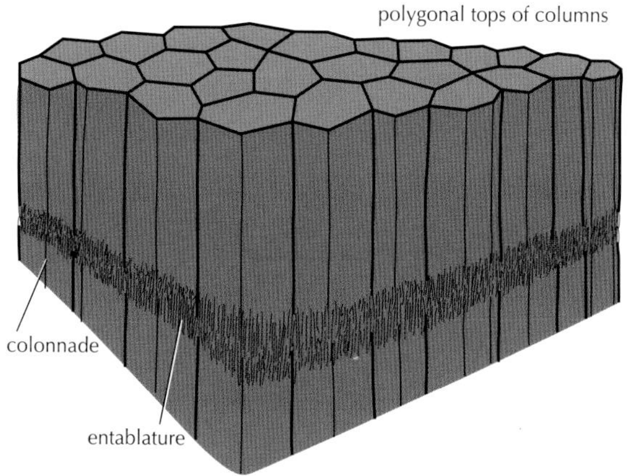

The Columbia River Basalt Flows came from vents that opened throughout eastern Oregon and Washington. Magma from an enormous chamber poured out of the vents and filled the landscape with eruptions for millions of years. In some places, the basalt rock today is three miles deep. Perhaps "eruption" is an inappropriate description because these flows were not violent, but rather more like a liquid oozing from multiple cracks in the Earth's crust to form a deep lake of molten basalt. The extension of the flows as far as the Pacific Ocean is evidence of the incredibly high temperatures of the lava.

The flows followed the Columbia River through a broad valley. Flow basalt is found today along the Clackamas River and further south. The west hills of Portland accumulated from several flows that traveled 200 miles from eastern Oregon. The basalt lining the Columbia Gorge (the river valley that cuts through the Cascade Range between the Deschutes and Sandy Rivers) is derived from 120 flows; a flow so voluminous that a highway of this rock seven feet thick and 100 feet wide would reach the moon.[3] The rock of the Blue Mountains, over 200 million years old, is covered by 16-million-year-old Columbia Basalt.

The Columbia River Basin in Washington and Oregon was first covered by the Grande Ronde Basalt Flows, 120 individual flows between 15 and 17

Basalt flows along the Deschutes River

million years ago. These were followed by fifty-five more basalt flows. All of these flows, which reached the Willamette Valley, are known collectively as the Columbia Basalt Flows.[4] Most of the prominent capes (for example, Tillamook Head) that mark the Oregon coastline are the most distant reaches of the great lava flows that occurred 6 to 17 million years ago. Large rocks off the Oregon coast (such as Haystack Rock at Cannon Beach) are remnants of Columbia River Basalt Flows. Some of the peaks in the coastal range (Saddle Mountain, for example) were formed by Columbia Basalt. The weight of the rock caused south-central Washington to sink, allowing lava pools up to two miles deep to accumulate. If confined to the State of Oregon and spread evenly, the total lava flows would have produced a layer 3,500 feet thick![5]

Most of the major eruptions stopped 6 million years ago, and rivers began to follow paths that are now familiar. At the time, eastern Oregon consisted of rolling, tree-covered hills. This world was full of animals, many of which would be recognized today. The continuing westward movement of the land and the eastward movement of the ocean floor began to

EXTENT OF COLUMBIA BASALT FLOWS

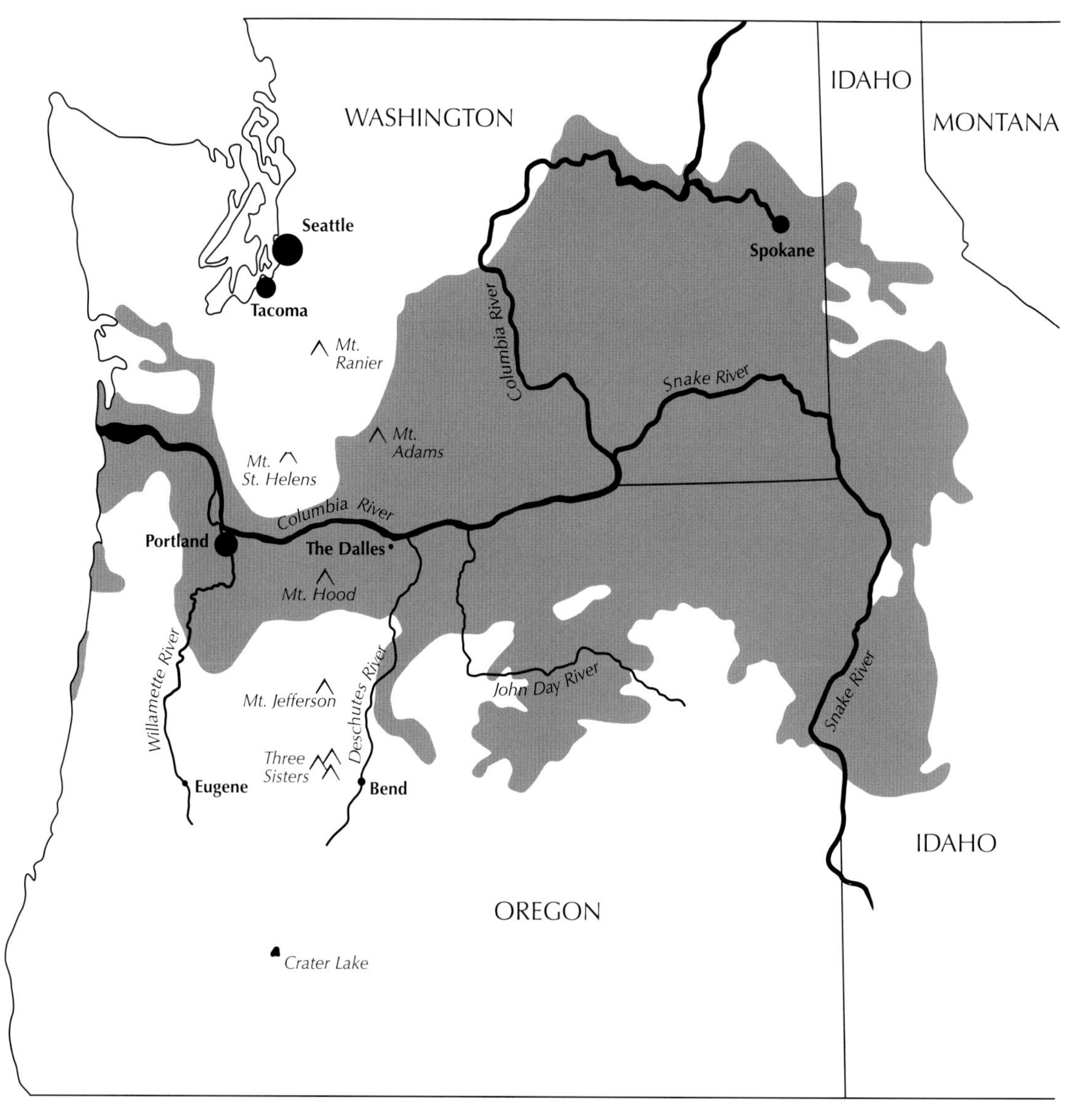

develop faults (in a process that is still on-going) producing the tilted mountains and the sunken basins we see today.

A "fault zone" is an opening from the deep interior of the Earth to the surface that can create volcanoes. The Brothers Fault Zone (making its appearance about 8 to 10 million years ago) extends diagonally across central Oregon from Burns through Bend to terminate between South Sister Mountain and Mount Bachelor, and allows a rotary movement that is ever so gradually westward. Fault zones uplifted the Blue Mountains and the Wallowa Mountains (establishing the Grande Ronde Valley), and created the Newberry Volcano. Mudflow and ash from this activity was carried by the Columbia River and deposited near Portland, a deposit called the Troutdale Formation (now an aquifer that is used by the city of Portland in times of low precipitation).

About 5 to 7 million years ago, the movement of the Pacific plate snuffed out the activity of the Western Cascades. The older rock (about 9 million years old) of the Western Cascades can be found near Mount Hood on the western slope between Zig-Zag and Government Camp. The new Cascade Range, called the High Cascades, became active 3 to 5 million years ago a little farther east.

The early High Cascade Range activity produced a lot of ash, and the eastern slope from the mountains to the Deschutes River is composed of layers of gravel and sand. From about 4 to 5 million years ago this eastern slope dropped several thousand feet along a fault. The canyons of the Deschutes and Crooked Rivers were carved about 2 to 5 million years ago, about the same time as Hells Canyon and the Grand Canyon.

A chain of volcanoes formed along the line where the sinking ocean crust reached a depth of sixty to seventy miles. It takes about a million years to reach a depth of sixty miles, and several more million years to build the heat and pressure to create volcanoes. It took 500,000 years for Mount Hood to rise to its peak height. The angle of the sinking crust determined the surface location where the new volcanoes erupted. A lower angle of sink from the new trench explains the location of the Cascade Range east of the old coastal volcanoes.

The Cascade Range carries the potential for eruptions of great magnitude. Crater Lake now exists where Mount Mazama stood before it exploded around 4,950 B.C., about 400,000 years after its formation. The crater of the lake was formed not by the explosion, but by the collapse of the mountain into the partially emptied magma chamber below it. Mount St. Helens, built mostly in the last 2,000 years, exploded in 1980. The exploded Newberry Volcano, the largest in Oregon, formed an oval caldera measuring four by five miles.

The Newberry Volcano began to contribute lava flows to the Deschutes Canyon and the canyon of the Crooked River about 1.2 million years ago. Newberry escaped modification by glaciers and continued to add ash and lava to the Deschutes basin for nearly a million years. Its most recent lava flow occurred only 1,200 years ago. The lava flow along the highway from Bend to Sunriver is 7,000 years old and came from Lava Butte, a small crater that was part of Newberry.

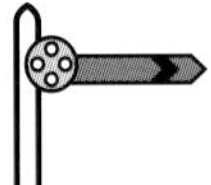

THE ICE AGES began 1.8 million years ago. From then till 10,000 years ago, the global climate cooled and glaciers advanced. It was during this time that the High Cascade Range emerged. Older volcanoes like Three Fingered Jack and Mount Washington were worn down by local glaciers, while younger mountains like Mount Hood and Mount Jefferson retained their classic shapes. The local glaciers were huge; one on Mount Hood reached Zig Zag at an elevation of 2,500 feet. The glaciers grew and retreated as many as twenty times, reaching their maximum extent 15,000 years ago and melting completely by 10,000 years ago. The massive ice sheet, which reached deep into the Midwest, stopped north of Tacoma and Spokane, Washington. This ice sheet moved back and forth many times over a million years. The sea level rose dramatically with this melting, then declined to its present level about 10,000 years ago.

Mount Hood is relatively young—about 600,000 years old with at least one lava flow dated to 7,700 years ago. Multiple eruptions occurred on Mount Hood 1,000 to 3,000 years ago, largely on the southwestern slope. The youngest eruption of ash and gas on Mount Hood occurred high on the southwestern slope, creating Crater Rock, in late 1781 or early 1782. Heat, steam, and ash have been periodically observed at Crater Rock over the last 150 years.

Mount Jefferson is about 300,000 years old, and Mount Bachelor and South Sister Mountain are also relatively young. All three escaped glacial scouring. The youngest lava flows in Oregon, 1,200 to 1,300 years old, came from South Sister Mountain and Newberry Volcano. A now-extinct volcano, northwest of Bend, the Tumalo Volcano, was active from 600,000 years ago to 280,000 years ago, contributing beds of ash along the Deschutes River.

Mount Mazama rose from multiple vents with eruptions that began 400,000 years ago and ended violently with the explosion 6,955 years ago that formed Crater Lake. Wizard Island in the lake was the last lava flow after the explosion. Heat and hot water in the crater indicate that Mazama is still alive. As the Ice Age ended, the Pacific Northwest was home to human settlements, and the explosion of Mount Mazama must have been witnessed by human beings.

Understanding Earth's geological history reveals a major inescapable lesson: this planet is constantly changing. The way it is now is not the way it is going to be. The ocean floor that is slipping under the land of Oregon continually moves irregularly, with stops, jerks, and lurches. A stop followed by a pressure-induced lurch is the mechanism for large earthquakes. Evidence indicates that such earthquakes occur every 300 to 600 years, and the last in the Northwest was in 1700.[6]

The Missoula Floods[7]

Like all scientific disciplines, geology is a combination of data and creative thought. The combination of new information and new ideas produces greater comprehension bringing new formulations and sometimes the correcting of conventional wisdom. The story of the Missoula Floods is a grand example.

The Missoula Floods, with depths greater than 400 feet and speeds over ninety miles per hour, traveled from Montana to the Pacific Ocean. These were deluges of massive proportions, consisting of water, ice, and rock. Doubling the velocity of a stream increases its ability to move material along the bottom sixty-four times.[8] The capacity of a flood, therefore, to move rock and sediment is enormous. Hundreds of feet of soil now in the Willamette Valley were moved by the floods from eastern Washington to Oregon, exposing the basaltic bedrock in eastern Washington. This bedrock was the result of the largest lava flows that occurred in North America, the Columbia River Basalt Flows, which were described earlier. The prehistoric Columbia River carved its path into this basaltic rock.[9]

The Columbia Basin was formed by the weight of this basalt depressing the Earth's surface over a period of 4 million years. The Columbia River carried gravel and silt into this area even before the lava flows had ceased; hence layers of sediment are found in the basalt rock. Low areas throughout the Deschutes Basin received sediment from other eastward flowing streams. The Dalles Formation is the basalt and sediment in the area of The Dalles, Oregon, (including Tygh Valley), which reaches to the mouth of the Deschutes River. Further upstream, these mixtures of basalt and sediment are called the Deschutes Formation.

During the Ice Age between 13,000 and 15,000 years ago, a glacial dam about 3,000 feet high impounded an enormous lake in what is now western Montana. The principal site of the ice dam was just upstream from where the Clark Fork River empties into Lake Pend Oreille. Here, a 2,500-foot-deep canyon provided the opportunity for glacial ice to back up the river and form Glacial Lake Missoula. This lake, derived from glacial melts, was over 2,000 feet deep behind the dam and covered over 7,700 square miles. The flood occurred when a 100-mile stretch of the glacial dam in what is now northern Idaho was weakened by the water behind it, releasing a huge amount of water in the relatively short time of two days. This volume of water would equal ten times the flow of all of the existing rivers on Earth today. The water flowed southwestward through the Spokane area, then turned south to pass through the Wallula Gap (a bottleneck the result of a mile-wide gap caused by the convergence of mountains on three sides just upstream of present day Lake Wallula behind the McNary Dam on the Columbia River).

We know there was more than one flood, probably dozens, because sediment layers indicate that the area was repeatedly filled as the glacier crept forward again and again retreated. The process was repeated every few years. Sediment layers at Missoula,

Pacific Northwest and the Missoula Floods

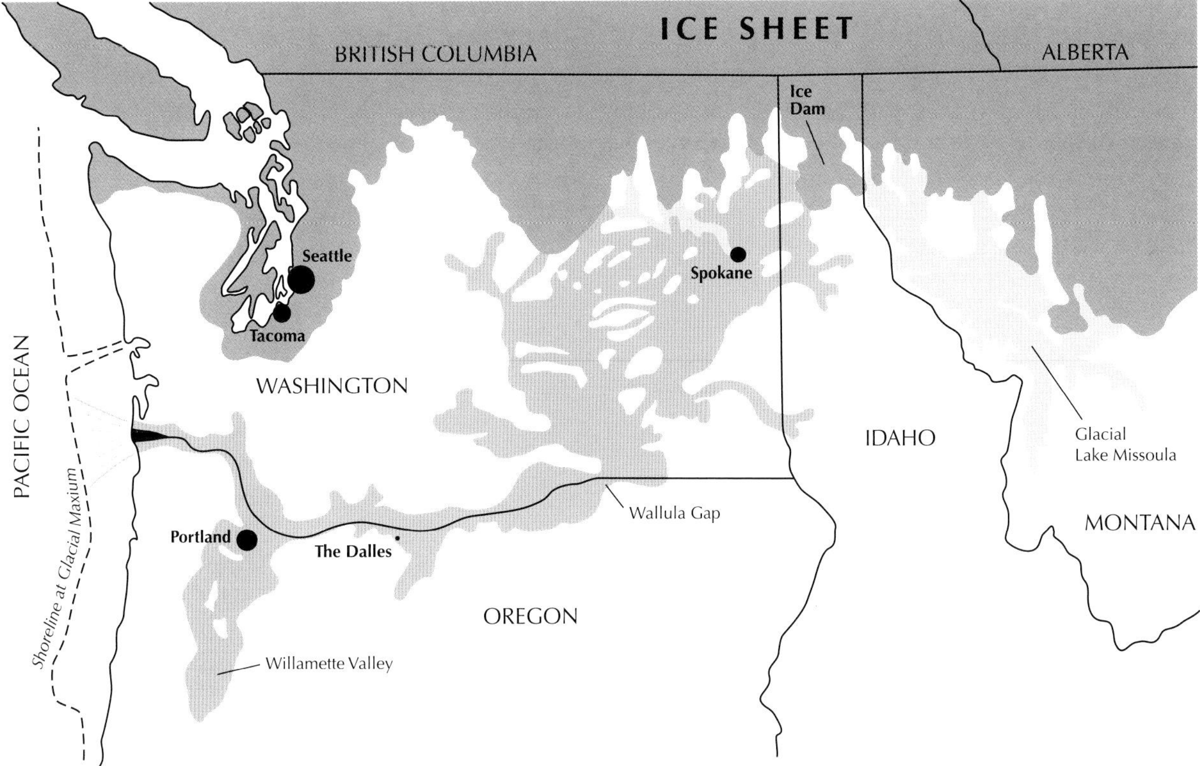

Montana, document thirty-six fillings and drainings of Glacial Lake Missoula.

The scarred channels, the dry stream beds left behind, are called the Channeled Scablands (after *ëscabsí,* erosion marks). The Scablands contain water-scourged coulees, giant gravel ripples, dry ancient waterfalls, basins and gouges (the remnants of plunge pools). Evidence of the floods can be seen in the hills west of Spokane, Washington. From the air these hills look like ripple marks—ripples that are up to thirty feet high and spaced 250 feet apart. Ripples in sand are the result of winds; the space between the ripples is the distance that sand particles are driven by the wind. In eastern Washington, the ripples were made of gravel driven by the flood waters. The accurate description of these ripples was made in 1940 by Joseph Thomas Pardee when he took aerial photos of the gravel ripples just east of the glacial ice dam, thereby giving credible support to the idea of the Missoula Floods.[10,11] These ripples are up to fifty feet high and 500 feet apart.

Scabland describes bedrock carved into canyons and buttes. The Scabland is filled with channels created haphazardly and acutely by gouging, not in an orderly slow way associated with a river's drainage basin (hence the name Channeled Scabland). The channels are connected and braided in a way that can be explained only by large volumes of water spilling over the sides of the channels.

The entire Columbia Gorge filled to overflowing. Many of the waterfalls in the Columbia Gorge (for example, Multnomah Falls) were originally tributaries that flowed down a moderate slope to the river at the bottom of a valley that was about a mile more narrow than today. The Missoula Floods blew those slopes away. The flow extended up the Deschutes River to near Maupin, evidenced by an erratic rock (rock transported by a glacier) found north of Maupin. By the time the flood reached Portland, Oregon, it was still over 400 feet deep and traveling eighty to ninety miles per hour. The wide Willamette Valley, flooded as far south as Eugene, absorbed some of the energy and slowed the flood's movement. The

Valley's rich soil (300 feet of sediment) came from Montana and Washington. Giant rocks in Portland originated in Idaho. Ridges in the Portland area, such as Alameda Ridge, are large gravel bars formed by the flood.

The Missoula Floods were first suggested by J. Harlen Bretz in the 1920s, who based his theory on studies of the geology of northeastern Washington. Bretz's ideas stirred up considerable disbelief and opposition. Bretz devoted much of his life to defending his explanation of the Missoula Floods. Born in Saranac, Michigan, in 1882, Bretz obtained his undergraduate degree in biology from Albion College. After graduating, he taught high school science in Seattle for four years. During his spare time, he pursued his interest in geology, mapping and naming the Ice Age lakes around Tacoma and Olympia. This early work helped him gain financial support to enter the University of Chicago, where he graduated with a Ph.D. in geology in 1913. He then became assistant professor of geology at the University of Washington. One year later, Bretz went back to the University of Chicago faculty, returning to the Northwest every summer on field trips.

Bretz's life work was precipitated by reviewing evidence of an enormous, ancient waterfall in the dry prairie land of eastern Washington. He was further intrigued by a second clue, the large number of rocks in the Columbia Gorge that obviously originated from a far distance. These sharp, angled rocks, some as large as a garage, are scattered throughout eastern Washington and Oregon. Bretz's third clue was the giant gravel bars, some 300 to 400 feet in height, deposited as ripple ridges throughout the Scabland and even in Oregon. Only large eddies could explain their origin. Bretz was the first to conclude that these large ice-borne rocks had been acutely deposited by floodwaters. His theory is a dramatic example of deductive reasoning, but what a creative imagination he had, to visualize from the ground huge gravel bars as ripples, ripples that could be appreciated only by viewing them from an airplane. Laboriously and with surprising accuracy, Bretz described this land based on his visual scouting by foot, a description easily made today by aerial and satellite photos.

It took years to link the great Glacial Lake Missoula to the floods and to the geological evidence. In 1965, a team of international geologists confirmed Bretz's conclusions, granting him recognition and congratulations before he died. Bretz was finally vindicated at age eighty-three, and his ideas were accepted as conventional wisdom when he was ninety. It took fifty years, but happily, still living and mentally alert, he could enjoy the satisfaction of recognition and awards. Bretz, age ninety-eight, died February 3, 1980, after a lifetime that still serves today as an example of scientific thinking buttressed by the courage of one's convictions.

Human beings in North America did not evolve from predecessors, but migrated from Asia via Alaska. These early Americans traveled great distances, reaching the distant parts of North and South America and the Caribbean Islands. Most believe these migrants crossed into North America about 25,000 years ago. It is still controversial whether people were living in the Pacific Northwest before the Missoula Floods because there is no definitive evidence for their presence. But it is likely that some were victims of the first Missoula Flood. A campsite that was buried before the floods has been discovered near The Dalles.[12]

The flood noise and the destruction were enormous. After the noise (heard at least thirty minutes before the flood's arrival), the wind came followed by the flood wall, a massive rush of water up to 500 feet tall. It's no wonder that ancient signs of human occupation (12,000 years ago and more) in the Columbia Basin are hard to find. The huge mammals dominant during the Ice Age disappeared after the floods over a period of about 7,000 years. The camel was the last to go, only 3,000 years ago. The new channels and rapids at Celilo became great fishing grounds for salmon.

THE LONG TUMULTUOUS GEOLOGICAL HISTORY of the Deschutes River makes it unique. Its rugged landscape would present tremendous challenges and problems for the railroad surveyors, engineers, contractors, and laborers who would work for the two railroads building along the river.

- CHAPTER TWO -

A Peculiar River

Utterly Impracticable for a Railroad

Lieutenant Henry Larcom Abbot, only twenty-four years old, explored the Deschutes River in 1855, searching for suitable railroad routes as part of the Pacific Railroad Survey.[1] He concluded that "the Des Chutes valley is mostly a barren region, furrowed by immense canyons, and offering very few inducements to settlers. Its few fertile spots, excepting those in the immediate vicinity of Fort Dalles, are separated from the rest of the world by almost impassable barriers."[1] "The route down the Des Chutes Valley to the Columbia River is considered utterly impracticable for a railroad. ...The whole difficulty consists in obtaining gradients."[2]

There was no doubt in Abbot's mind. "We were encamped in a narrow part of the canyon, and as its steep sides were crowned by vertical walls of columnar basalt, it would have been impossible for a pack mule to get out of it, in most places. ...This river canyon is very remarkable. ...The entire absence of life, the dull sound of the river rushing over its rocky bed, and the dark green of the stunted cedars and pines clinging to the precipices which confined it."[3] "The road could be built at a moderate expense, with a descending grade of 13 feet per mile, from the place where we first reached the Des Chutes river, to the point where my party rafted it, a distance of about 29 miles. ...A short distance below this point, the river enters the great canyon. It is not considered practicable, without enormous expense, to construct a railroad from this place to the Dalles, either in this canyon, or upon the eastern or western side of the valley. ...The canyon, which in many places is more than 1,000 feet in depth, extends, without doubt, to the mouth of the river; a distance of about 140 miles. It abounds in rapids and short bends, which would render numerous tunnels and deep cuts through a kind of basaltic rock of exceeding hardness, indispensable. There would also be the constant danger of avalanches of earth and stone, from the precipitous sides."[4]

The Deschutes River

On their way to the Pacific Ocean, Lewis and Clark called the Deschutes River by an Indian name that meant "the river on which the Snake Indians live," *Towarnehiooks.*[5] On their return journey, they renamed it Clarks River, but the fur traders called it *Riviere des Chutes* or *Riviere aux Chutes,* the River of the Falls, which evolved into Deschutes. The falls referred to by the fur traders were those nearby on the Columbia River at Celilo. Deschutes also became the name for a post office established in July 1868 at the site now known as Sherars Bridge.[6] Joseph H. Sherar became postmaster at this site in January 1872 and officially changed the name to Sherars Bridge in February 1888.

The Deschutes landscape reflects a geomorphic history that includes volcanic discharges, tectonic movements, landslides, and periodic floods. As rivers go, the Deschutes has unique characteristics because of its geology, topology, and climate (so unusual, it has been called "a peculiar river"[7]). The geology of the Deschutes River mutes its response to extreme climatic events (for example, there is more than 150 inches of precipitation per year in the Cascade

Range, and in the arid east, precipitation is less than 9.8 inches). As landscapes go, the contrast between eastern and western Oregon is striking. To the west, the Cascade Range provides a physical barrier to the moisture generated from the ocean and moved by the prevailing westerly winds. To the east, relief from unending clouds and rain in western Oregon can be found in the *magic of eastern Oregon* — prevailing sunshine in a semi-arid landscape encountered after a trip over the mountain.

The constant flow of the Deschutes River in central Oregon (about four miles per hour) is the result of abundant moisture in western Oregon moving through the highly permeable, layered lava flows in the southwestern part of the Deschutes Basin.[8] The Deschutes River drains the side of a relatively young uplifted volcanic land. The high permeability of multiple lava flows results in little surface runoff, and the young, unweathered rocks produce little sediment. Eighty percent of the average flow of the Deschutes River is from spring-fed groundwater. This groundwater is responsible for a remarkably uniform flow, more uniform than that of any other river of its size.

There are three dams in the Pelton-Round Butte Dam Complex. The farthest upstream dam is the Round Butte Dam. About ten miles downstream from Round Butte is the Pelton Dam, and about two miles further downstream is the Regulating Dam (100 miles upstream from the Columbia River). The dams were constructed by Portland General Electric between May 1956 and August 1964 and generate 427 megawatts of power. The purpose of the Regulating Dam is to balance the fluctuations in water released by the upstream dams, maintaining a constant downstream flow. In 1982, a nineteen-megawatt powerhouse was installed on the Regulating Dam by the Confederated Tribes of Warm Springs.

The original license for dams issued by the Federal Power Commission expired at the end of 2001. Relicensing of the Pelton-Round Butte Hydroelectric Project raised the question, What effect has damming had on the Deschutes River? Seven years of research produced a somewhat surprising answer: there has been little change to the lower river despite approximately fifty years of upstream damming because of remarkably constant flow and low sediment production.[7]

The Deschutes Drainage Basin

The drainage basin can be divided into three sections.[9] (1) In the southwestern section of the basin, volcanism and tectonism have produced a lava-covered landscape with water originating in the Cascade Range precipitation and emerging from the ground. Drained by the Deschutes and Metolius Rivers, the southwestern section is bounded by the Cascade Range on the west and the lava flows from the Newberry Volcano on the east. The young volcanic rocks are covered in the southern portion by pumice from Mount Mazama, which exploded to form Crater Lake. (2) In the eastern section, volcanic and sedimentary rocks have weathered into a landscape with *uplifts* sloping into valleys, a landscape with great density, but seasonal runoff is limited by the arid climate. The eastern region is largely drained by the Crooked River flowing from the Ochoco Mountains and over the plains of lava flows and volcanic tuff laid down 20 to 55 million years ago. This section is the oldest in the Deschutes basin with more than 10 million years of weathering. (3) In the northern section, the land is late Cenozoic in origin with varied elevations and the greatest density (meaning it has the highest capacity for runoff during precipitation). The canyons of the northern section are etched into young basalt flows. In the recent floods of December 1964 and February 1996, half the flow at the mouth of the Deschutes River was derived from the northern section.

The Deschutes River drains about 7 million acres of north-central Oregon (this is its "basin"). It first flows east from the Cascade Range, then north for nearly 200 miles, joining the Columbia River 100 miles east of Portland. Its principal tributaries are the Crooked River, which joins at 115 miles upstream, and the Metolius River, which joins at 112 miles from the confluence with the Columbia River.

The basin is formed by sedimentary, igneous, and metamorphic rocks that range in age from 1,300 years to more than 250 million years. Most are volcanic rocks less than 65 million years old. The rocks in the eastern basin (the Ochoco Mountains and the Mutton Mountains) are weathered remnants from volcanic activity 20 to 55 million years ago. This rock is different compared with the Columbia Basalt Flows. Rather than an oozing forth into a lake of hot rock, the rocks of the Ochoco and Mutton Mountains, as well as that of the Tygh Ridge, are

DESCHUTES RIVER BASIN

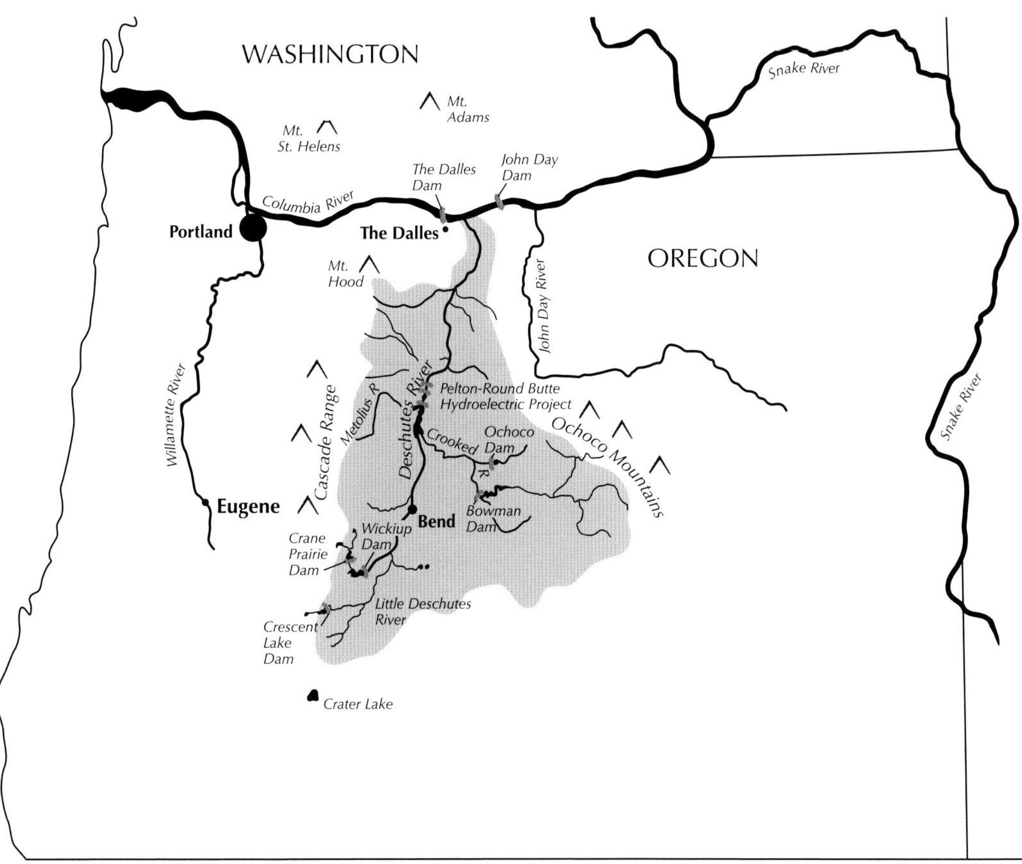

older, the results of explosive eruptions from volcanoes that amalgamated other rock into a dense, hard composite. These are the rocks of the John Day and Clarno Formations, underneath and older than the Columbia Basalt Flows.

Elevation of the land into mountains is the result of uplifting, and the uplifted area is called an anticline. The ongoing encounter between the continent and the Pacific trench is producing a pressure that is not limited to an east-west direction. The meeting of the two forces is actually oblique, producing a north-south effect over the last 4 million years. This results in a folding of the land, lifting the pressure points that we recognize as the anticlines called the Mutton Mountains and the Tygh Ridge. It is this pressure that has caused (and is still causing) the twisted and leaning positions of the basalt, movement from the original vertical columns created by cooling.

At the site of North Junction seventy-three miles upstream on the Deschutes River, the end of the Mutton Mountains (named for wild sheep that later were extinguished by the diseases of domestic sheep) reaches the river. The rock of the Mutton Mountains is older than basalt, hence its jumbled, weathered look. The composite nature of this volcanic extrusion with a mixture of lava, ash, and rocks picked up during the flow makes it harder in contrast to the polygonal, homogenous structure of the softer basalt, with its fissures alongside the uniform columns produced in cooling. Thus, the basaltic rock downstream from North Junction, because it is softer, would prove easier for the railroad workers to blast and move. But at North Junction, the railroad had to cross the river to avoid rock so hard it could not be easily blasted or penetrated.

Underlying the eastern and northern sections of the basin are the layered basalt flows of the Columbia

River Basalt Flows that covered southern Washington, western Idaho, and northern Oregon 6 to 17 million years ago. The basalt flows in the eastern section originated from vents in the John Day River Basin (the John Day Formation). Additionally, basalt flows in the northern section came westward from vents in eastern Washington, eastern Oregon, and western Idaho, filling the area with about 2,000 feet of lava. One other basalt flow, known as the Prineville Basalt, erupted near Bowman Dam in the central basin and flowed north along the path where the current Crooked River meets the Columbia Basalt Flows.

By 17 million years ago, the present overall configuration of the northern Deschutes Basin was in place. Between 4 and 15 million years ago, deposits accumulated of sediment and airfall tuffs (compacted deposits of volcanic ash), both derived mostly from the emerging Cascade Range on the west with a smaller contribution from the volcanic land in the east. South of Trout Creek these deposits are known as the Deschutes Formation. Similar deposits between the Tygh Ridge and Mutton Mountains and again near the Columbia River are known as the Dalles Formation.

Geological analyses indicate that the course of the Deschutes River 4 to 7.5 million years ago was similar to the present course.[10] Initially, the river was spread over a broad plain, several hundred yards higher than the present water level.[11] Basalt flows near Maupin and north of Madras indicate that about 4 million years ago the Deschutes River was flowing at an elevation approximately equal to the present-day canyon rims.[12] At that point, the river began a slow but steady and inexorable etching into the earth. Westward, the older rocks are covered by the effluent of the active volcanoes of the Cascade Range, less than 2 million years old. About 0.5 to 1.2 million years ago, lava flows south of Bend from Newberry Volcano, partly filled the Crooked, Metolius, and Deschutes River Canyons. Analyses of these flows indicate that by 1.2 million years ago, the Deschutes River had incised the earth near to its present level. Similarly, analyses of the lava flow along the Columbia River indicate the river level at the confluence has been about the same for the last 1 million years. Thus between 1 and 4 million years ago, the Deschutes River descended about 900 feet, about four inches per year.

THE DESCHUTES RIVER has two natural reservoirs: the mountain snow pack and the large aquifer in the permeable rock of the upper river. The largest portion of surface water in the Deschutes Basin is derived from the high rainfall and deep winter snow pack in the Cascade Range. Before dam regulation, the flow at the mouth of the Deschutes River in late summer was one-sixth that of the maximum flow in early spring. This compares to a thirty-fold difference on the John Day River and a ten-fold difference on the Willamette River. After dam regulation, today there is only a 1.5-fold difference between the minimum and maximum flow on the Deschutes.[13] Even the maximal flow in response to flood conditions is tempered; the flow in the February 1996 flood was four-fold greater than the average flow (compared with twenty-fold differences on the John Day and Willamette Rivers).

Most of the rain and snowmelt enters the permeable volcanic fields in the eastern, western, and southern parts of the Deschutes Basin. This water emerges later in large springs at the head of the Metolius River, along the Crooked River, and along the Deschutes River 100 to 120 miles upstream. Thus there is minimal seasonal or monthly variation in the flow of the upper Deschutes River. The total volume of flow in the east is low, contributing only a little to the lower Deschutes River. Thus seasonal and climatic increases in flow found in the lower Deschutes River are affected by runoff only in the northern section of the basin, especially by the Cascade Range tributaries (Shitike Creek, Warm Springs River, and the White River).

THE SOUTHERN AND SOUTHWESTERN REGIONS of the basin are relatively young and unweathered, and thus lack sediment. The low superficial drainage in these areas produces little in the way of sediment transport. Sediment in this area, therefore, is attributed to volcanic eruptions and the glaciers during the Ice Age. Glacial deposits evident along the eastern side of the Cascade Range contributed sand and gravel to the Metolius and Deschutes Rivers only in the distant past, thousands of years ago.

Ash and pumice fallout from eruptions west of Bend, including Mount Jefferson and Mount Mazama, covered much of the Deschutes Basin over the past 500,000 years. The fallout was heaviest around the upper Deschutes and Metolius Rivers. These were not mere coverings of the ground; indeed, a thickness greater than thirty feet has been measured west of Bend, and the Mazama pumice from 7,000 years ago covers over 62,000 acres.[14]

The eastern region, because it contains older and more weathered material, is more erodible, and over time it has contributed considerable sediment into the Crooked and Deschutes Rivers. Prior to the building of dams, the greater variation in seasonal and climatic flow in this area delivered significant sediment to the Deschutes River. Now, there is very little sediment available to be deposited in the river. Most of the sediment in the Deschutes River is the result of pulses delivered over time by the deposits of volcanic pumice and ash, glaciation, and landslides.

IN THE FIRST DECADE of the twentieth century, the forests on the eastern slopes of the Cascade Mountains were pristine, barely touched by invading lumbermen.[15] Higher elevations were dominated by firs, pines, and cedars, but as the forest descended into the arid valley, at about 4,000 feet elevation, the prevalent trees became ponderosa pine interspersed with junipers. Prior to the availability of the railroads, this pine forest consisted of magnificent, huge trees awaiting harvest, providing an instant temptation to any lumberman.

The ponderosa pine (*pinus ponderosa* or western yellow pine) is a hardy tree. The ponderosa pine received its name from David Douglas, the Scottish botanist who discovered the tree in 1826 and named it for its ponderous (heavy) wood. It grows in any soil and in areas with precipitation from less than ten inches per year to more than 100 inches. The

Ponderosa pine forest

bark of the ponderosa found in Oregon is distinctive, a rough orange-pink to red-brown surface, with long and irregular, vertical, dark junctions that give the appearance of crocodile skin. A mature forest is a beautiful sight, with widely spaced trees that allow the sunlight to be brilliantly captured by the colorful bark. Many trees reach a height of sixty to 130 feet with a ten-foot circumference and a diameter of two to four feet; a few are taller than 200 feet with circumferences greater than fifteen feet. The large trees in the virgin forest of the early 1900s filled the lumberman's mind with images of wall studs, floors, and window frames.

The Upper Deschutes River

The dam complex divides the river into the lower Deschutes, 100 miles below the dams, and the upper Deschutes, the river above the dam complex. Lake Billy Chinook (named after a Wasco Indian who was the chief scout for John Fremont's U.S. Army expedition to the Rocky Mountains in 1842), is the reservoir behind the most upstream dam, the Round Butte Dam, collecting the water from the inundated confluence of the Deschutes, Crooked, and Metolius Rivers. As the ground elevation decreases, the ground water emerges, discharging along a ten-mile stretch above the lake, accounting for most of the flow of the upper Deschutes River.[16,17] In this stretch, the rivers have cut deeply into the permeable rock, producing innumerable springs in the canyon walls. The lower Deschutes River (now below the Pelton Dam) had to cut into impermeable rock, and there is no significant ground flow contribution. The impounded lake behind the Pelton Dam is named after Pipsher Simtustus, who was also a Wasco scout for the U.S. Army.

Ingenious studies using oxygen and hydrogen isotopes have documented that elevation is the primary determinant of isotope composition. The isotope composition in canyon spring water is similar to that of snow cores and water obtained at higher elevations, a fact that documents that the source of the spring water is the precipitation absorbed by permeable rock, the water originating from as far away as thirty-one miles. This water percolates through the rock and resides in deep aquifers for as long as a few years to several decades or several hundred years as the elevation decreases (and the distance from the crest of the Cascade Range increases).[18] The permeability of the upper basin extends to great depths. According to temperature studies, it reaches 328 feet to 1,640 feet deep, providing a vast reservoir for water.[19,20]

Lake Billy Chinook

This large capacity and retention time impose a stable flow for the Deschutes River despite the highly seasonal nature of the precipitation. The size and the depth of this system allow major fluctuations in the water level to be absorbed without affecting the discharge flow of groundwater. Thus, for flooding to occur on the lower Deschutes River, a meteorologic event, such as the rain-on-snow episodes in 1964 and 1996, must affect the lower basin. A rain-on-snow storm results from the South Pacific dumping of large amounts of warm rain on deep snow packs, causing rapid melting and runoff. Today, leaking from unlined irrigation canals also contributes to the groundwater. About half of the irrigation water in the area of Bend and Redmond finds its way back to the groundwater emerging in the spring.[21]

The Lower Deschutes River

The lower Deschutes River is a congressionally designated Wild and Scenic River. It descends 1,250 feet in a channel that averages 240 feet wide, with its narrowest width being twenty-seven feet at Sherars Falls and its maximum width being 600 feet. This portion of the river has over 100 islands that are 75 percent alluvial, except for bedrock at two points (river miles 40 to 50 and 0 to 10).

The lower Deschutes now flows through its own product, a canyon, which at its greatest depth is 2,000 feet deep. The canyon is deepest where the river crosses the Mutton Mountains, about seventy miles upstream from the mouth, and again where it crosses the Tygh Ridge at forty miles upstream. The canyon is shallowest just below the dam complex eighty-five to 100 miles upstream, near the town of Maupin fifty miles upstream, and at the confluence with the Columbia River.

Throughout the lower basin, the river runs through the Columbia River Basalt Flows, hard enough rock, but not as hard as that to be encountered by the railroad builders farther upstream. Sixty to 100 miles upstream from the Columbia River, volcanic flows (the John Day and Clarno Formations) are found just below the rim of the canyon. These flows lift the Columbia basalt to higher elevations while the even older rock is pushed upwards by a folding effect of the pressure created as the continent meets with the

TIMELINE

Years Ago	Event
40 to 50 million	Clarno Formation
17 to 40 million	John Day Formation
12 to 17 million	Columbia Basalt Lava Flows
4 to 7.5 million	Deschutes River Established
10,000 to 1.8 million	Ice Age
1.2 million	Deschutes Canyon Established
200,000 to 1.2 million	Newberry Lava Flow
600,000	Mount Hood
300,000	Mount Jefferson
13,000 to 15,000	Missoula Floods
6,955	Mount Mazama Explodes

TOPOGRAPHY OF THE DESCHUTES RIVER CANYON[22]

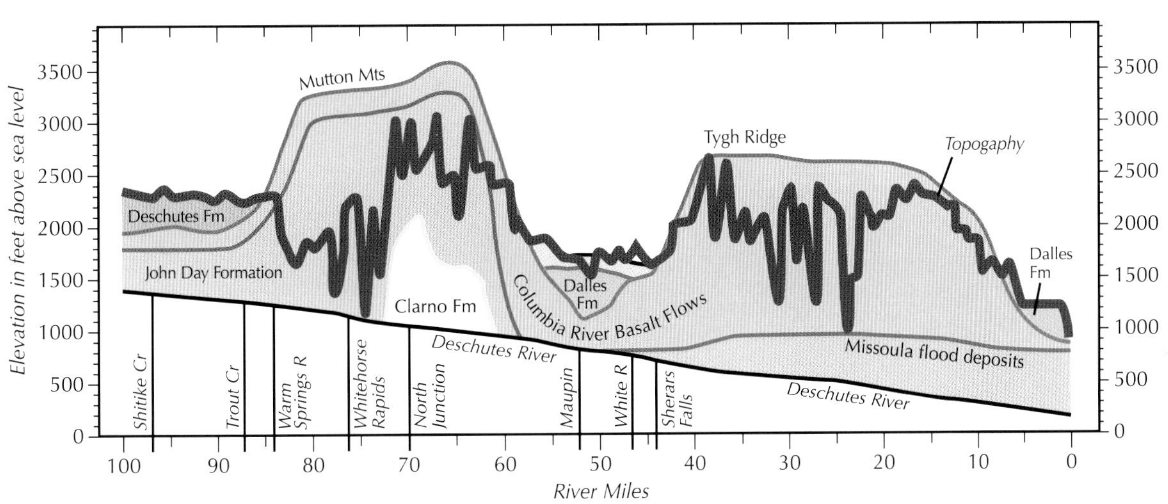

Pacific trench. From the dam complex to the eighty-five mile mark, the John Day rock is exposed at the banks of the river's edges. The canyon walls reveal that the John Day Formation is overlain with about 500 feet of Columbia River basalt that is in turn covered by many feet of younger basalt flows. But it was the composite, hard rock of the John Day and Clarno formations that would prove to be the most difficult to blast.

From sixty miles to eighty-five miles upstream, the river flows through the Mutton Mountains where the canyon walls expose rock of the John Day

The Deschutes River Canyon, looking downstream from Beavertail, 31 river miles north to the Columbia River

Formation, which overlays rock from the Clarno Formation. At the very top of the canyon is a cap of Columbia basalt. The John Day and Clarno Formations are vulnerable to landslides, especially between river miles 65 and 85 because the John Day rock has been lifted to the heights of the Mutton Mountains. Landslides occur in these formations because, as the land is being thrust upward, the river erodes it, thereby weakening support and allowing the land to shift downward toward the river.

In some places, the true canyon rim is up to fifteen miles from the river. Severe landslides have created this width, covering this distance and reaching the river. The width of the canyon ranges from 115 feet to 700 feet, with points as wide as 2,500 feet.[22] The Deschutes River in this stretch, therefore, winds through a mixture of hard, volcanic bedrock and displaced jumbo rocks and sediment from landslides.

Downstream from river mile 60, the canyon is formed of gradually thickening layers of Columbia Basalt, and the width is consistently less than 700 feet until river mile 30 where it widens to about 1,640 feet. At river miles 40 to 50, where the White River enters the Deschutes, and around Sherars Falls, the river bottom and river edges are bedrock; thus the river is at its minimal width. From the mouth of the river to forty miles upstream, the Columbia Basalt is covered by sand, silt, and clay left by the Missoula Floods.

River mile 109, just above the Round Butte Dam, marks the farthest downstream remnant of lava flows from the Newberry Volcano. When lava flows filled the river canyon at this location, the river simply resumed its relentless carving and recreated the canyon. In the lower river, two similar remnants of lava flows originating from Gordon Butte about 1 million years ago are exposed on the east side of the river, between river miles 4.5 and 4.0, and 2.6 and 2.2.[23] At the time the lava flows entered the river, the river elevation was fifty-six feet higher than it is currently.

Evidence of a white, pyroclastic flow which came from Mount Jefferson about 100,000 years ago, is found just below the Pelton Dam. This large lehar (a flow of debris of volcanic origin) covered most of the lower canyon at a time when the river was eighty-two feet higher than it is presently. The canyon walls in this area indicate layers of volcanic debris, pumice, and ash. This eruption of Mount Jefferson spread falls of ash as far away as Idaho. Its flows reached downriver partly because the eruption occurred at the time of glaciers (during the penultimate Ice Age 74,000 to 59,000 years ago), and significant melt water carried the debris downstream. A more recent deposit (around 1781) flowed from Mount Hood, down the White River, reaching the Deschutes at river mile 46.6. Downriver, the flows are capped by Missoula Flood deposits and loess (a fine covering, the residue of ground up ancient rocks).

Massive landslides occurring sometime between 10,000 and several hundred thousand years ago produced temporary damming of the river at Whitehorse Rapids (river mile 76) and Dant (river mile 64).[24] The Whitehorse Rapids landslide is the youngest, a movement of land that covered a semicircular shape of the eastern slope. When this landslide moved west, it completely blocked the river for over a half-mile. The rock in the landslide is uniformly from the John Day Formation. An older, even larger landslide preceded the Whitehorse landslide, reaching from Whitehorse to river mile 85. The height of the dam created by this large landslide was 115 to 500 feet above the water level at Whitehorse Rapids, producing a lake that reached eighteen miles upstream to Trout Creek. This blockage lasted long enough to deposit thirty-two feet of sand and gravel on the valley bottom. Whitehorse Rapids (a drop of forty feet in 0.6 miles) is the result of the river continuing to carve its way through this landslide (the large rocks in the river were placed there by the landslide and are not the result of erosion). It is estimated that the river has another twenty-five feet to go before it carves to the elevation it held before the landslide.[25]

PERLITE, a rapidly extruded and solidified volcanic glass, light gray to nearly black in color, that differs from obsidian by containing more water,[26] was discovered in the cliffs on the west bank of the Deschutes River, sixty-four miles upstream from the Columbia River and nine miles south of Maupin in 1945. These perlite deposits are found within the Clarno Formation. Mining was developed by Dant and Russell of Portland, Oregon, to produce a

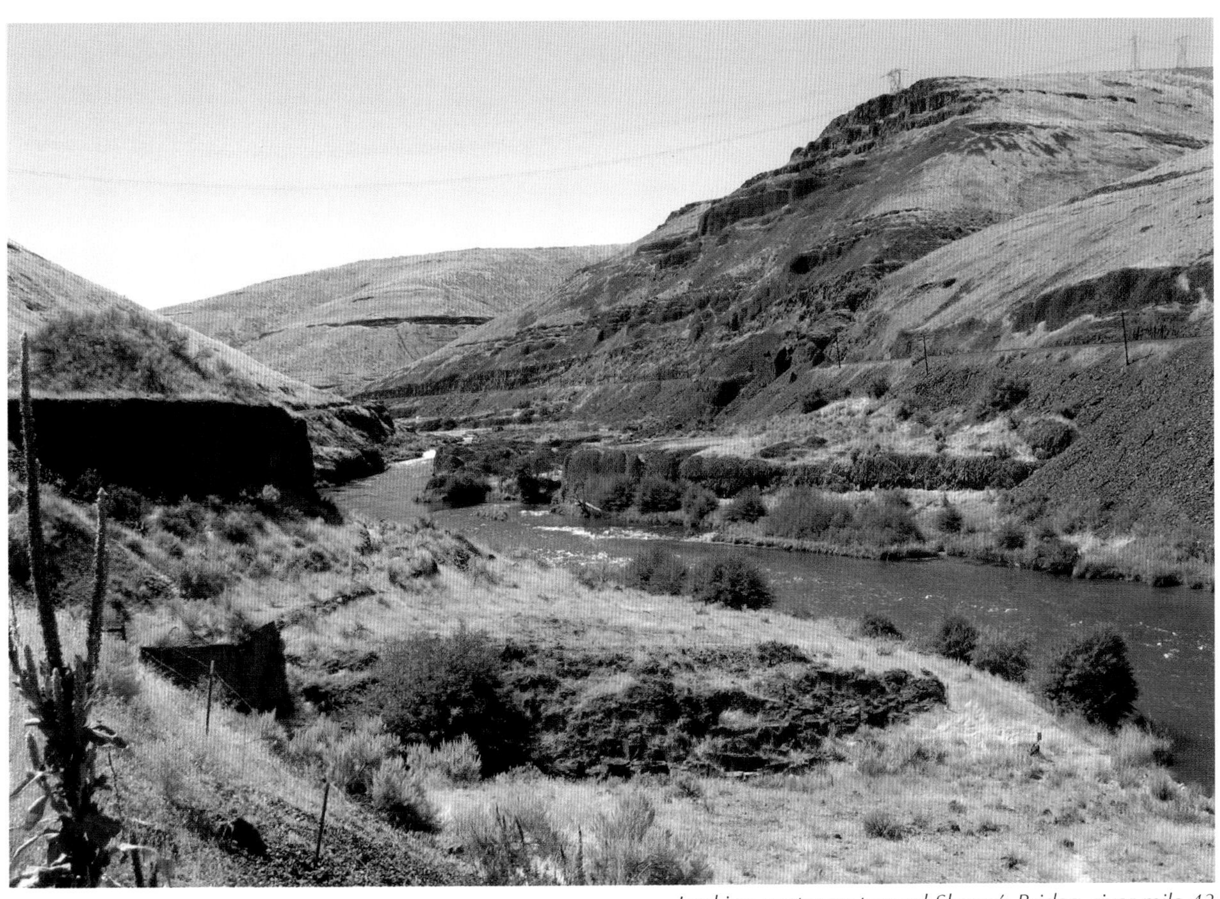

Looking upstream toward Sherar's Bridge, river mile 43

Looking downstream from Horsehoe Bend, river mile 40

product named "Dantore," used in plasterboard and acoustical tile.[27] The Dant and Russell Company changed the railroad name for the stop at this site from Frieda to Dant in 1950. The community of Dant is located at river mile 64. A massive landslide of John Day Formation rock from the west slope immediately downstream of the present day community blocked the Deschutes River for about 0.3 miles. The railroad tunnels under this flow. The old mine, called the Lady Frances, had about 1,500 feet of tunnels. Its entrance is visible 500 feet up the west bank above Dant. The perlite at the opening to the mine is about 150 feet thick.[28] The Oregon Trunk built a spur to service the mine, delivering the perlite about 200 miles to the Dant and Russell plant in St. Helens, Oregon. Dant and Russel quit the perlite business in 1952, and Dant is now occupied by private homeowners as a fishing camp. The mine was operated for only one more year by the Henry J. Kaiser Company, which elected not to exercise its option to purchase the property.[29]

THERE ARE TWENTY-THREE RAPIDS larger than Class 2 on the lower Deschutes River. The greatest drops are at Sherars Falls (15.4 feet) and Whitehorse where the river descends 26.2 feet in less than one-third of a mile, and then another 13.8 feet in the next one-third of a mile. Fourteen of the major rapids are located where the river meets the bedrock at miles 20 to 40 and miles 0 to10. Twelve of the major rapids flow over ledges of basaltic bedrock. The remaining eleven were created by the major floods, landslides, and tributary floods. Buckskin Mary was formed by the Dant landslide, and Four Chutes just downstream from Buckskin Mary was formed from debris when the Dant landslide was breached. Over the last 100 years, there have been no major changes in these rapids, except for an occasional boulder moved by floodwaters. Three smaller east slope landslides of Columbia River Basalt at river miles 53 to 44 produced Boxcar Rapids and Wapinitia Rapids.

Deschutes River Rapids in Bedrock[30]

Name	Class	River Miles from the Mouth
Wapinitia	3	54.7
Oak Springs	4	74.3
Upper and Lower Rollercoaster	3	45.6
Osborne	3	45.0
Sherars Falls	6	44.0
Sherar's Bridge	3	43.6
Wreck	3	40.0
Jet Pump	3	15.5
Gordon Ridge	3	5.9
Rattlesnake	4	2.7
Moody	3	0.8

Deschutes River Rapids Formed by Events[30]

Name	Class	River Miles	Event
Upper Trout Creek	3	87.0 m	Large flood
Lower Trout Creek	3	86.9	Large flood
Whitehorse	4	76.1	Landslide
Buckskin Mary	3	63.8	Landslide
Four Chutes	3	63.4	Landslide
Boxcar	3	53.7	Landslide
White River	3	46.3	Large flood
Bull Run	3	18.4	Large flood
Harris	3	11.4	Large flood
Washout	4	7.8	Tributary flood (1995)
Colorado	4	4.2	Large Flood

IN THE LOWER SIXTY MILES of the river, deposits and loess from the Missoula Floods have covered the valley with many feet of silt and clay. Weather erosion has created rills and gullies in this covering, a process increased by the rerouting of drainage by rail and road construction. The Deschutes alluvial surfaces, boulders, and gravel bars have been formed in large part by major floods, both meteorological and those associated with the breaching of landslide dams. These deposits form the rapids downstream from the major landslides: the Trout Creek Rapids, the riffles and rapids downstream of Whitehorse, and Buckskin Mary and Four Chutes Rapids just downstream of Dant.

The Missoula Floods were cataclysmic releases of the ice-dammed Glacial Lake Missoula (Chapter 1). At the mouth of the Deschutes River, the largest flood was about 800 feet deep, reaching upstream of the Deschutes to river mile 60, depositing clay, silt, and sand as high as 900 feet up the canyon slopes.

Meteorologic floods are the result of snowmelt or precipitation, with the largest floods following rain-on-snow storms. A meteorologic flood that occurred between 2,800 to 4,100 years ago has been named the Outhouse Flood because of the observation that Bureau of Land Management outhouses have been placed on the bars of boulders deposited by this flood.[31] This flood was approximately twice as great as the 1964 and 1996 floods (the largest in 100 years of recording). This flood also formed the largest islands made of coarse gravel and large boulders, accounting for 39 percent of the total island area. These are Harris Island at river mile 11.7, Airstrip Island at 22.8, Cedar Island at 30.9, Doe Island at 40.6, and Peanut Island at 88.9. The large rock deposits from this flood are of such a size that they have resisted erosion. Thus, the major consequence of the floods during the last 100 years has been the accumulation and erosion of silt and sand on banks away from the main channel. There has been little change in the river's channel.

There are 272 tributaries entering the lower Deschutes River below the dam complex.[32] The major drainage on the west comes from Shitike Creek, the Warm Springs River, and the White River; on the east, from Trout Creek, Buck Hollow Creek, and Bakeoven Creek. These six tributaries cover 78 percent of the lower river drainage basin, but contribute only 20 percent of the river flow (10 percent in late summer).[33] All of the tributaries, however, are important during floods when they contribute flow and sediment to the Deschutes. There are eighty-four alluvial fans associated with tributaries in the lower Deschutes River. A good example of a major alluvial fan is Washout Rapids at river mile 8, the consequence of debris from a tributary flood in 1995 in Mud Springs Canyon.

Whitehorse Rapids

RAILROAD CONSTRUCTION has not resulted in changes in the river channel or in the river banks.[34] The streamside location of railroad ballast represents deliberate placement to prevent river erosion of the railroad roadbed. As a result, most riverbanks and islands have been in the identical locations for the last 100 years; the river channel has changed very little.[35] Most island changes have been in the form of small accumulations and erosions of gravel deposits. A few small islands have been created and a few have disappeared, as a consequence of major floods.

The Deschutes River Fish

The coldness of the deep groundwater sources of the Deschutes accounts for the abundant trout that otherwise could not survive in the eastern arid landscape. The habitat is robust enough to support at least twenty-six species of fish in the Deschutes River Basin. Seven species belong to the family Salmonidae, including steelhead/rainbow trout, Chinook salmon, and sockeye salmon. Seven species are non-native and are known to have been introduced (including brook trout, brown trout, and bass).

River fish follow four different life-history patterns:

Anadromous — juvenile fish migrate to the ocean and return as mature fish to spawn (salmon and steelhead trout)

Fluvial — migration between the large river and smaller tributaries (rainbow and bull trout)

Adfluvial — migration to lakes (rainbow and bull trout)

Resident — no migration (rainbow trout, Kokanee sockeye salmon)

The Deschutes River fish spawn in gravel beds. A redd is a nest constructed by the female by arching her body and turning on her side, directing a downward flow of water. The female releases her eggs into this depression, and this is immediately followed by the release of sperm from the male. The female moves upstream and creates another depression, causing gravel to cover the egg-filled redd. Survival and development of the fertilized eggs require an undisturbed redd that has been appropriately constructed to maintain a flow that delivers oxygen and removes metabolic waste. The juvenile fish may emerge in less than sixty days (rainbow trout) or take as long as 160 to 190 days (bull trout).[36]

Anadromous salmon enter the ocean early in life and return to the location where they were hatched after two to three years to spawn in October or November. Fall Chinook return in late summer or fall, and, once hatched, the juvenile fish return to the ocean within a few months after leaving the redd. Spring Chinook, which are smaller than fall Chinook, enter fresh water during the late spring and hold until spawning in the fall, and the juvenile fish remain in the river for over a year before migrating to the ocean.

Spring Chinook salmon used to spawn in the Crooked and Metolius Rivers, and as far upstream as 130 miles from the mouth of the Deschutes. Fall Chinook salmon never passed Sherars Falls, forty-four miles upstream, until fish ladders in the 1920s enabled them to reach the confluence of the Metolius, Deschutes, and Crooked Rivers. Today, spring and fall Chinook salmon do not pass the Regulating Dam, 100 miles upstream. The Deschutes fall Chinook are the only remaining population of a gene group that included the now-extinct inhabitants of the John Day, Umatilla, and Walla Walla Rivers.[37]

Steelhead trout return to their natal sites after one to two years in the ocean. Historically, steelhead reached most of the Crooked River and its tributaries, but today their passage is blocked by the dams, and they are found only below the Regulating Dam. Most steelhead spawn in side channels or along the edges of the main river. Resident rainbow trout are present in great numbers below the dam complex.

Bull trout migrate between the larger rivers and small streams. Once widely distributed in the Deschutes Basin, bull trout are today present in small numbers in the Metolius River, the western tributaries of the lower Deschutes, and the lower Deschutes River. These areas are suitable for bull trout spawning, but optimally they prefer the colder water of high spring-fed streams.

The fish population is affected by water flow (amount and variation), water temperature and chemistry, and river bottom sediment. The key to survival of juvenile fish is the water temperature. As noted, the course of the lower Deschutes River has been remarkably stable; the river channel has changed little during surveys over the last 100 years.[38] About 25 percent of the approximately 150 islands are formed of bedrock and likewise have changed little. The remainder grow and diminish with floods, but their size and location have also changed little over the last century. This stability is believed to be an important factor in the maintenance of the large resident rainbow trout population.

Upstream and downstream passages using fish ladders and fish lifts have not been very successful. Big Falls, 132 miles upstream, was the historical upstream limit for all anadromous fish on the Deschutes River. These falls formed 300,000 to 700,000 years ago in response to lava flows from the Newberry Volcano. They were formed when the river cut through the lava flow and encountered a hard basalt flow. Sherars Falls, forty-four miles upstream, is where the river encounters the hard basalt of the Columbia Flows. Sherars Falls, formed when the river cut into the earth during the last 10,000 to 100,000 years, blocked the upstream movement of large salmon until fish ladders, constructed between the 1920s and 1940s, allowed some passage. Downstream passage of juvenile fish was especially adversely affected by water temperature and current changes caused by the dam complex. The dam complex now prevents upstream passage beyond 100 miles from the mouth of the river, and therefore, spring Chinook salmon and steelhead are produced in the Round Butte Hatchery to provide fish to the upper river.

Downstream flow in the Deschutes River is derived from the deep water exiting from Lake Billy Chinook behind the dams. The Crooked River has the warmest water and fills the upper layer of the water in the reservoir. The Metolius is the coldest, and its denser water moves to the bottom of the reservoir. The Deschutes water lies in the middle. Juvenile steelhead and salmon travel with the prevailing current at the surface.

The intake of the Round Butte Dam is deep, and this, combined with the temperature differences, produces unusual surface currents. The three rivers produce counter currents that do not guide the fish downstream. Beginning in the late 1990s, a plan was developed to reestablish downstream passage of juvenile fish. This plan includes altering the Round Butte Dam so that water will be taken from the surface from fall to June of the following year. Successful mixing of the warmer surface water and colder deep water is required in order to maintain the cooler temperature favored by the fish. Taking water from the surface layer will allow the reservoir to fill from the bottom up with the colder Metolius River water. If successful, the plan will restore salmon, mainly Kokanee, sockeye salmon, in the Metolius River and steelhead to the upper Deschutes River and Crooked River.

AS WE WILL SEE, the problems in the Deschutes River Canyon for railroad construction and the points of conflict between the Hill and Harriman lines were to be determined by the geology of the river. What at first seemed impossible yielded to human ingenuity and drive. Perhaps human folly also played a role because not one railroad, but two railroads would be built along the Deschutes River. But first, to understand and appreciate the Deschutes railroad conflict, it is helpful to learn how a railroad is built.

- CHAPTER THREE -

BUILDING A RAILROAD

A DYNAMIC MIXTURE OF FORCES

Large construction projects inspire awe, respect, and appreciation; the Egyptian Pyramids, the Golden Gate Bridge, and the Empire State Building are good examples. Railroad tracks are often simply regarded as part of the landscape, not meriting a second look. The massive size of a railroad requires imagination because the vastness of a railroad extends horizontally and out of view. It takes a moment of reflection to understand that a railroad reaches out to connect to all corners of the land.

The history of railroads began in England. During the seventeenth century, horse-drawn tramways traveled over oak rails and ties and carried coal from mines to ships.[1] The roadway between the rails was graveled to provide good footing for the horses. As the railways evolved, the oak rails were replaced by iron ones, first cast in 1767 in three-foot lengths. The idea of coupled cars to make a train was born when these first iron rails proved to be too light for large carts or wagons. To keep the cars on the tracks, smooth and level rail tops and flanged wheels were introduced in 1789.[2] Almost immediately, it was recognized that wheels of railroad cars required one-inch flanges on the inside of the wheels to counteract the forces that pushed the cars laterally. Even today, there is about three-fourths inch of clearance between the flange on the wheel and the rail when a car is riding on a straight track. The iron chair (now called a tie plate) was invented in 1797, the piece attached to the tie to which the rail is fastened. Iron joining bars bolted in place to unite the ends of two rails emerged in 1847. Locomotives were introduced in the 1830s, and as engines and cars increased in size and weight, the size and weight of rails had to increase.

There have been several important American contributions to railroad development.[3] The swiveling truck (also called a pilot truck because it refers to the wheels at the front end of an engine that can turn), first used in 1832, allows engines to maneuver sharper curves. Swiveling trucks were also placed at each end of railroad cars. Equalizing levers provided greater stability by placing the greatest weight on three of the driving wheels.[4] Switchbacks, a back and forth zigzag course, allowed the ascent and descent of a steep grade.[5] A contemporary and noteworthy example of switchbacks designed by American engineers is the railroad from Cuzco to Machu Picchu in Peru.

PARTS OF A RAILROAD

A railroad track consists of steel rails held in place by spikes passing through steel tie plates into treated wood ties resting on a ballast that is supported by the land of the right-of-way. Standing on a track or looking at a track leading off to the horizon, it appears heavy and inert. But the optimal function of a railroad track requires a delicate and dynamic balance of weights and forces.

A segment of straight track is called a tangent. There are few tangents along a river because any railroad track that follows a river has to carry trains around curves. The sharpness of a curve is measured in degrees, the angle between two points 100 feet apart on the curve. Increasing degrees of curvature (increasing sharpness of a curve) indicate an increasing angle through which the track turns in 100 feet. The sharper the curve, the more energy it takes for the train to make that curve. Every degree of curve adds the energy requirement needed to climb a 0.04 percent grade.[6] The extra energy required to make a curve is not great, but wear on wheels and rails can be an expensive result.[7]

Railroads try to avoid curves greater than 1° or 2° because greater curvature requires slower speeds. Centrifugal force must be met by raising the outer rail on a curve, usually no greater than six inches, thus tipping the cars inward. Six inches of elevation compensates for the centrifugal force created by a train traveling forty-five miles per hour on a 5° curve.[8] Every curve has an optimal speed. Speeds too slow rapidly wear the flanges on the inner wheels. Speeds too fast excessively stress rails and ties. To minimize damage, a track with many curves must be built so that maximum and minimum speeds are not too far apart. The first part of a curve coming into or out of a tangent is called a "spiral curve of easement." This is the area of gradually increasing curvature and increasing elevation of the outer rail that allows adjustment of the train to the curve or the straight-away. In the effort to avoid great curvature, compromise is necessary when building a railroad in the mountains because greater curvature is usually unavoidable in order to avoid excessive grades.

Rails themselves underwent an evolution of improvements. Originally, the railroad tracks along the Deschutes River used rails that weighed either seventy-five (the Des Chutes Railroad) or ninety (the Oregon Trunk Railway) pounds per yard.[9] Today, rails weigh from 112 to 145 pounds per yard.[10] With increases in rail weight and improvements in track construction, today's rails last as long as seventy years. Rails develop fatigue cracks over time and, in the past, rails were empirically replaced periodically to prevent breakage and derailment. Beginning in 1926, detection cars passing over the rails found flaws using magnetic measurements, and today, detection of defects is further enhanced by the use of ultrasound. In the 1930s, improvements in producing steel rails reduced fatigue cracks to a very low incidence. In recent years, even further improvements have been required because freight cars have become increasingly heavier. Railroad grinding uses a special equipped train to correct irregularities in the rail surface and has further increased the durability and length of service for modern tracks.

For many decades, the standard length of a rail was thirty feet. When the length of railroad cars was extended to forty feet, longer rails could be carried, and the length became thirty-nine feet. In the early railroads, rails were bolted together with joint bars (also called fish plates) allowing a calculated space for heat-induced expansion, the cause of the familiar clickety-clack of a moving train. These joints are less rigid and are subject to greater stress, requiring periodic tightening of the bolts and tamping of the ballast. Today, these problems are eliminated by making rails longer, often welded together.

Because the top of a rail, only 2¼ inches wide, provides a small area of contact with wheels, it is subject to high pressures and stress. By the 1890s, rails initially made of iron gave way to steel (iron with impurities removed in a blast furnace), as increasingly heavy loads required greater strength and durability. In addition, heavier and stronger rails reduced the wear and tear on the steel driving wheels of locomotives.

Rails remain upright, even on curves, mainly because of the downward direction of the wheel's force. The purpose of the spiking is to prevent sideways shifting. Trains also cause rails to creep lengthwise, a movement that is countered by anchors attached to the rails and abutting the ties.

Though it may seem common sense that ties should be constructed of more durable material than wood, it was rapidly discovered that stone did not allow the cushioning of forces necessary to keep a track in line. Rails are not rigid but are depressed ever so slightly under the wheels as they pass over. To compensate for rail distortion, wooden ties must be of sufficient hardness to hold the rails in place, but able to compress and bend in order to transmit the load to the ballast and absorb the impact of the steel wheels. To prevent crushing and cutting of the wood by the rail the steel tie plate spreads the load over a wider area of the tie. To further prevent damage to the wood, railroad ties today are pre-drilled with holes and treated to increase their lifespan to twenty-five to thirty years.[11]

Turnouts divert a train from one track to another, using a switch and a "frog" (the assembly that allows the flanged wheels to cross over the opposite rail). Frogs also allow crossings and crossovers of other tracks.

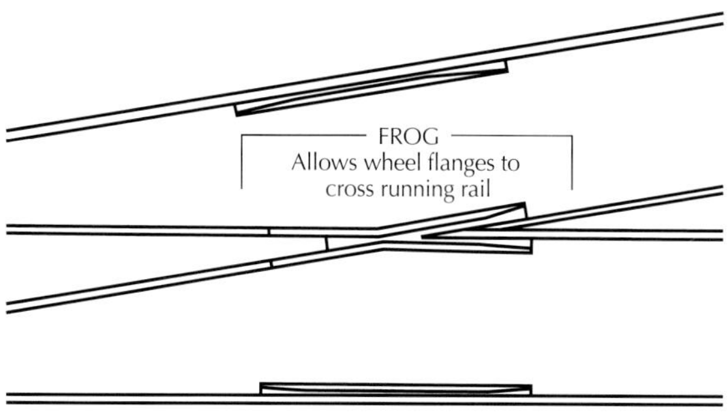

Individual locomotives and railroad cars can be turned on a turntable, but whole trains require the use of a wye. A wye is an extended triangle of tracks with a Y-shaped switch in each corner. Moving forward and backward, trains of any length can be turned. Most locomotives today are bi-directional and do not need to be turned, but the old steam locomotives required turning.

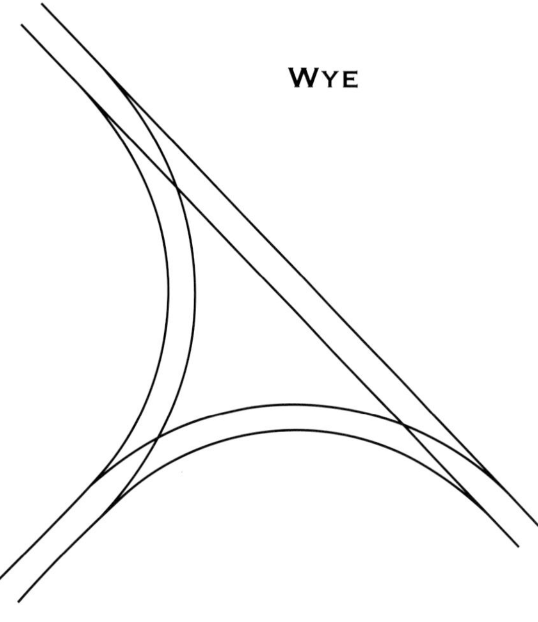

All the components of railroad tracks eventually wear out and must be replaced, a process that is performed as needed without interruption of train travel. In the past, this work was handled by small crews working on small segments of a track. Today, special machines (even laser-controlled machinery to produce accurate alignment and smoothness) and large gangs of workmen combine to renew lengthy sections at a time. Specially instrumented cars generate data for computer analysis to evaluate and correct tracks. The Railroad Safety Act of 1970 gave the Federal Railroad Administration the authority to establish and maintain track quality.[12] Construction, inspections, and speed limits are now established according to minimal federal standards.

"Tractive force" is the force a locomotive generates at its driving wheels to move a load.[13] To prevent slipping, the weight of the locomotive must be several times the tractive force. The adhesion of the wheel for the rail is affected by the rail condition, including the effect of the weather on the rail surface. Locomotives blow dry sand on the rails to increase the coefficient of adhesion, thereby increasing the tractive force. When a single locomotive cannot generate sufficient tractive force to overcome a grade, helper locomotives are added either at the front or at the back to act as pusher engines.

Gradient or grade is the uphill rise in a track; 1 percent grade would be a one-foot rise in 100 feet length, equivalent to 52.8 feet in a mile. The "ruling grade" dictates the limit of weight that can be hauled, determined by the combination of grade and curve resistance on a line that provides the greatest challenge to the locomotive. The power requirements (as measured in horsepower) vary with the weight to be hauled, the weather, quality of the track, grade, and curves.

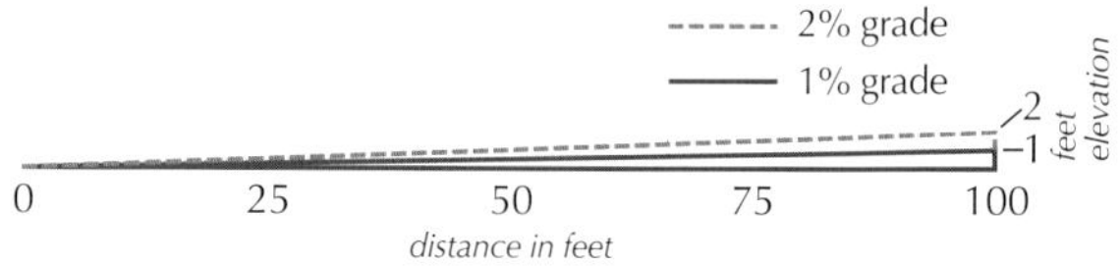

Grade has a major impact; a train powered at 1.5 horsepower per ton can travel sixty miles per hour on a level track, but will slow to twenty-two miles per hour on a 1 percent grade and to ten miles per hour on a 2 percent grade.[14] More importantly, revenue is affected because the tonnage that can be hauled decreases with increasing grade. Railroad engineers aimed to maintain grades less than 2 percent, but the transcontinental lines encountering difficult sections in the mountains were forced to build grades slightly greater than that.

The inventor of the locomotive, Richard Trevithick, died in poverty, but not before he made a key modification in 1804 that allowed the steam locomotive to become powerful.[15] Trevithick directed the steam leaving the engine after it had pushed against the single cylinder, up a smokestack to create the puffing, choo-choo action that drafted air through the firebox. The harder a steam locomotive worked, the greater this action, burning more fuel and making more steam. This mechanism provided power and speed, but was simple enough to be operated by only two men. It was not until 1930 to 1950 that steam locomotives were replaced by diesel engines that now range from 2,500 to 6,000 horsepower.

In the early years of U.S. railroading, cars were coupled by various "link and pin" systems.[16] This simple method required a man to drop a pin in place through the link, a dangerous maneuver which too often resulted in the loss of fingers, hands, and lives. In 1893, the Federal Safety Appliance Act required air brakes and couplers that could work without requiring an individual between two cars. The coupler designed and patented by Eli H. Janney in 1873 was selected to be the standard, and modern couplers continue to be versions of this design.[17] The principle behind the coupler is one of "clasped fingers," with the open fingers on each coupler closing under the open fingers of the other coupler when the cars are pushed together. Uncoupling requires pushing the cars together and removing a locking pin by hand. Slack and impact are moderated by cushioning systems to avoid breakage of cars.

Prior to air brakes, trains were stopped by braking the locomotive and hand-braking the cars individually. In response to a signal whistle from the locomotive, brakemen jumped precariously from car to car to turn brake wheels on the top of each car. George Westinghouse's first patent for an air brake was filed in 1869 when he was only twenty-two years old.[18] He improved his invention in 1872 with a valve system that allowed the setting of brakes with a charge of air and a release of brakes when air was drained. By 1900, air brakes had replaced the mechanical system. The air brake system allows equal pressure to be applied to every car throughout the train, and provides a fail-safe system to stop cars if breakage or loss of pressure occurs.

Railroads require a signaling system to prevent the simultaneous use of a track by two trains. The block system of signaling originated during the Civil War.[19] The interval between a tower with an operator working a semaphore and the next tower was designated a block. When signals were operated by hand, the operator at a signal tower would raise the red danger arm when a train passed and raise the safety signal only when the operator at the next tower informed him that the train had passed. At night, lanterns with red and green lights were used. This hand-powered system was replaced with an automatic block system triggered electrically by the passing trains, a system invented by William Robinson in 1872. The system provides a fail safe because an electrical failure prevents the display of the clear signal.

It is often more economical for a railroad to take a short-cut through a tunnel than it is to take the long way around an obstacle. Until compressed air drills, nitroglycerin, and dynamite were introduced, tunnels were built by hand. "Mucking" referred to the removal of the excavated material using handcarts or small cars on rails. Tunnels were temporarily lined with timber, which was replaced by a permanent lining that could also be made of timber, but was often brick, and later concrete. Tunnel-drilling machinery and dynamite were available by the time railroad tracks were being built along the Deschutes River in Oregon, but costs and the inaccessibility of the location dictated the use of hand power and black powder.

Railroads require the periodic placement of freight-handling facilities, known as freight yards.[20] A freight yard was constructed at Wishram on the north bank of the Columbia River in 1910 to 1912 to serve the connection of the Spokane, Portland & Seattle Railway with the Oregon Trunk up the Deschutes River. The purpose of a yard is to assemble and disassemble trains to provide efficient transportation of carloads of freight to and from diverse origins and destinations. These movements are accomplished by switching cars among parallel tracks using small switching locomotives and incorporating humps in the line to make use of gravity. Over the years, the steps in these procedures that required manual operations were replaced by automatic technology and eventually computerized controls. Today, the largest automated yard is the Union Pacific yard at North Platte, Nebraska, handling 10,000 cars per day.[21]

Building a Railroad

The first step in building a railroad is the choosing of a pathway. Obviously, the ideal path is a straight one. This ideal remains the goal while surmounting the problems of geography and cost. To ensure the best path is chosen, the initial reconnaissance of the country to be traversed is not done by surveyors but by an engineer whose skill by experience and training permits the selection of a route that yields the best grade and curvatures at the most reasonable cost. It was the engineer's responsibility to estimate the nature and size of excavations, bridging and fills, water supply, availability of wood for ties and trestles—all important information to enable accurate estimates of cost. Early engineers traveled on horseback and on foot, using hand instruments that included a barometer, a compass, drawing instruments, and a hand level. The engineer was helped immeasurably by the maps produced by government surveys; in unsurveyed land, the engineer calculated distances with a pedometer or an odometer. Surprisingly, the greatest errors in location were made in flat land or in foothills when an "obvious" route cut short further exploration.[22] The functions of the exploring engineer were incredibly important; thus, the quality of the individual could not be overrated. John F. Stevens, an important man in the Deschutes River story, was one of the best.

A surveyor with his instruments and his assistants then lays out the precise route under supervision of the chief engineer. This party measures not only the route, but the precise elevations of the ground, the high and low water levels of streams, and intersecting private property. In addition, they assessed land to the right and left of the railway for roads and buildings. In the rocky canyon of the Deschutes River, surveyors calculated lines by lowering instruments and assistants from the top of a cliff or by triangulation from opposing sides.[23] Surveyors paid careful attention to the grade and tangents at the ends of curves to ensure stability of a train prior to entering and after leaving a new curve. These measurements culminate in the maps that provide railroad management with the information required to gain government approval and financial backing and that provide the master blueprint for construction. The chief engineer reviews the maps at the completion of each twenty miles of the route. The engineers and surveyors stake out a path at least every 100 feet, marking the roadbed of the railway. The company must secure legal entitlement to a right-of-way 100 feet in width before construction can begin.

A division engineer supervises construction over a length of forty or more miles, and assistant engineers are responsible for four to six miles of roadway. These engineers check the work of the surveying party then stake out the excavations (cuts) and filled embankments (fills) that will be required. A single track requires a filled embankment fourteen feet wide. A cut for a single track is twenty feet wide in earth and sixteen feet wide in rock. Embankments are protected by rip rap, broken stone no less than two feet thick on an earth bank to protect against the action of water. Tunnels and cuts are never level, to allow drainage. The size of culverts and bridges often depends on the experienced judgments of the engineers. The engineers also establish supply points and arrange for the delivery of materials.

A level roadbed requires cutting elevations in the earth and filling low points. Material for fills less than ten feet high is taken from each side of the embankment, a "borrowpit."[24] Deep fills require the hauling of material that is of uniform, dense quality from each end to the encroaching embankments. Fills built with small carts or wagons (the method used by the workers along the Deschutes River) suffer the most from settling; this settling was compensated for by building embankments higher than the required level, the size determined by experience and judgment. The top of the embankment is the full width of the railway roadbed and the bottom sides are established by stakes that determine the slopes. Cuts in the earth can provide material for fills, but often are located in sites that do not allow for practical transport. Blasted rock can be used for embankments, but must be tamped by hand to prevent excessive settlement. The roadbed is outlined by stakes before rails and ballast are placed into position. Grade stakes are placed five feet to each side of the center stake. On curves, the inside of the roadbed is lowered equal to the height of the outside and increases with increasing degrees of curvature. The roadbed is now ready for the laying of track.

There is a sequential series of events in the track-laying process that generates an organized cadence. Construction trains bring track-laying material to the end of already-laid track. Small cars carry tie plates (metal plates under the rail on top of the tie, with extensions on the bottom surface to grip the tie and resist movement), bolts, and spikes to the front where the work gang distributes them along the rails. The men push full cars up the track past freshly emptied cars that have been thrown off the track. Empty cars are put back on the track and reloaded. Men put the rails in place by hand or use special machines for this purpose. Spikers spike the rails sufficiently to temporarily support the construction train, and half-bolt the joints using a variety of two- to four-foot-long rail joints. The construction train moves forward, and the process is repeated until the construction train is emptied of rails. Then the train moves backward and is either reloaded or its empty cars are pushed into a siding to be replaced with full cars. Often, only a sufficient number of ties were placed to bear the construction train, and the rest of the ties were inserted under the rails at a later time. Specialty gangs of men carried out each step: tie unloaders, rail unloaders, distributors of fastening pieces, and spikers. The construction train carried rails, tie plates, bolts, and spikes in the front cars (usually a sufficient number for a day's work). The next set of cars carried ties, and the final set of cars provided food and bunks for the men.

The competing railroads building along the Deschutes River were the last to be constructed without mechanized tools. But, the Oregon Trunk Railway did use the Harris track-laying machine.[25,26] The Des Chutes Railroad used the McCoy track-laying machine, a variant of the Harris machine, invented by L.C. McCoy, the assistant engineer in charge of track laying.[9] "Machine" is a somewhat disingenuous term applied to these contraptions that appeared to be jerry-built from available materials. These machines were powered by donkey engines (so-called because they replaced the work of animals), and they did make the work easier. A donkey engine is a small steam engine of one to four horsepower, invented by John Dolbeer in 1881 to provide power for multiple

Harris track-laying machine

Harris track-laying machine

tasks in logging. Mounted on a railroad car, the donkey engine became a small crane.

A gang of men operated a track-laying machine. The Harris machine consisted of several platform railroad cars with thirty-foot rails spiked to five ties attached to each car. The men stacked ties crosswise on the rear cars of the construction train and delivered them to the site of construction with a small car rolling forward across the rails on the track-laying machine. Each tie car had a movable top that allowed the ties to be dumped crosswise across the roadbed, and each car carried enough ties for two lengths (sixty feet) of rails. On the Deschutes River, this method of laying ties was replaced by a method that utilized a long channel of rollers along the right side of the cars. The men delivered the ties one-by-one just ahead of the newly laid rails.

In contrast to the Harris machine, the track-laying machine designed by McCoy on the Deschutes River was of cheaper construction and required fewer men to operate it. A gang of thirty-five to forty-five men laid a mile of track per day using the McCoy machine. The Harris machine was faster, averaging two miles of track per day, but it required about 100 men to work to its capacity.[27]

The ordinary railroad spike has stood the test of time, changing little since its first use. Its square cross section gives it holding power; its L-shaped head provides just enough room to receive a hit from a railroad

McCoy track-laying machine

maul. A good spiker could drive the six-inch-long spike with three blows. There were about 12,000 spikes per mile of track, and the Deschutes railroads were able to lay one to two miles of track per day. On a straightaway the rails were spiked to three ties, and on a curve, to four ties, allowing the construction train to move forward to repeat the process.

Complete spiking, bolting, and alignment of a track could only be completed once the train moved forward and out of the way. To hold the rails in place, workers used shims placed between rails to provide room for expansion (the size of the opening was determined by the current temperature). The next gang removed the shims after spiking and bolting were completed. Follow-up workers would return to tighten down the nuts a second and even a third time days later.

The Oregon Trunk construction train along the Deschutes River, for each half-day of work, needed five railcars with seventy-six rails per car, five railcars of ties with 270 ties per car, ten more railcars of ties for placement after the tracks were laid, a tool car, a car with telegraph material, and a caboose.[28] The working crew consisted of about 140 men, with

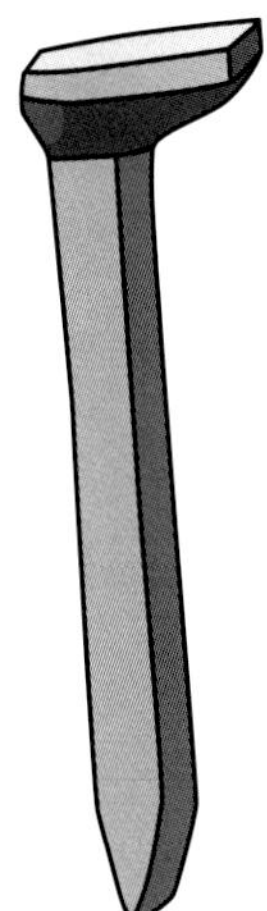

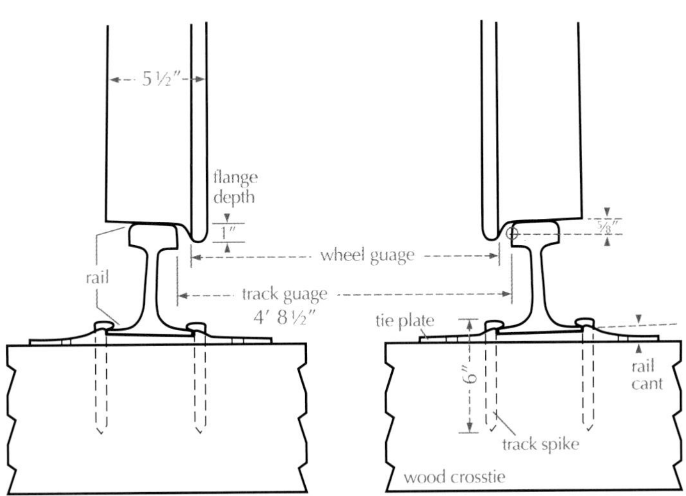

twenty men on the cars handling the ties and rails, thirty-five men working in front of the Harris machine, fourteen men placing ties behind the train, and seventy men finishing the spiking, bolting, lining, and surfacing. Fifteen men placing thirty poles to a mile made sure that a telegraph line kept pace with the track. Last came the carpenters to build depots, platforms, and warehouses. Supporting the working men with food, water, and a place to rest was an important obligation for the foremen and supervisors. Obtaining water and fuel supplies for locomotives was just as important.

The telegraph line was critical in the days before radio communication became available. Stationmasters would receive "orders" by telegraph from a dispatcher. The orders specified at what sites trains traveling in opposite directions would meet and further instructed which train would move to a siding to let the other clear the mainline. Once he had orders, the stationmaster would signal an approaching train with a yellow signal or lantern. As the train slowed, the stationmaster raised a basket containing the orders on a pole. The fireman would lean out of the locomotive cab, grasp the basket, and give the orders to the engineer. This system was operating along the Deschutes River until the mid-1980s.

Ballasting a newly constructed line with earth used a crown design. A crown design means that the earth between the ties was level with the top of the tie between the rails sloping down to the bottom of the tie at each end. This design was essential for good drainage, but care had to be taken to avoid covering ties with dirt, a condition that led to rotting of the wood. The earliest western railroads were built rapidly using this design with dirt, as was much of the Des Chutes Railroad along the Deschutes River.

Ballast has four jobs: holding the ties in place, preventing lateral movement, absorbing and spreading out the load under the ties, and allowing drainage of rainwater. Crushed rock, crushed slag from blast furnaces, or hard lava rock make the best ballast.

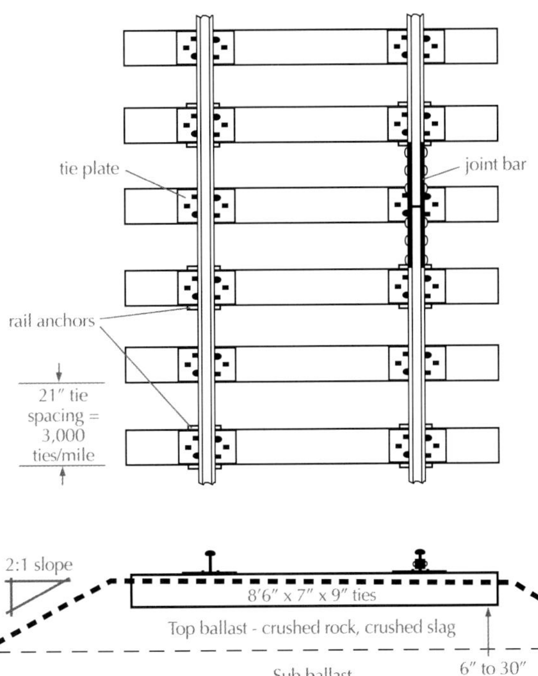

The best ballast is durable, allows drainage, and resists movement.[29] Plain earth, therefore, is inferior to hard stone.

Ties are best placed on approximately a ten-inch layer of stone crushed to a size of one to two inches, often with a layer of larger stones underneath. The ties are then ballasted with stones level with the top of the tie and extending two feet outside of the rails. Sometimes railroads had to make do with what was available. Other materials used for ballasting included slag (cinder from blast furnaces), burnt clay (clay exposed to high heat), gravel, and sand. Along the west bank of the Deschutes River, the Oregon Trunk Railway was ballasted with gravel and burnt clay. The entire Spokane, Portland & Seattle line, including the Oregon Trunk along the Deschutes River, was re-ballasted with crushed stone during World War II.[30]

The wood used for ties often reflected what was available nearby, including oak, pine, cedar, hemlock, and even redwood. A good tie will not split when spiked, will not bend excessively under the pressure of a rail, and will not require frequent replacement (at 3,200 ties per mile of track, this can be a major expense). The average life of an untreated tie is from five years (with softer wood) to twelve years (with hard oak).

Removing the sap and water from wooden ties inhibits fermentation and decay. For the last 150 years, manufacturers have been treating the wood with a preservative, most often with creosote. Coal tar creosote, which is carcinogenic, contains hundreds of chemicals that are highly toxic. Creosote is produced by distilling coal tar, the by-product of high-temperature treatment of coal to make coke or natural gas. Another preserving method (one used by the Union Pacific in building the first transcontinental railroad) is Burnettizing, saturating the wood with zinc chloride. Treating a wooden tie increases its lifespan by two to four times.

In recent years, concrete railroad ties have become more common because of their long durability. This is not the stiff and rigid concrete typical of a road or wall. Modern concrete ties are heavily reinforced with steel and made of a cement-impregnated fiber that yields the needed flexibility. These ties sit on resilient tie pads held in place by heavy steel clips. Concrete ties are expected to last more than fifty years.

Welded rails and concrete ties on the Oregon Trunk at Gateway—2005

A LONG TRAIN is not a simple string of pulled cars. It is a constantly changing dynamic mixture of forces: the effects of curves, the varied weights of the cars, the weather, and the forces of one part of the train differing from another (for example, the end of the train may be going downhill and the head of the train starting uphill). These forces together with the complex integration of engine power, track adhesion, grades to be overcome, and the desired operating speed determine the load that can be hauled by a locomotive. Today the sophisticated engineering analysis of these forces is accomplished rapidly by computer programs. But 100 years ago, it was done with pencil and paper. The railroads along the Deschutes River were built without the aid of powered tools; the locomotives were steam engines, the ties were untreated, and the trains were regulated by telegraph orders delivered by hand.

Building a railroad is complicated, but learning how to build a railroad is easier than understanding the finances. Some railroads, like the two along the Deschutes River, were built with money earned by established lines. However, the first railroads in the West were financed by the land-grant system, used to sell bonds to wealthy capitalists. The first transcontinental railroad was a good example of both the advantages and the abuses of this method.

- CHAPTER FOUR -

THE FIRST TRANSCONTINENTAL RAILROAD

NAIL IT DOWN! GET THE THING BUILT! WE CAN FIX IT LATER

Any consideration of western railroads must begin with the story of the first transcontinental line. It is a story of massive proportions, physical challenges, human achievements, and the power of money. The transcontinental line followed the pattern and blueprint already established for railroad building and financing, but on a new enormous scale that would guide western railroad development. The first transcontinental line had to be largely rebuilt because it was built on one principle: build it fast and worry about the quality later. This standard of construction was the result of the fact that completing the line was a legitimate race between two companies, a consequence of the conditions established by federal legislation to finance the construction.

THE PACIFIC RAILROAD SURVEYS

Military commanders throughout the world understood the need for good topographic maps, and the American Army was no exception. In response to this need, the U.S. Army formed the Corps of Topographical Engineers, which existed from 1813 to 1863.[1] On a federal scale, the Corps was truly small, never exceeding thirty-six officers. The officers of the Corps were trained as engineers at the United States Military Academy at West Point. These heroic soldier-explorers, beginning after Lewis and Clark with John C. Fremont's expedition to the Rocky Mountains in 1842, were the first to chart the vast westernmost parts of the United States. They had multiple obligations: political, military, and scientific. They recorded the West, collecting scientific information on plants and animals, making maps, and writing descriptions of the land.

The location of the first transcontinental railroad was hotly debated in Congress with Southerners pitted against Northerners. After years without a decision, it was hoped that nature would resolve the argument. Congress ordered the Pacific Railroad Surveys with an expectation that a dispassionate, scientific assessment of potential routes would resolve the deadlock between Southerners and Northerners.[2]

In 1853, Congress directed the Secretary of War, Jefferson Davis, to search for a railroad route from the Mississippi River to the Pacific Ocean using the Corps of Topographical Engineers. Four major routes were being advocated: (1) between the forty-seventh and forty-ninth parallels; (2) between the thirty-eighth and thirty-ninth parallels; (3) the thirty-fifth parallel; and (4) the thirty-second parallel. The Corps of Topographical Engineers was charged by Secretary Davis with reconnoitering all routes simultaneously, assessing elevations, grades, and climate.[3] The military personnel were to be accompanied by expert scientists, and a total of $150,000 was appropriated for expenses. Ironically, the first transcontinental railroad would be built along a route different from any of the routes being championed in Congress prior to the Civil War.

Isaac I. Stevens, the new governor of the Washington Territory, was given command of the northern expedition, marching west in 1853 from St. Paul. Relying on the journals of Lewis and Clark, the northern expedition identified several passes across the Rocky Mountains, but missed the best route for a railroad, Marias Pass, found in 1889 by John F. Stevens (Chapter 5). Robert S. Williamson was assigned the task of exploring California, including a path to connect California with the Columbia River, and a route along either the Willamette River or the Deschutes River was suggested. But Jefferson Davis's instructions to the Corps stated that "Along Des Chutes River, the character of the country is such as to render it improbably [sic] that a practicable route can be found."[4] Henry Larcom Abbot, twenty-four years old and less than a year out of West Point, where he was second in his class, reported to Williamson as second in rank. Abbot became commander of the party in the field in Oregon when Williamson became ill.[5,6,7]

Besides the two military men, Abbot and Williamson, the expedition to Oregon included a geologist and botanist, a physician, an engineer, a mathematician, a draftsman, and nineteen men to tend to the equipment and mules.[8] The force was augmented by a military escort of about 100 men. Newberry Crater in Oregon is named after the accompanying geologist, John Strong Newberry, who was professor of geology at the School of Mines, Columbia College in New York.

The expedition entered Oregon from California and separated into two parties; Abbot's party followed the Deschutes River to the north. Reaching the Columbia River, armed with a sextant, barometer, thermometer, and a compass, Abbot explored both upstream and downstream. He visited the military post at The Dalles. Returning up the Deschutes Canyon, the party explored the area around Mount Jefferson and finding no pass, they returned to the Deschutes River, turned to the north and explored around Mount Hood, crossing to the Willamette Valley through Estacada (southwest of Mount Hood).

Abbot marveled at the beauty of the Deschutes Canyon and encountered Indians, miners, and an occasional ranch. At Fort Dalles on September 11, 1855, he wrote his parents and said, "I never conceived of so wild and rough a country. The streams were sunk about 1,000 feet below the general level of the land, & they were bordered by banks almost vertical."[9] Over and over, Abbot concluded that railroad construction would be so expensive it would be "impracticable."[10]

Abbot served with distinction in the Civil War, and after the war, developed a school of engineering for graduates of West Point. He received an honorary degree from Harvard in 1886, retired from the Army in 1895 with the rank of brigadier general, but continued to bring distinction to his life by being instrumental in the routing of the Panama Canal. Abbot was a member of the board appointed by Theodore Roosevelt to select the type of canal, voting against the majority that favored a sea-level canal. His last service came at the age of eighty-four when he visited the Panama Canal to assess the landslides in the Culebra cut. Finally retiring to Cambridge, Massachusetts, Abbot died on October 1, 1927, at the age of ninety-six.

The Pacific Railroad Surveys accumulated large volumes of useful and important information (twelve volumes published between 1855 and 1861), but failed to accomplish the objective assigned by Congress.[5,11] A conclusive route for the first transcontinental railroad was not designated, and the debate over its location continued until after the Civil War, when Northern interests were freed from Southern opposition.

RAILROAD LAND GRANTS

The land extending beyond the original thirteen states was designated as public land by the Constitution, owned and administered by the federal government. The Land Ordinance of 1785 established the system for the surveying and selling of this public land. As a result, land was divided into townships six miles square, with one-mile square sections containing 640 acres, and quarter sections consisting of 160 acres. In 1800, the Harrison Land Law Act allowed the purchase of 320 acres, and four years later, the minimum purchase was lowered to 160 acres. In 1820, the minimum purchase was reduced even further to eighty acres at a price of $1.25 per acre.

In 1841, for the first time, squatters on public land were granted the opportunity for purchase, and in 1854, the Graduation Act allowed people to purchase land that had remained unsold for thirty years for 12.5¢ per acre. In 1862, pressure to provide free land to settlers resulted in the Homestead Act, granting 160 acres to individuals who agreed to live on the land for at least five years. In 1909, the size of the homesteads was increased to 320 acres in several western states, and in 1916, to 640 acres.

To be sure, these federal acts benefited many families, but large ranchers, mining companies, and timber companies benefited the most. This rapidly became a mechanism for entrepreneurs to make money and to gain political favors. In the early years, the major accomplishment for the government was revenue; in later years, political apportionment became dominant.[12]

The original motivation in granting land to railroads was to ensure the building of lines into the West and to provide land for migrating families. Using the land grant system, western railroads received the odd-numbered sections on each side of the railroad right-of-way, at first extending ten miles to each side, and then twenty miles. Soon, the system became a way of doing business, a method to make sure the railroads could afford the price of construction and equipment. It was understood that the railroad corporations would sell this land to meet their expenses and even to make a profit.[13] The land in question was selected by the railroads according to their preferences for routing. The land grant was then requested from Congress or the states. Right-of-ways through Indian reservation land was acquired either by federal decision-making or by negotiated purchases from individual tribes for small sums of money. Railroads went into the real estate business, advertising the sale of their surplus land throughout the U.S. and Europe. More money was earned by transporting the buyers and the goods produced and required by the settlers.

It has been argued that land grants to railroad companies involved land of little value, that only after the building of the railroad did the value increase. It has been further argued that this was an egalitarian method that promoted development. There was another option that could have given the railroads the land they needed. The land could have been leased to the railroads, maintaining a negotiated arrangement that would benefit both the railroads and the public.[14] But the effect of lobbying efforts and stock options provided to legislators cannot be underrated. In addition, western politicians were sensitive to their constituents, who demanded development to expand local wealth and the tax base. Keep in mind that in the years of railroad expansion, there was no large bureaucracy in Washington to regulate the flow of land and money. Thus, railroad entrepreneurs could exert their influence by meeting frequently and personally with key legislators and even the president.

Originally rooted in an objective aimed at increasing farms, the land-act legislation also allowed disposal of public lands for roads, canals, and land for schools and buildings. Ultimately, twice as much public land was transferred without purchase in the land grant system (including the free homestead acts) than was actually sold. The bulk of the grants went to homesteads, amounting to almost 592 million acres. The next largest amount of land was awarded to railroads, about 131 million acres.[15,16] The third largest grants were for education (most of the land was sold by the states to generate revenue, some of which went for schools that became land grant universities).

THE BIG FOUR AND THE CENTRAL PACIFIC RAILROAD

Theodore Dehone Judah was one of the first men, if not the first, with the energy and perseverance to pursue a transcontinental route and to promote the fundamental method to finance the transcontinental railroad: selling public lands to finance it as you go, the land grant method. Judah was born in Bridgeport, Connecticut, in 1826, and graduated from Rensselaer Polytechnic Institute with an engineering degree. He worked on several railroads in the East, then in 1854 crossed Nicaragua and arrived in Sacramento to work for the Sacramento Valley Railroad. Convinced of the importance and value of a transcontinental railroad, Judah, exploring alone except for his horse, confirmed that a route suggested by a Dutch Flat druggist named Daniel W. Strong was the best route (avoiding a grade over 2 percent) over the Sierra Nevada through the Donner Pass and the Truckee River Canyon. Three times, Judah made the slow, arduous trip back to Washington to lobby the federal government for his transcontinental route.

Judah convinced four merchants in Sacramento to finance his definitive survey of a railroad route over Donner Pass. One of the four merchants was Charles Crocker. Born in Troy, New York, in 1822, Crocker went west in the gold rush of 1849, choosing to go overland. Collis P. Huntington was born in Litchfield Hills, Connecticut, in 1821, and he too went to California to seek gold, but he chose to cross Panama. Mark Hopkins, born in upper New York near Lake Ontario in 1814, joined the gold rush, but he came around Cape Horn. All three men made it to Sacramento and decided to be merchants. Hopkins and Huntington opened stores next to each other and then became partners.[17] Leland Stanford was the fourth man in what came to be called "The Big Four." He was also a storekeeper in Sacramento, but soon was involved in politics and eventually, in 1861, he became governor of California.

The Big Four incorporated the Central Pacific Railroad on June 28, 1861, with total assets amounting to about $160,000.[18] Eager to provide supplies to the miners in Nevada, the Big Four also organized the construction of a road over Donner Pass that would prove lucrative until the railroad was operating. With the backing of the Big Four, Judah returned to Washington with complete engineering plans for a Central Pacific Railroad over the Sierra Nevada Mountains and was successful in influencing the congressional passage of what would be known as the Pacific Railroad Bill of 1862.

The Pacific Railroad Bill

The Pacific Railroad Bill of 1862 established the Union Pacific Railroad. The bill directly ordered the creation of a new corporation, and without Southern opposition in the midst of the Civil War, attached "Union" to the name.[19] The bill directed the Union Pacific to build west from Omaha on the Missouri River and the Central Pacific to build east from Sacramento.

The Pacific Railroad Bill also authorized the granting of thirty-year government bonds for every mile of track in place, with the amount increasing from $16,000 per mile in flat lands, to $32,000 in foothills, and $48,000 in the mountains.[20,21] The railroads would have to sell the bonds and repay them with 6 percent interest in thirty years, but any railroad services provided to the government, such as the transportation of mail and troops, could be deducted. The precedent for this method of railroad financing had been established in 1850 with the Illinois Central Railroad.[22] An important component of the Pacific Railroad Bill was the requirement that all ironwork be of American manufacture (an amendment added by Thaddeus Stevens who owned a foundry in Pennsylvania).[23]

The intent of the Pacific Railroad Bill was to allow the railroads to raise money to pay the costs of construction. The initial land grants amounted to ten square miles for each mile of track, distributed in checkerboard fashion (every other square mile on each side of the track). The land grants were in addition to the 400-foot right-of-way. The Pacific Railroad Bill of 1864 doubled the land grants to every other section extending twenty miles on each side of the tracks per mile of track, about 12,800 acres per mile of track.[24,25] And most importantly, the railroads now gained full rights to minerals underneath the land (eventually a source of great wealth for the Union Pacific when oil and coal were discovered under railroad land). In addition, each company could now issue bonds in an amount matching the government bonds, providing another mechanism to raise money. The land itself became useful as collateral when money was borrowed for expansion or development. However, the width of the right-of-way was reduced from 400 to 200 feet. The Pacific Railroad Bill of 1864 also gave the Central Pacific Railroad permission to cross the California border into Nevada.

For many years, track gauges on American railroads ranged from two feet to six feet. Narrow gauge railroads have a distance of three feet between rails. In signing the Pacific Railroad Bill of 1864, President Lincoln approved of Omaha as the starting point for the Union Pacific and set the standard gauge of U.S. tracks at four feet, eight and one-half inches, the distance the English Parliament established as standard gauge in 1846. It is argued that this distance was chosen because it was the distance between the wheels of Roman chariots in England, and a good distance for hitching horses to a carriage or wagon.[26]

In 1866, permission was granted to continue building on the transcontinental railroad until the Central Pacific and the Union Pacific met; hence, there was great competition by the two companies to cover as many miles as possible in order to acquire as much land as they could. The Union Pacific eventually received more than 11 million acres and $27 million in bonds, the Central Pacific, eight million acres and $24 million in bonds.[27] When the bonds were repaid in 1898 and 1899, the government received a good return, about $168 million from a total loan of about $65 million.[28]

The Union Pacific Railroad

The Pacific Railroad Bill created the Union Pacific, with a board of commissioners to organize the company. Thomas Durant, a physician who never practiced medicine, chose the financial world instead and was one of Union Pacific's first stockholders, as was Brigham Young, who was eager to see a railroad come west.[29,30] The Union Pacific was anxious to enroll Grenville Dodge as chief engineer, but he was occupied as a general commanding troops in the Civil War, although many of his activities involved creating and maintaining effective railroad service for the Union. After the war, Dodge served under William T. Sherman, the commanding officer of troops west of the Mississippi, in the Indian campaigns. But it was Dodge who had surveyed the westward route from Omaha through the Platte River Valley and over the mountains, and finally, in 1866, he became the chief engineer of the Union Pacific. His friendships with Lincoln and the Union generals would prove to be a great asset for the Union Pacific.

Durant rapidly became the chief financial officer of the Union Pacific and organized the method of paying for construction and the mechanism for creating huge profits for the investors, a method that was simultaneously used by the Central Pacific (the stock in the Central Pacific's Credit and Finance Company was secretly held by the Big Four and E. B. Crocker, Charles Crocker's brother).[31] Durant purchased a Pennsylvania holding company and renamed it the Crédit Mobilier of America, offering stock to investors. This organization became the Union Pacific's construction company, earning large profits for the investors, who also were the directors and principal owners of the Union Pacific.[32] Thus, no matter the quality and operations of these railroads, large amounts of money would be made in the construction. Eventually, public exposure of the method of financing, along with the fact that many elected officials were given stock, created a great financial scandal in the 1890s, although the Central Pacific escaped scrutiny because its books were lost in a suspicious fire.[33]

This financial system affected construction because money for actual construction was always hard to come by. Any extra money was siphoned off as dividends to the investors in the construction companies. In the beginning, the Central Pacific made its way using loans and the money of the Big Four. But as the track began to accumulate miles, government bonds could be sold, and speed of construction became essential in order to acquire the government-backed bonds. Fueled by the competition for land and government-backed financing, the motto became, "Nail it down! Get the thing built! We can fix it later."[34] Tracks often followed a less desired route, simply to add extra miles and gain more government bonds.

The Race to the Finish

In Sacramento, the Central Pacific began construction on January 8, 1863. Huntington was sent to New York to be the money and supply man, while Crocker sold his store and became the chief engineer and contractor. Hopkins was a financier behind the scenes. Stanford became governor of California. Of course these men became enormously wealthy, and it is easy to view their gains with cynicism, but don't forget they were willing to gamble literally everything they had with no guarantee of success. Judah was left out (probably because he had no significant money to contribute).

Upset over being removed from ownership of a railroad that was his idea and dream, Judah once more traveled to the East Coast. His purpose was to influence the financial arrangements of the Central Pacific (perhaps to persuade wealthy eastern railroad men to purchase the Central Pacific). Stricken with yellow fever during his crossing of Panama, Judah died in New York at age thirty-seven, ironically the same week the Central Pacific laid its first rails running east out of Sacramento.

The Central Pacific had trouble finding and keeping laborers. It was hard work paying only $3 per day plus board. Crocker tried immigrants and attempted to get Confederate prisoners of war and freed slaves. Even when he had a sufficient number of men, they stayed only long enough to accumulate enough money to get to the Nevada silver mines. The Central Pacific continued to struggle to find a workforce, until, finally, Crocker turned to Chinese labor hired locally for about $30 per month. By the end of 1865, there were 7,000 Chinese at work, doing unskilled dangerous work, including grading through old-growth forests and blasting through the rock cliffs and moutainsides.[32] One year later, the Central Pacific employed over 10,000 men, 8,000 of whom were Chinese.

The Union Pacific began construction on December 2, 1863, and had similar difficulties finding laborers, until the project attracted Civil War veterans—young men accustomed to hard work and, importantly, accustomed to discipline. In addition, young immigrants, many of them Irish, came from Europe and all parts of the U.S. to work on the Union Pacific. Grenville Dodge organized the work on a military basis, a method that became very acceptable to the Union Pacific laborers, who were significantly influenced by the war veterans.

The roadbed was graded by hand, with shovels, picks, scrapers, and wheelbarrows. Rock was blasted using hand drills and black powder (potassium nitrate, sulfur, and charcoal—gun powder). The use of nitroglycerin, introduced in the last stages of construction, was avoided because of its instability and tendency to explode unexpectedly. The tracks were ballasted with rock only when it was available from blasting; most of the line was ballasted with dirt and sand that was vulnerable to washouts with storms and floods.

Alfred Nobel began producing dynamite in 1865. Nitroglycerin is an explosive liquid made by treating glycerol with nitric and sulfuric acids. Nobel mixed nitroglycerin with silica, making a paste that was more stable than nitroglycerin and required a blasting cap for detonation. Dynamite was not yet available to replace the black powder used in building the first transcontinental railroad. Nobel's fortune, of course, has funded the Nobel Prizes since 1901.

The Central Pacific had the tougher job, with slow progress through the Sierra Nevada Mountains. It took a year for the Central Pacific to leave Sacramento and reach its major challenge, the summit of the Sierra Nevada. Besides tight curves and gorges, there was the granite rock that had to be tunneled thirteen times. The largest tunnel was the Summit Tunnel at Donner Pass, about 1,700 feet long and 125 feet below the summit. The blasting required hundreds of barrels of black powder. The supplies needed to conquer this mountain terrain occupied up to thirty ships at a time traveling from the East Coast to the West Coast.

Blasting used three-man teams. One man held and rotated the drill, while the other two alternately struck the drill with heavy sledgehammers. The number of finger and arm injuries must have been enormous. The twelve- to eighteen-inch depth of the drilling hole was critical; if not deep enough, the explosion fired out of the hole like a blast out of a cannon, injuring the workers. It took an eight-hour shift to drill four inches in the hardest rock; the process was faster in softer rock.[36] Once drilled, the hole was filled with black powder or nitroglycerin and capped. Nitroglycerin was more powerful, did a better job and avoided the ventilation problem of the smoke produced by black powder, thereby allowing more rapid tunneling. But its use was limited by the constant threat of unexpected detonation. With three or four teams working at the face in shifts around the clock, tunnels progressed at the rate of six to twelve inches every twenty-four hours.[37] Tunneling was started at each end of the tunnel, and amazingly, the sixteen-foot diameter shafts would meet within a few inches of each other.

Both lines had the same supply problem. Everything they needed had to come from the East Coast, by train and wagons for the Union Pacific that had to cross the bridgeless Missouri River, and by ship to Panama, across the isthmus, and by ship to the West Coast for the Central Pacific. There was no wood or water available crossing the plains. Wood for Union Pacific ties and trestles had to be shipped from the East. Soft wood, cottonwood and pine, had to be treated by a huge machine in Omaha called the Burnettizer, dehydrating the wood in a vacuum and replacing the water with a zinc solution.[38] Water was hauled many miles by train and wagons. Pre-fabricated bridges for the Union Pacific came from Chicago.

The Union Pacific had to contend with raiding Indians who intimidated workers and required armed workers and military personnel. The U. S. Indian Peace Commission was created in 1867 by Congress to address the Indian "problem." Negotiations with tribes were placed in the hands of a group of civilian and military leaders who had the authority to meet with chiefs and create treaties. A primary aim of the negotiations was to secure safe conditions along the railroad lines being constructed throughout the West, as well as the trails used by settlers and merchants. Huge amounts of land in the western half of the United States were considered to be unoccupied. Thus American Indians were seen as a problem, but not as occupiers who lived there. The problem was resolved by the creation of the reservation system, concentrating the Indian population in small areas, a procedure made easier for the federal government by the drastic reduction in the Indian population by repeated waves of epidemics. The major treaty with the southern tribes in the West was signed at Medicine Lodge Creek, Kansas, in October 1867, and with the northern tribes at Fort Laramie in 1868.

The Central Pacific had to work in the snow. The winter snows of 1866–1867 were record-making; at the summit the depth averaged eighteen feet.[39] The Chinese worked and lived in tunnels and rooms in the deep snow. Precious time was lost to shoveling snow, and the snow and cold provided another danger as men were lost to avalanches and the freezing cold. Eventually the Central Pacific built snowsheds, covering about forty miles of track, first of wood then later replaced by concrete.

There was a rhythm to the construction, involving thousands of men. First came the surveyors, then the engineers to lay out the exact line. Bridge gangs came next, erecting trestle bridges within a week's time. The fillers and diggers came next, smoothing out hills and gorges. Track layers followed in an orchestrated series of steps. Horses pulled the wagons carrying the rails to the end of the tracks. Five men on each side grasped the iron rails and, at the command of "down," placed rails on the ties at a rate of a rail on each side every thirty seconds.[40,41] The gauger made sure the separation between the rails was exact, the men settled the ties, to be ballasted later, and dropped spikes for the spikers, who, with three strokes for each spike, inserted ten spikes to a rail, and the bolters joined the rails. Following gangs provided the final structure with about 2,250 ties and 9,000 to 10,000 spikes per mile of rail.[42] The track laid was immediately used to bring supplies forward. Emptied trains were shunted to a spur to let the full trains pass by. The construction train and wagons covered a distance of twenty miles.[43] Finally, the carpenters arrived to build depots, repair facilities, and camps.

Construction of the first transcontinental railroad was associated with a phenomenon known as "Hell on Wheels." As the line progressed, makeshift villages would sprout, providing gambling, prostitution, and saloons. Murders were a common occurrence as the young workers spent their hard-earned money and often quarreled. As the track moved, the villages moved with them, often within a day's time, leaving only rubble behind. Some villages grew into towns that persist today, such as Cheyenne, Wyoming.

The American public was captivated by the race, with practically minute-by-minute reports appearing in the daily newspapers. By the end of 1866, the Central Pacific was within twelve miles of the Sierra Nevada summit. They had completed twelve tunnels by early 1867, and the Summit Tunnel (1,660 feet long) by September 1867. The workers grading the roadbed leapfrogged the tunnels and extended the line eastward; surveyors were way ahead in Utah. In 1868, the Central Pacific line connected its two segments running through the Summit Tunnel, and by the summer passengers could travel between Sacramento and Reno.

By the end of 1867, the Union Pacific was 500 miles from Omaha. When both lines entered Utah, the race was truly on. The two companies were energized to capture as many miles as possible to gain the government-backed bonds, but it also became a true competition for the sake of winning.[44] The competition stimulated the crews to set records for miles of track in place in one day—first eight miles by the Union Pacific then ten miles by the Central Pacific.

The competition led to the two companies laying track side-by-side in the last days, while they awaited a federal decision on the definitive meeting point. When the two lines met, the grading crews ignored each other and kept working. More than 200 miles of parallel roadbed was constructed (a waste of about $1 million) as each company strove for the land grants associated with the tracks.[45] When Ulysses S. Grant became president, he ordered the two companies to reach an agreement on the meeting point, which was soon accomplished on April 9, 1869, by Grenville Dodge of the Union Pacific and Collis P. Huntington of the Central Pacific.[46] The meeting

Transcontinental Railroad

– 1869 –

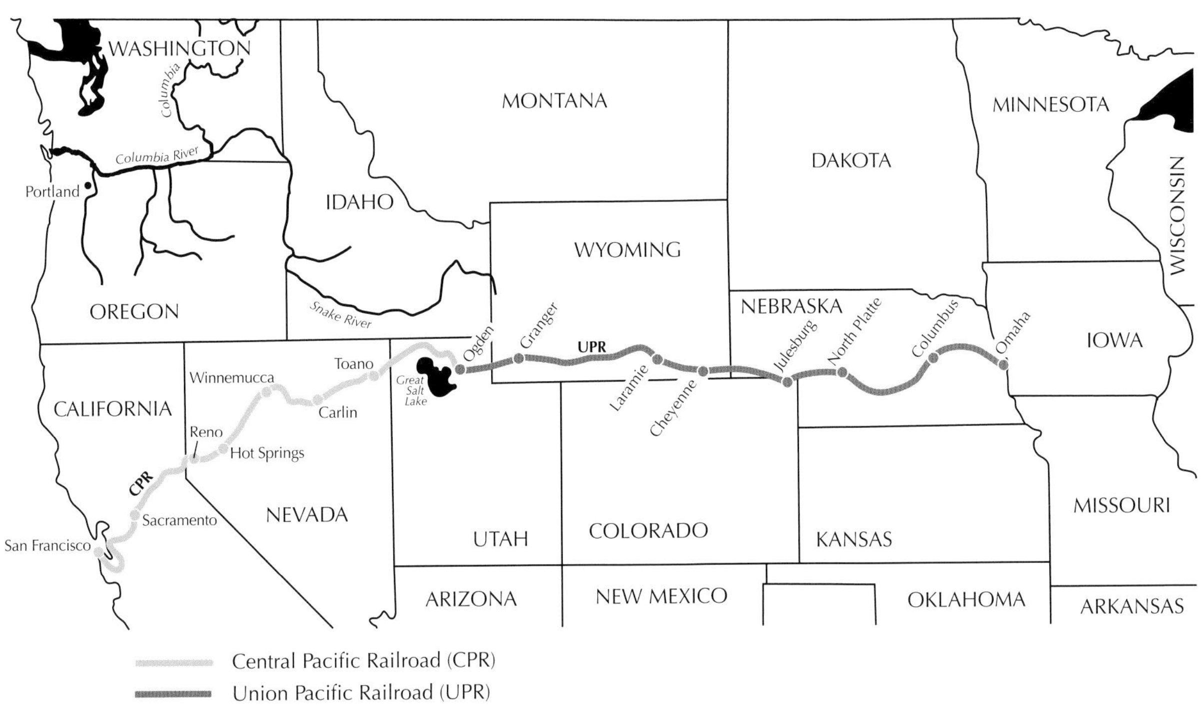

point was determined to be about in the center of the parallel rails at Promontory Point in Utah. At the same time, it was recognized that Promontory Point was unsatisfactory as a junction point and it was agreed that the Central Pacific would purchase the line to Ogden, the permanent junction point. Ogden marked the eastern terminus at 742 miles for the Central Pacific and the western terminus at 1,038 miles for the Union Pacific (abandoning about sixty excess miles of line built by the Central Pacific and 222 miles by the Union Pacific).

THE GOLDEN SPIKE CEREMONY, which celebrated the completion of the first transcontinental railroad, took place on May 10, 1869, at Promontory Summit, about thirty-seven miles north of Promontory Point and fifty-six miles west of Ogden.[47] A friend of Leland Stanford arranged for a jeweler to construct a golden spike, using about $350 worth of gold. Engraved on four sides were aphorisms and the names of the officers of the Central Pacific. The San Francisco News Letter Company donated a second golden spike. Nevada provided a silver spike, and Arizona donated an iron spike with gold on top and silver on the sides. Using a silver plated maul, the four spikes were gently tapped into pre-drilled holes. The spikes were immediately replaced with iron spikes; the fourth iron spike was wired to a telegraph line (when struck with a wired hammer, the message "D-O-N-E" was transmitted along the lines). Today, the first golden spike, the silver maul, and Nevada's silver spike are in the Museum of Stanford University. Arizona's spike is in the New York Metropolitan Museum. The second golden spike disappeared.

Crocker continued to build railroads with the Southern Pacific Railroad and the California and Oregon Railroad from San Francisco to Portland. He died a wealthy man at age sixty-six in 1888. Huntington remained active in railroading with the Southern Pacific, and Stanford became a U.S. senator.

Hopkins remained the treasurer of the Central Pacific until his death in 1878. Forced off the board of the Union Pacific in 1869, Durant died in 1885, neither rich nor famous. Dodge also continued to work on railroads, his last being the Cuba Railroad. He died a wealthy man in Council Bluffs, Iowa, on January 3, 1916, at age eighty-five.

NO ONE CAN dispute the place of railroads in American history. The railroads brought immigrants to the land, carried commerce to points of need and distant ports, and created the linkage necessary for a national economy. The railroads have been big business, making many individuals incredibly wealthy, providing work for thousands, enduring the lifecycle of business: growth and shrinkage, profits and bankruptcy. The size and growth of railroads led to government regulation, the emergence of labor unions, and the development of corporate programs like safety, retirement, and insurance.

Railroads created the system of time we use today. Prior to railroads, travel was slow and at the mercy of the weather and seasons. Railroad travel was fast regardless of weather and season and, when every geographical area in the country established time by the position of the sun, trains had to travel through hundreds of local times. Keeping two trains from using the same piece of track at the same time was just one of the difficulties. In 1883, the railroads instituted "standard" times, creating the four time zones in each of which every clock reads the same. Although this was not officially established by the U.S. government until 1918, the country quickly adopted railroad time zones to regulate commerce and social behavior.

Railroads gave us the well-known phrase, the real McCoy.[48] In 1972, Elijah McCoy, a black American, invented a lubricant for the moving parts of a locomotive. The lubricant was so superior that soon railroad men demanded "the real McCoy."

In railroad history, there are thousands of human stories, of triumphs, and tragedies. The names of the leaders are recorded in our histories, but their wealth and stature depended on the contributions of countless workers who are the real heroes of the railroads. We will meet some of those workers, men who worked on the Deschutes railroads and brought to reality the plans of the two competing moguls, James J. Hill and Edward H. Harriman.

- CHAPTER FIVE -

The Protagonists

The Bear and the Terrier

James J. Hill and Edward H. Harriman have been labeled in American history as moguls, giants, tycoons, entrepreneurs, and capitalists. These two men rescued American railroads in the nineteenth century and prepared them for the twentieth century. They became massively wealthy in the process, but totally within the legal and social boundaries of American society at that time. The competition between Hill and Harriman was a major driving force in improving American railroads. The last major confrontation between the two men was the Deschutes River Railroad War.

The Bear: James Jerome Hill

James J. Hill shared many characteristics with Edward H. Harriman. They were both short, blunt and direct, and hard-working men who took little time off, but who were still highly devoted to their families. They dominated their respective business operations, each man committed to strategies that produced better-built railroads using the best equipment available and delivering greater volumes of freight at lower cost.

Hill was always neatly and fashionably dressed, initially in a black Prince Albert coat then later in tailored, dark suits. In Hill's later years, the adjective "grizzled" was often attached to his description; he did give the impression of a bear with his loud voice, thick body on short legs, topped with a large, bald head, and a rather wild, untrimmed beard that became progressively whiter after age fifty.

James J. Hill

Hill was a fisherman. Fishing for Atlantic salmon every June became a treasured and protected time in his life. In 1899, he purchased the exclusive rights to fish the St. John River in Quebec. Hill built a large, seven-bedroom lodge on the river, and his financial and railroad friends were his companions in fishing accomplishments that counted salmon by the hundreds.[1]

Hill and Harriman were dedicated to the constant growth and improvement of their railroads. The railroad line that stood still withered. If there is a motto they would have shared, it is this: The shortest, the straightest, and the best line. Both men directly supervised every aspect of the construction, building, and improvement of their railroads. Both men had difficulty delegating authority, something each endured only when absolutely necessary. Both men were allied with giants in the banking world who became prominent railroad financiers—Hill with J.P. Morgan and Harriman with Jay Gould.

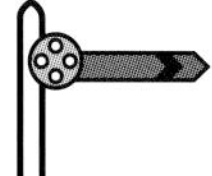

JAMES J. HILL married Mary Theresa Mehegan, who was born in New York City on July 1, 1846, into a Catholic family who migrated to Minnesota in 1850. In 1864, James J. Hill, who was eight years older, was engaged to Mehegan, and three years later, they married. Hill weighed 135 pounds on his wedding day, but soon grew to a stocky figure of 166 pounds that did not project an overweight image, rather one of strength.[2] The family grew steadily, eventually gaining nine children over the next twenty years.

One daughter, Mamie, married an unrelated Hill, Samuel Hill, a lawyer in Minneapolis who became wealthy working for James J. Hill. In 1889, the couple provided James J. Hill's first grandchild, Mary. Sam and Mamie eventually lived apart, Mamie in Washington, D.C., and Sam in Seattle.[3] Sam Hill established Maryhill, a museum of art named after his daughter, Mary, in a castle-like chateau high on the north bank of the Columbia River about six miles east of the Deschutes River. The 6,000 acres purchased in 1907 and the concrete and steel mansion were intended to be Sam Hill's estate, but the site was converted to a museum even before Hill's death in 1931. The site also contains Maryhill's Stonehenge (a full scale replica of England's Stonehenge), a monument built by Sam Hill to local soldiers who lost their lives in World War I.

The large James J. Hill family functioned very well in large St. Paul mansions. The largest mansion, and Hill's home for the rest of his life, was completed in 1891; it contained thirteen bathrooms, twenty-two fireplaces, 36,000 square feet and an army of servants. Hill always had sufficient funds to provide private education, interesting family trips, and family vacations. Although Hill himself was not very religious, Mary Hill conducted a strict Roman Catholic household.

JAMES J. HILL was born September 16, 1838, in the Village of Rockwood, an area northwest of Toronto in Ontario, founded by Quakers in the mid-1830s. The son of poor immigrant farmers from northern Ireland, Hill wanted to be a physician. His future plans were altered following two major events: the loss of sight in his right eye at the age of nine (the snap of a bow propelled an arrow backward into his eye and injured the optic nerve, although the eyeball and its movement were preserved), and the death of his father. His father died in 1852, four years after the family left their farm and opened an inn and tavern, leaving no money to pay for an education. In retrospect, it is unlikely that the eye injury would have hindered a medical education and practice, as Hill never demonstrated any evidence of a visual constraint in the remainder of his life.[4]

Hill clerked in Rockwood stores during his teenage years until age eighteen, when having saved $600, he traveled by train to New York then visited the eastern seaboard cities.[5] He then went to St. Paul, Minnesota. St. Paul, located at the head of navigation on the Mississippi River, was the starting point in the mid-1850s for travel into the Pacific Northwest and the Far East. Hill knew that neighbors in Rockwood had acquired good paying jobs in St. Paul. It was still a frontier town and in the era of the steamboat. Hill's first job was as an agent for a steamboat company. The railroad had not yet reached out from Chicago.

St. Paul became a center for the storage, milling, and shipping of flour. With his administrative skills and love of hard work, Hill came to understand the economics of farming and transportation, as well as the importance of railroad transportation in marrying the two. Working for the Northwest Packet Company, Hill acquired the knowledge and money to form his own company in 1866, providing a storage depot to link the transport of goods from river boats to the railroad.

Hill's next success was based on fuel, first the transport of wood, then coal as a source of fuel and energy. Hill formed the Northwestern Fuel Company, which yielded profits that allowed Hill to fully enter the railroad business. With a select group of partners, he purchased in 1877 the bankrupt St. Paul & Pacific Railroad. He and his associates extended this line north from St. Paul to Winnipeg, Canada. In acquiring this railroad, Hill's organization also acquired its land grants, a source of further profits as the land was sold to immigrants settling in northern Minnesota. This railroad was a substantial purchase requiring over $5 million and involving about 2.6 million acres of land (which soon sold for $13 million). The method of purchase became the blueprint for railroad expansion in the next decades: a little bit of cash, investments from foreign capitalists, and the selling of bonds. Hill's railroad swiftly returned a handsome profit from its freight and passenger traffic, and in 1879 it was reorganized as the St. Paul, Minneapolis, & Manitoba Railway Company (often called the Manitoba for short), with Hill as general manager and then president. By 1880, Hill was a wealthy American citizen, although his business strategy often found him in debt and short of cash.

Until 1883, Hill was very involved in aiding the Canadian Pacific Railway to reach Vancouver, and in so doing, he realized that the future required his Manitoba line to have its own road to the Pacific. By 1880, the Union Pacific was reaching from its main line in Utah into Montana, and the Northern Pacific was advancing through the southern part of Montana. The Northern Pacific, as did the Union Pacific, reached the West Coast in 1883 by joining to the Oregon Railway & Navigation Company, the line developed by Henry Villard. The Union Pacific's extension to the Northwest with its own junction with the Oregon Railway & Navigation Company was called the Oregon Short Line. The Union Pacific owned a large interest in the Oregon Railway & Navigation Company, and thus, this was the first true transcontinental line that was wholly owned by the Union Pacific.

The next decade saw a rapid expansion in railroads, with construction reaching to all parts of the land, mostly as the uncoordinated result of competition among multiple small companies. A major depression beginning in 1893 would plunge these lines into financial crisis, out of which Hill and Harriman would emerge as the dominant figures.

John F. Stevens and Hill's Route to the Pacific

Hill concluded that a better route to the Pacific than had been previously built would traverse northern Montana. A major obstacle to the construction of Hill's railroad to the Pacific was that it required crossing of multiple Indian reservations. Hill was counting on the eventual federal granting of a right-of-way. Indeed, in 1887, such legislation was passed and signed by President Cleveland. With this obstacle overcome, the Manitoba road began laying track, and by mid-1888 in Hill's fiftieth year, rail traffic could reach the Pacific by traveling the Manitoba; but doing so required the use of a connection with the Union Pacific in Butte, Montana. To deliver goods to the east, the Manitoba went into the steamship business from its railroad terminals on Lake Superior to Buffalo, New York, on Lake Ontario.

The story of the Hill lines reaching the Pacific Ocean features a remarkable man, John Frank Stevens, a self-educated engineer who established the Great Northern route through the Rocky Mountain and Cascade ranges. Stevens was born in Maine in 1853, and died ninety years later in North Carolina on June 2, 1943. His engineering career began at age twenty-one, when he was employed by the Minneapolis City Engineer's office. In 1882, he was hired as an engineer by the construction contractor of the Canadian Pacific Railway. On Januray 1, 1895, Stevens became the chief engineer of the Great Northern, with offices in St. Paul. Eight years later he resigned to become chief engineer and later vice-president of the Rock Island Railroad. From 1905 to 1907, Stevens worked in Panama as chief engineer of the Isthmian Canal Commission.

Stevens was instrumental in recognizing that a sea-level canal in Panama was impractical. An international panel of European and American engineers had recommended a sea-level canal despite the problems of deep cuts, flooding rivers at the times of torrential rains, and the tides of two oceans. After two

GREAT NORTHERN RAILWAY

Great Northern Railway

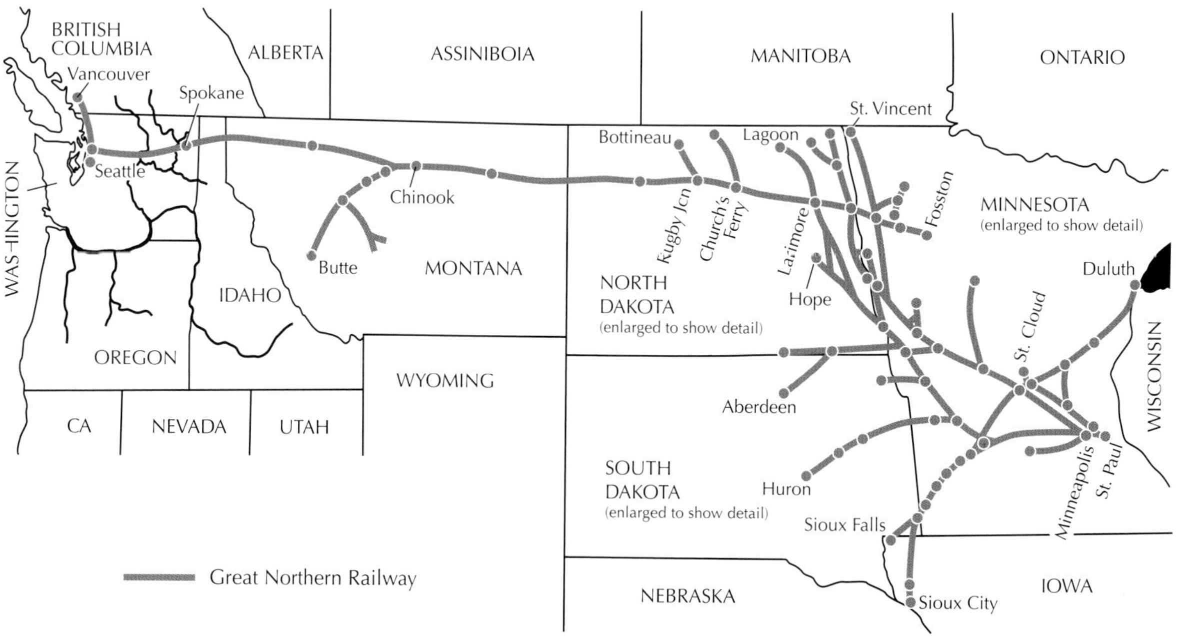

days of testimony before a Senate committee, a lock-type canal was narrowly approved, based on Stevens' recommendations.[6] Stevens was responsible for the initial organization of the canal work, the care of the workers, and the sanitation measures needed to eliminate yellow fever. George W. Goethals, Stevens' successor as Chief Engineer of the Panama Canal, said this of his predecessor: "Frankly, it is a fact, that Mr. Stevens devised, designed and made provisions for practically every contingency connected with the construction and subsequent operation of that stupendous project. …My effort was to see that the project, as conceived, designed, laid out, and duly recorded, was carried out accordingly."[7]

After leaving Panama, Stevens became a vice-president of the New York, New Haven and Hartford Railroad Company until he rejoined James J. Hill to work in Oregon where he was in charge of building the Oregon Trunk Railway along the Deschutes River. In 1911, Stevens went out on his own, establishing a private practice in New York as a consultant for engineering projects. During World War I, Stevens was dispatched by the government to Russia to operate the railroads to keep Russia in the war. After the Russian Revolution, he became president of the board that operated the Trans-Siberian and Chinese Eastern railways.

But in the summer of 1882, Stevens was supervising Canadian railroad construction over 125 miles of line at a time, driving thirty miles to and fro and learning to sleep in a bouncing buckboard. Despite all this, Stevens did find time to experience the excellent trout fishing in the Bow River.[8]

In addition to his intrinsic engineering common sense, Stevens was a very tough man. Late in the fall of 1883, while working for the Canadian Pacific, he was surveying in Kicking Horse Canyon, trapped by deep snow. Trying to escape to the east, he found the trail impassable; all fifteen pack horses were lost, slipping off the trail into the canyon. Returning westward to his camp, Stevens and one volunteer set out up an unknown creek to an eastern pass to seek help. Snowshoeing across the pass with little food in below-zero weather, Stevens encountered a relief party that ultimately went on to bring out the rest of Stevens' men. Returning home, Stevens discovered that family and friends had thought he was lost.[9]

Later that same year, Stevens returned to find a route for the Canadian Pacific Railroad across the Columbia River through the mountains in British

Columbia. Traveling by train and boat, Stevens found himself at the foot of the Gold Mountain Range without the promised pack animals. His party of about twenty-five men hoisted their supplies on their backs and began to cut a path to the west, producing a trail over the mountains to the Columbia River. "I can see myself yet, with a tumpline across my forehead toiling up a muddy trail carrying a pack made up of a grindstone and a sack of flour, and trying at the same time to absorb what I could of the topography of the country through which we were traveling. ...It was a hard trip, some of it through deep snow, over immense logs and through swamps which we had to corduroy before we could walk across them."[10] Later, the Canadian government built a wagon road along this trail. Stevens' salary in those days was approximately $125 per month.[11]

In 1889, Elbridge H. Beckler was appointed chief engineer for the extension of Hill's railroad, now known as the Great Northern, to the Pacific Ocean. Stevens was then unknown to James J. Hill, and it was Beckler who invited Stevens to Montana, requesting that he find the best route for the Great Northern through the Rocky Mountains.[12] At that time, the Northern Pacific crossed the Rocky Mountains through Mullan Pass, just west of Helena, Montana. The high point of the crossing was a tunnel at 5,563 feet elevation, and the grades were 1.9 percent eastbound and 2.2 percent westbound. The aim of the Great Northern was to reach the Kootenai River over a lower elevation requiring less of a gradient, but the only known route was a complex one, placed too far south, adding 100 miles and severe gradients to the east-west line. It was common knowledge that the Blackfeet and Kalispell Indians talked of a pass directly to the west, at the head of one of the streams flowing into the Marias River (named by Meriwether Lewis in 1805 after his cousin, Maria Wood). Flathead and Kootenai Indians followed this route, crossing from the west to hunt buffalo in Blackfeet country. However, violent retaliations by the Blackfeet discouraged use of the pass, and both Indians and white mountain men began to use safer passes to the north and south.[13] Eventually the pass was overgrown and lost to memory. Merriweather Lewis tried but failed to find the pass on his way back from Oregon in 1806.

A federal exploration party, part of the federal Pacific Railroad Survey, led by Isaac I. Stevens, governor of the Washington Territory, was seeking a route for a railroad to the West Coast in 1853–1854. W. W. Tinkham, a member of this party, accompanied only by a Flathead guide, explored a path through the Rocky Mountains and called it Marias Pass.[13] Tinkham had mistakenly followed another tributary (the Cut Bank) of the Marias River. Tinkham's pass, now known as Cut Bank Pass, was high, above the summer snow line (7,600 feet elevation), and would require a 2.5-mile-long tunnel that would still leave a steep descent on the western side.[14] Hill studied the twelve volumes and maps of the Pacific Survey; he knew there long had been talk of a pass at a lower altitude, and by mail he urged John F. Stevens to find it.

Stevens set out from the military post at Fort Assinniboine, and traveled by covered wagon 180 miles to the Blackfeet Indian Agency.[15] At the Blackfeet Agency, Stevens convinced a Flathead Indian, who said he had traveled through the pass to accompany him.[16,17] Pushing west, they followed Two Medicine Creek, until two- to four-feet-deep snow forced them to send the mule team back and to use their homemade snowshoes. It was soon apparent to Stevens that his Indian companion had never been very far west of the Agency. Reaching high ground on December 11, 1889, Stevens left the Indian in camp with a fire and went on alone. Snowshoeing another six miles, he crossed the Continental Divide. To be sure, he pressed onward until he was certain that the stream he was following, Bear Creek, was flowing westward. By the time he returned to the summit, it was dark. Unable to build a fire, he tramped back and forth in a 100-yard track all night to keep from freezing.[16] The next morning, he found the Indian still in camp, nearly frozen in front of the cold ashes of the fire. Stevens revived the Indian, whose name, Coonsah, has been given to a creek and a false summit just before the true summit found by Stevens. Back at the Agency, Stevens discovered the temperature was 36° below zero (at an elevation of 1,600 feet, causing him to estimate that it was 40° below zero at the summit).[18]

The Great Northern would travel through the Marias Pass without a tunnel at an elevation of 5,214 feet, shortening the overall distance to the west by

100 miles and achieving a 1 percent grade (increase in height per 100 feet of track) westbound and 1.8 percent eastbound. Although the pass does not bear his name, the canyon that leads westward from the pass is named the John F. Stevens Canyon.[19] Beside the track, where Stevens tramped back and forth through the night to stay alive, there stands his statue, dedicated on July 21, 1925. At the dedication of this statue, Stevens spoke highly of James J. Hill and the Great Northern Railway:

> For clearness and tenacity of purpose, for vision and accuracy of judgment, he far surpassed any other man whom it has been my fortune to know during an active business life of more than fifty years, and I have come in contact with many whom the world calls great. ...It is a common truism that corporations have no souls. But I think that you will all agree with me that one corporation has a soul, and that it is wonderfully shown here today, and that besides soul, this one has lasting memory. I have neither the brain nor the tongue to give expression to the appreciation for what the Great Northern Railway has done for me. If I should attempt to do so, my feelings would drown my feeble words. I shall go down from this spot with a deeper appreciation of human brotherhood, and the feeling that a life of work and the knowledge that such work carries its own reward, and that I can count as not the least among my friends those whom it has been my lot to serve, in the years which are so rapidly receding.[20]

STEVENS' NEXT TASK was to find the best route through the state of Washington from Spokane to Puget Sound. The major challenge was to choose the best crossing over the Cascade Range. Stevens personally explored every inch of the territory in the summer of 1890, and discovered Stevens Pass, at the head of two creeks, one flowing into the Wenatchee River to the east, and on the other side of the pass, the other flowing into the Snohomish River. The Great Northern initially crossed Stevens Pass using multiple switchbacks with 4 percent grades. Stevens chose to build switchbacks only because he knew that they could be eliminated later with a short tunnel. The passage through the Cascades demanded a tunnel but racing against time, Hill approved the building of a switchback crossing. Seven years later, when Stevens was chief engineer, the Great Northern built a 2.5-mile-long tunnel at an elevation of 3,348 feet.[21] And even later, following another recommendation by Stevens, this tunnel was replaced by a 7.7-mile-long tunnel that opened in 1929.

Amazingly, Stevens first met James J. Hill face-to-face when Hill came west to personally examine the switchback route over the Cascade Range. Hill was so impressed with Stevens' decisions that he immediately raised his salary.[22] In May 1902, Stevens became general manager of the Great Northern.

Pushed to accept positions of high management dealing with operations, Stevens repeatedly declined. He knew that his training and temperament made him unfit for such positions, but he had no trouble running a dozen or more engineering projects simultaneously.[22] After his experience in Panama, Stevens supervised the modernization of the New Haven Railroad until Hill sent him to Oregon to begin the confrontation along the Deschutes River.

The building of the Great Northern Railway from Montana through the Rocky Mountains and Cascade Mountains was a massive project involving thousands of workers, but it was completed without government funding. Specifically, the line was built without government land grants, contrasting with the 40 million acres granted for the building of the Northern Pacific.[23] The 900-mile length was completed in three years, just in time for the economic depression of the 1890s. The last spike was driven on January 6, 1893, linking the eastern and western segments at a site that today is the west opening of the Cascade Tunnel at Stevens Pass. Hill's devotion to the best line over the shortest route never abated. After the depression of the 1890s, the Great Northern continued to make improvements, providing such upgrades as replacing wooden bridges and trestles with steel structures.

The Terrier: Edward Henry Harriman

Edward H. Harriman

Edward H. Harriman made his impact on American railroads in the short decade that began after his fiftieth birthday. Together with Hill, he made major contributions to the modernization of the railroad industry, bringing about changes in the tracks and equipment, efficiency in business operations, and even improvements in safety records.

If Hill resembled a bear, Harriman reminded one of a Jack Russell terrier: small, hyperactive, and tough. A short (5 feet, 4 inches), intense, unremarkable-looking man, whose mind worked at a feverish speed, Harriman appeared ruthless and abrasive when he repeatedly failed to explain his thinking to those slower and duller. His small stature contained a strong athleticism that he combined with an aggressiveness that made him combative and impatient. But in his private life, he was kind, considerate, and devoted to family and friends. He was called Henry by his family, but at work he was called Ed or Ned and later by his initials, a deliberate policy to separate family and work. His appearance in his later years was most marked by a prominent forehead, topped by sparse hair combed to the side. His thick, wire spectacles perched above his second major feature, a bushy mustache that drooped shaggily over his lip. Although he looked like a lowly clerk, he was an energetic and competitive athlete who enjoyed outdoor activities. He learned how to box, shoot a rifle, and play billiards. He was a gymnast, and he loved horses and camping in the woods. At the same time, he frequently participated in the New York social scene, belonging to several fashionable clubs. He was a regular at formal dinners. In business, society, and in play, Harriman was the small underdog who emerged victorious by the grit of his determination, energy, and intellect.

Harriman was born February 25, 1848, on Long Island to Orlando and Cornelia Harriman, an upperclass couple who struggled to make ends meet. Harriman began his business career as a broker, quickly establishing a reputation for cautious reliability. He started as an office boy at age fourteen with a Wall Street firm. At the age of twenty-two, Harriman borrowed money from his uncle and purchased a membership on the New York Stock Exchange for approximately $5,000. The aristocratic contacts he made through his family provided good clients, wealthy men who valued an honest, reliable, and energetic broker. Harriman was conservative and made his money on commissions from the speculations of others.

Harriman found a match in his intellect, his upperclass background, his business interests, and his outside passions in Mary Williamson Averell, three years younger. They were married September 10, 1879. Mary was the daughter of a banker and businessman in Ogdensburg, a small town in northern New York on the banks of the St. Lawrence River. Her father was also the president of the Ogdensburg & Lake Champlain Railroad.

Harriman and his wife had two sons. W. Averell Harriman, their first son, was president of the Union Pacific from 1920 to 1946 and was the acclaimed diplomat of the twentieth century who brought honor to the family name with a distinguished career in business and government service. Roland Harriman, their second son, was a successful banker. After her husband's death, Mary Harriman inherited and controlled Harriman's estate, valued at $70 to $100 million (twenty to twenty-five times that amount in 2006 dollars). Brought up in an environment of charitable work, she personally administered the charitable activities funded by the Harriman estate until her death in 1932.

By 1885, Harriman was ready for another project. In the midst of great demand and expansion, railroads in the 1880s attracted the attention of American venture capitalists. Railroad investments were a major component of New York Stock Exchange activity, and Harriman had no choice but to learn about railroad finances. His father-in-law, William Averell, provided first-hand experience by appointing Harriman to the board of his small, 118-mile railroad, the Ogdensburg & Lake Champlain. Harriman joined other socially prominent capitalists who were interested in railroad investing (including Stuyvesant Fish) on this board. He was instrumental in restructuring the line's finances, but soon Harriman left the board to join an effort that acquired another short line running between Oswego and Rochester, New York.[24] Taking advantage of the competition between the Pennsylvania Railroad and the New York Central, Harriman sold the line after less than a year to the Pennsylvania Railroad for a handsome profit. Next, Harriman's brokerage company acquired the bond business for the Illinois Central, the first land-grant railroad and the only major north-south line at that time. When the Illinois Central became embroiled in management difficulties under the leadership of Harriman's old friend, Stuyvesant Fish, Harriman was recruited and appointed to the board of directors.

DURING THE 1890s, railroads were in trouble. There was a profound nation-wide recession that lasted until 1897. There were many causes for the downturn in the economy. Railroad expansion suddenly ceased and entered a period of contraction. The national trade balance had abruptly changed with an excess of imports. Agriculture accounted for a decreasing share of the national wealth and was experiencing a decline in crop prices and thus decreasing purchasing power for farmers. Foreign investments were being withdrawn from the U.S. because of European banking problems, and the public lost confidence in American banks and the U.S. Treasury's gold standard. By the end of 1893, banks and businesses were closing. Massive unemployment generated significant labor unrest throughout the country. The downturn in the economy and intense competition lowered railroad revenues. Overbuilding of railroads was often followed by bankruptcy.

Money for improvements and expansion of railroads now came from issuing bonds at lower and lower rates. Harriman became adept and successful in this process for the Illinois Central. He also became active in bargaining for and acquiring new lines for expansion. Harriman was in the right place at the right time to usher in a new era in railroading, highlighted by the emergence of giant, more efficient systems. Harriman saw the need for, and became forceful and skillful in the promotion of, the development of the best route and physical condition of tracks to allow the hauling of bigger loads at lower cost.

In the 1890s, Harriman turned to the West and the Union Pacific Railroad. The Union Pacific was the larger part of the first transcontinental railroad, but by 1896 it was in receivership. Its branch lines had gradually been lost to foreclosure. Because it was built under a federal charter, Congress was in charge of its future, but the main line awaited financial reorganization, a job that would require a giant in the field. The government insisted on a cash sale, rejecting federal funding. J. P. Morgan was not interested, but Kuhn, Loeb & Company, under the leadership of Jacob H. Schiff, proposed a financial reorganization syndicate, that ultimately included Harriman as a member of the supervising executive committee. For a brief period, Jacob Schiff, the director of Kuhn, Leob & Company, was an important financial backer of Hill, but although their

friendship was maintained, Schiff, in 1897, began backing Harriman. Harriman himself invested several million dollars,[25] and on November 1, 1897, the Union Pacific was purchased and free of federal government involvement. Harriman immersed himself in reorganizing the Union Pacific, earning his appointment, at age fifty, as chairman of the executive committee on May 23, 1898.

At this point in time, James J. Hill observed, "Now, who the hell is Harriman?"[26]

The Union Pacific in 1898 was a typical western railroad that had been built cheaply to handle light traffic, with "light rails, little or no ballast, heavy grades over mountain ranges, and light equipment."[27] After touring the line, Harriman became convinced that heavy investment in improvements was necessary. He wanted straighter lines with heavier rails, lower grades, new bridges, and new depots to handle longer trains with heavier and larger cars. This was accomplished by an investment of $160 million and prodigious feats of construction with thousands of workers in dozens of bleak and difficult locations over the next ten years.[28]

UNION PACIFIC TO THE NORTHWEST
– 1900 –

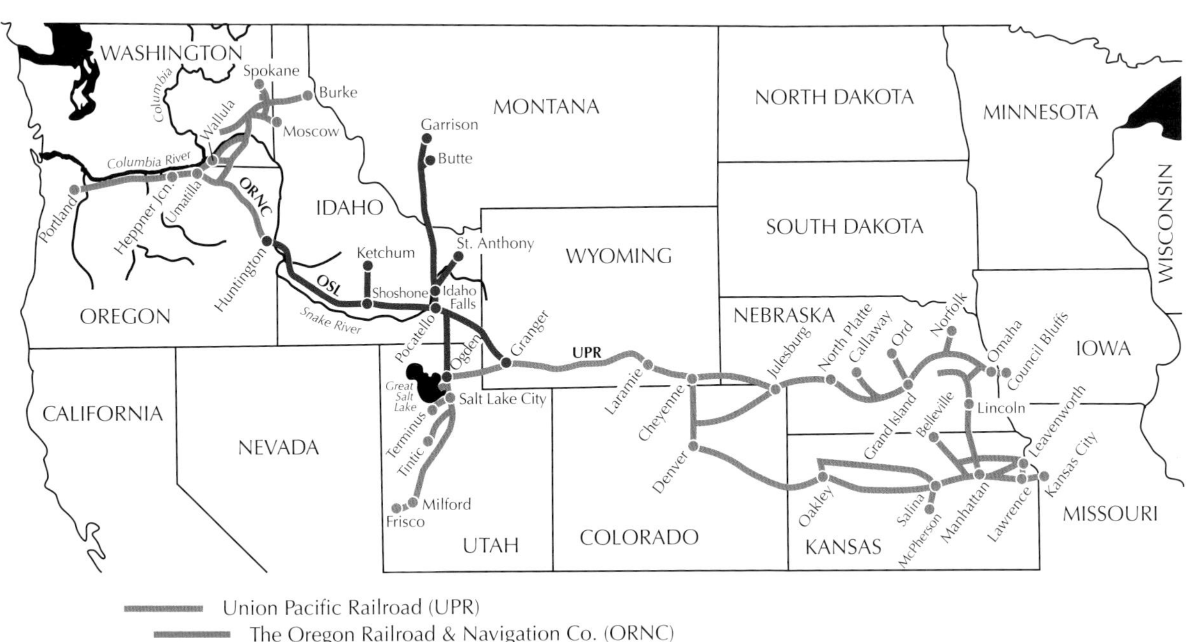

JAMES J. HILL planned to unite the Northern Pacific and the Great Northern, but the Northern Pacific began to thrive under independent ownership linked with J.P. Morgan. The picture was further complicated by Harriman's emergence, and by 1898, the Union Pacific under Harriman's leadership had re-acquired the Oregon Short Line, a branch from the main line at Salt Lake City to Huntington, Oregon, with an extension to Butte, Montana. The Oregon Railway & Navigation Company, using rail and steamers, extended from Portland to Huntington at the Oregon-Idaho border. A voting trust composed of the three competing railroads (Union Pacific, Great Northern, and Northern Pacific) controlled the Oregon Railway & Navigation Company. Each railroad desired the best route into Portland, the one held by the Oregon Railway & Navigation Company line along the south bank of the Columbia River, and thus the Oregon Railway & Navigation Company was used by all lines. Heading east, the Oregon Railway & Navigation Company branched at Umatilla, the northern branch connecting to the Northern Pacific and the southern branch

OREGON SHORT LINE RAILROAD

Oregon Short Line Railroad (OSL)
Oregon Railroad & Navigation Co. (ORNC)
Union Pacific Railroad (UPR)

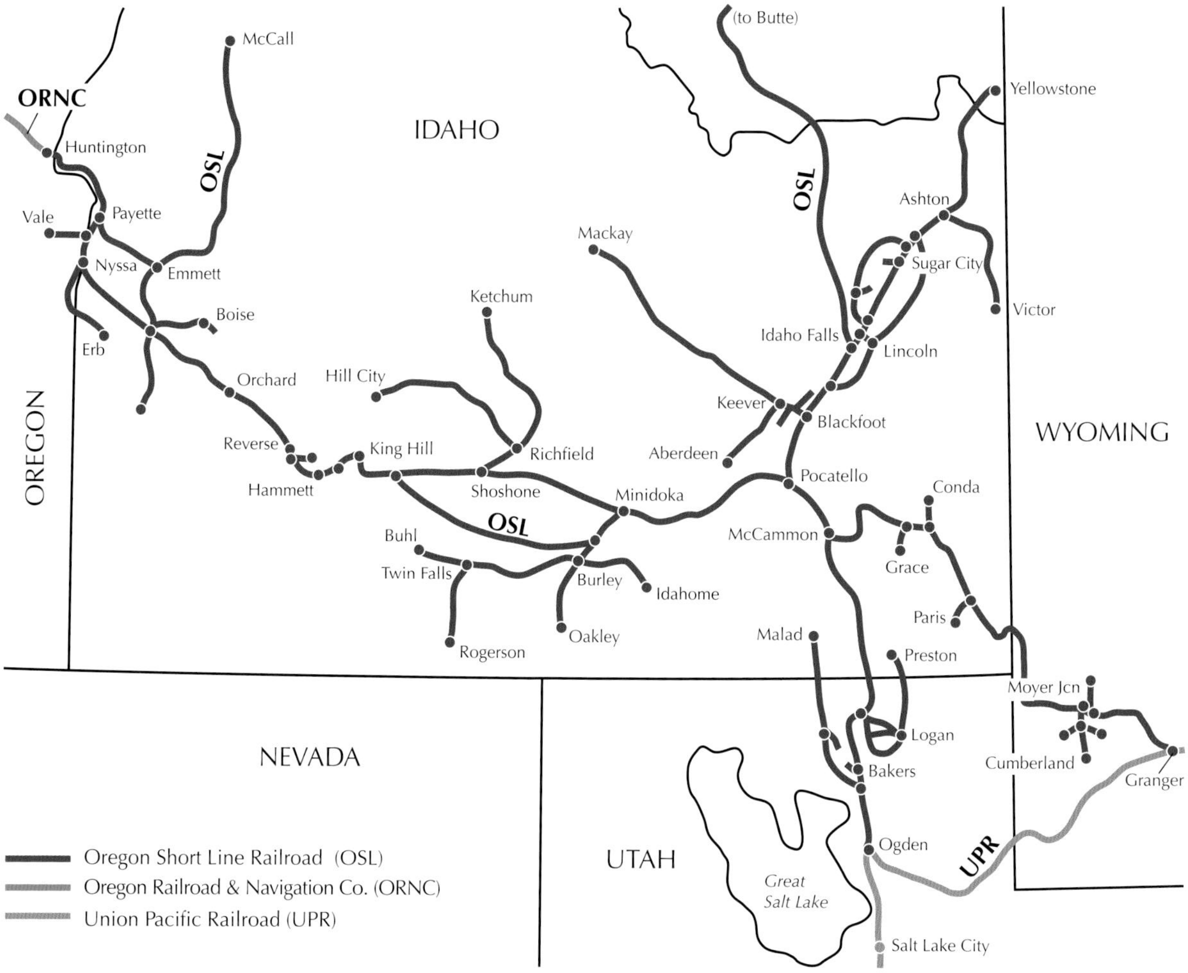

to the Oregon Short Line. The uneasy truce in the voting trust was superficial, covering confrontations and competitive desires.

As the Oregon Railway & Navigation Company became more and more successful, control shifted to the owners of common stock. By 1900, the Union Pacific, owning a majority of the common stock, brought the Oregon Railway & Navigation Company under the control of Harriman. The Oregon Railway & Navigation Company and the Oregon Short Line were soon modernized and functioning within the standardized Union Pacific system.

The route to Portland, Oregon, was Harriman's first true Union Pacific transcontinental route. The first transcontinental line was in 1899 still a joint effort of the Union Pacific and the Central Railroad; and because it was a joint effort, the Union Pacific had to hand over its westbound traffic to the Central Pacific at Ogden, Utah, and vice-versa for Central Pacific traffic going east.

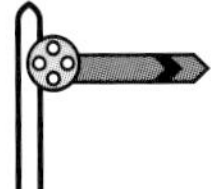

IN THE MIDST of these railroad changes and competitions, Harriman undertook his most amazing "vacation," a scientific expedition to Alaska, a three-month trip that highlighted Harriman's strengths: energy, organization, and commitment.[29] At the end of May 1889, he and fifty passengers embarked on a refitted old steamer, the *George W. Elder*. In addition to the Harriman entourage that consisted of his wife, children, two secretaries, three maids, a brother-in-law, a chaplain, and two physicians, there were twenty-three scientists from twelve different fields, two photographers, three artists, and two taxidermists. The scientists, recruited by recommendations from recognized authorities in the fields, were brought by Harriman to Seattle in a special train. The baggage, including horses, chickens, turkeys, sheep, a milk cow, and a piano, weighed the ship down.

During this expedition, Harriman's enthusiasm, stamina, and desire to see everything were unmatched (the rest of his family were no different). This was no leisurely vacation. The group explored by hiking many miles (one covered twenty-four miles). The hikers were often roped together, crossing glacier crevices. On several occasions, Harriman manned the oars for daring rescues of stranded scientists. Not one person was lost or seriously injured despite several close calls and damage to their steamer's propellor. A measure of the man is the fact that every passenger, including John Muir who had never met him before the trip, developed both admiration and affection for Harriman. The success of the voyage produced the first public awareness of Harriman beyond business circles. The resulting scientific information took many years to organize and publish, reaching a total of thirteen volumes.

AFTER HARRIMAN returned from his Alaska expedition, he would have ten years left to live. These last years were dominated by an intense competition with James J. Hill in the Pacific Northwest that culminated in the Deschutes River Railroad War.

- CHAPTER SIX -

HILL AND HARRIMAN IN THE PACIFIC NORTHWEST

COMPETITIVE FINANCIAL SHENANIGANS

The history of railroads in the Pacific Northwest is a tangle of personalities linked to financial schemes at the national level. A brief review of this history is helpful in understanding the motivations of James J. Hill and Edward H. Harriman in their battle along the Deschutes River.

The Oregon Steam Navigation Company existed from 1860 to 1880, controlling steamboat transportation on the Columbia and Snake Rivers and earning large profits.[1] Transportation up the Columbia River encountered two major obstacles: the "Cascades," six-mile-long rapids on the Columbia River about forty-five miles upstream of Portland, and difficult water upstream at The Dalles extending for several miles to the quiet water above the falls at Celilo. The first railroads in Oregon, in 1851, were very short lines (six miles on the Washington side at The Cascades and 14.5 miles on the Oregon side around Celilo), acquired in 1862 by the Oregon Steam Navigation Company. These tracks provided portage around The Cascades and Celilo Falls. Until 1862, these portage railroads had wooden tracks and used cars pulled by mules.[2]

In 1864, Congress chartered the Northern Pacific to complete a route across the West into Oregon and Washington, including a line down the Columbia River into Portland. Lacking financial support, the Northern Pacific did nothing until Congress reauthorized the charter and included land grants along both sides of the Columbia River. The Northern Pacific then purchased the Oregon Steam Navigation Company from its owner John C. Ainsworth in May 1872, but the sale did not include the portage railroads around The Cascades and Celilo Falls. Over the next few years, Northern Pacific finances were problematic, and Ainsworth was able to regain control of his company.

HENRY VILLARD was the key figure in the early development of two railroads, the Northern Pacific and the Oregon Railway & Navigation Company. Born Ferdinand Heinrich Gustav Hilgard in Germany in 1835, he changed his name to Henry Hilgard Villard when he came to the U.S. in 1853.[3] Villard returned to Germany and cultivated connections among German bankers and investors. His charming personality was an important factor in his success; he was a man of "most engaging and genial manners with nothing of the hard selfishness or avaricious grasp of the typical rich man."[4] As a measure of his regard, when he purchased control of the Northern Pacific in 1881, Villard invited his friends to invest $8 million without revealing his plans or purpose; they invested $20 million!

In 1872, a short railroad line, the Oregon & California Railroad, between Portland and Roseburg in southern Oregon, defaulted on $11 million in bonds held by German capitalists, who sent Villard to Oregon to gain control of the line. Villard became known to the major capitalist behind the Union Pacific, Jay Gould, and learned of the Union Pacific's plan to build north into Idaho and then to Portland.

Planning to thwart the Union Pacific, Villard purchased the Oregon Steam Navigation Company and its portage railroads in 1879 and renamed it the Oregon Railway & Navigation Company, raising the money from German investors.[5] Villard thus gained control of commerce on the Columbia River and also acquired land transportation to Walla Walla, Washington, because the Oregon Railway & Navigation Company also owned a short railroad line, the Walla Walla & Columbia River Railroad. In addition, the Oregon Railway & Navigation Company owned extensive real estate in Portland. Villard's immediate objective was to use the revenue and assets of the Oregon Railway & Navigation Company to build a railroad along the south bank of the Columbia River.

Villard was a financier, not a railroader. His aim was to build quickly and make as much money as possible. Construction initially extended the portage line on the Oregon bank of the Columbia River from Celilo to Wallula (now flooded behind the McNary Dam), and eventually connected it to the Union Pacific's Oregon Short Line by running from Pendleton to Huntington, Oregon, on the Idaho-Oregon state boundary. In 1879 and 1880, the Oregon Railway & Navigation Company was reaping large profits and Villard's reputation soared. But, being so focused on money, Villard directed little revenue to improving his railroad. His lack of foresight would prove disastrous to him later on.

Knowing that the Northern Pacific had a charter to build to the West Coast, Villard negotiated an agreement to establish a connection with the Northern Pacific at Wallula. Villard's overall goal was to acquire the Northern Pacific. With support from the blind investments of his friends, who were stimulated by the success of the Oregon Railway & Navigation Company, Villard purchased sufficient stock to gain control of the Northern Pacific in 1881. Under Villard's control, the Northern Pacific was building its line to the west, and at the same time, the Oregon Railway & Navigation Company was building its connection to Portland, and east to Idaho. The quality of construction was poor, and the expenses were high. Supervising these multiple projects was complicated, requiring the hands-on presence of an experienced railroad man. Villard was not such a man. Nevertheless, the Oregon Railway

NORTHERN PACIFIC RAILROAD

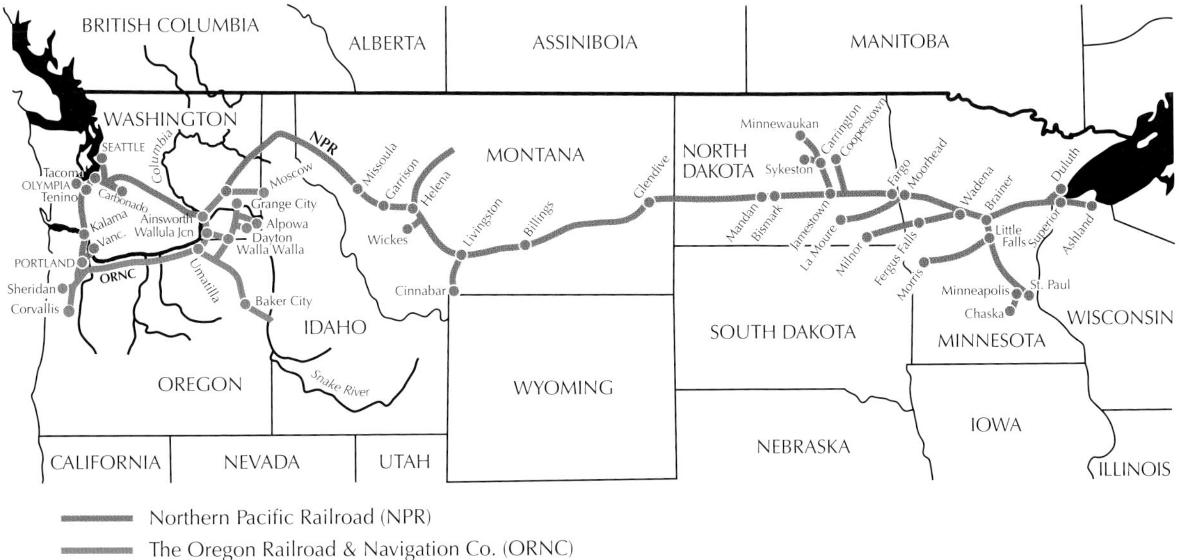

& Navigation Company completed its construction, and 212 miles of railroad service from Wallula to Portland began in November 1882. In September 1883, the Northern Pacific line from St. Paul to Wallula was completed, connecting to the Oregon Railway & Navigation Company, making Portland a western terminal for a transcontinental line. The cost overruns of this construction led to falling stock prices, prompting stockholders to call for Villard's resignation in December 1883. He moved back to Berlin in early 1884.

AFTER VILLARD LEFT THE COUNTRY, management of the Oregon Railway & Navigation Company was placed in the hands of a board of directors controlled by the eastern investors. The story that follows is one of complicated financial dealings and personal interactions.[6]

THE OREGON RAILROAD & NAVIGATION CO.

– AROUND 1900 –

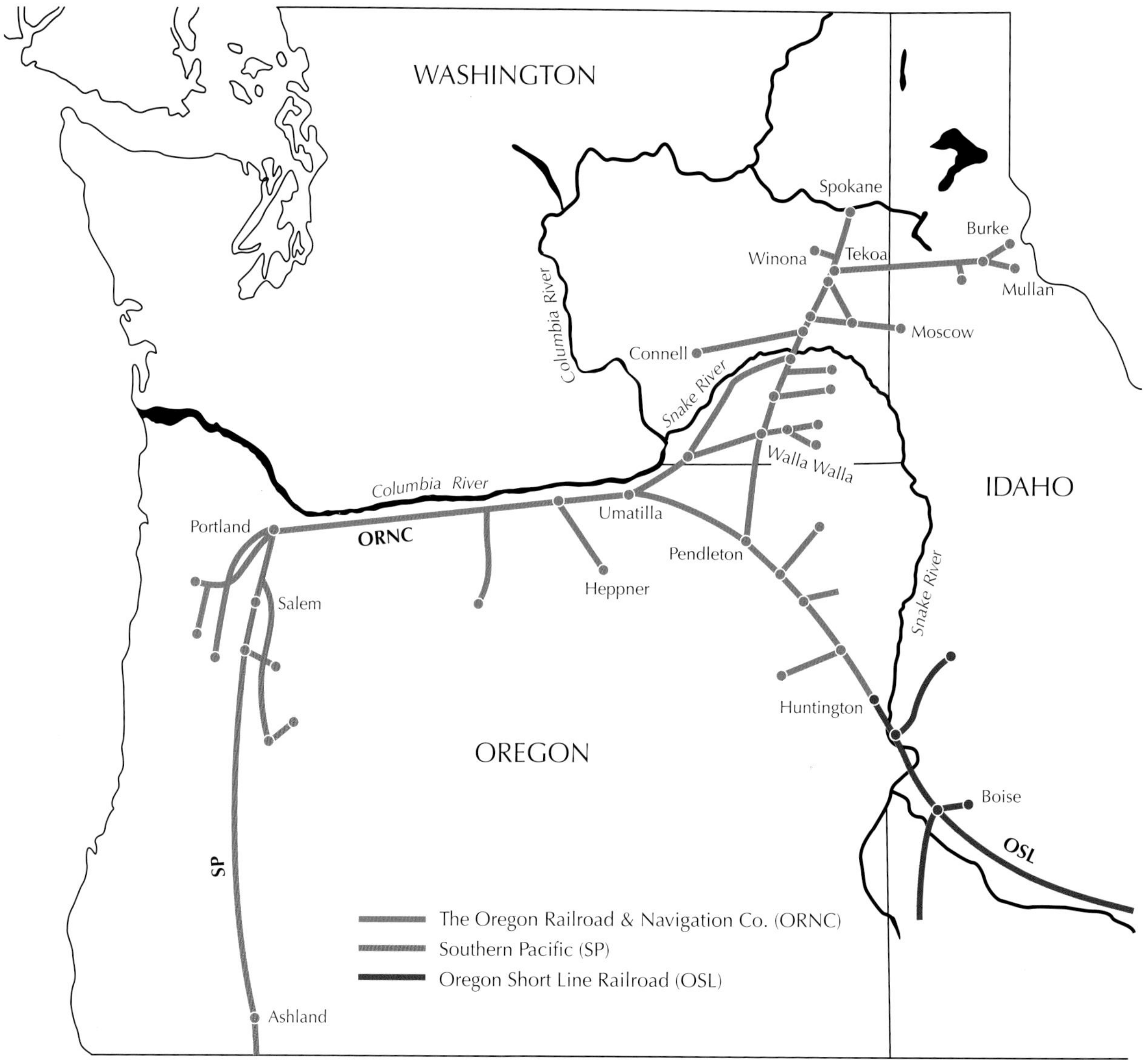

WASHINGTON
Spokane
Winona
Tekoa
Burke
Mullan
Moscow
Connell
Columbia River
Snake River
Walla Walla
IDAHO
Columbia River
Portland
ORNC
Umatilla
Pendleton
Heppner
Salem
Snake River
Huntington
OREGON
Boise
OSL
SP
Ashland

The Oregon Railroad & Navigation Co. (ORNC)
Southern Pacific (SP)
Oregon Short Line Railroad (OSL)

Construction of the Oregon Railway & Navigation line eastward to Huntington continued through La Grande and Baker, reaching Huntington in November 1884, completing the second transcontinental route. In 1887, the Union Pacific, through the Oregon Short Line, officially leased the Oregon Railway & Navigation Company with its 463 miles of mainlines and 289 miles of feeder lines, a move that solidified finances and traffic for the Oregon Railway & Navigation Company.[7] An inspection of the Oregon Railway & Navigation line easily revealed poor routing and construction, problems that were corrected when the Union Pacific gained control.

In 1887, the majority of the Oregon Railway & Navigation Company stock, and a large segment of the Northern Pacific, were owned by Villard's old company, the Oregon & Transcontinental Holding Company. The loans for the construction over the previous ten years required payment, and in desperation the Boston investors turned to Henry Villard. Once again using European investors, Villard returned to the U.S., paid the loans and became a director of the Northern Pacific. He attempted to create joint ownership of the Oregon Railway & Navigation Company with the Northern Pacific and Union Pacific, but this failed, and he sold his interest to the Union Pacific in 1889.

In the midst of the depression and financial panic in 1893, the Union Pacific filed for bankruptcy when it could not meet its loan payments. The Oregon Railway & Navigation Company went into separate receivership, terminating its lease with the Union Pacific. In 1896, with the reorganization of the bankrupt railroads, the Oregon Railway & Navigation Company, with just a slight change in name, became an independent company, the Oregon Railroad & Navigation Company.[8] It was James J. Hill who insisted that this company remain neutral so that its tracks would be available to all three major lines, the Great Northern, the Northern Pacific, and the Union Pacific. In 1897, the Great Northern purchased sufficient shares of Oregon Railroad & Navigation Company stock to gain representation on its board of directors. But the Union Pacific had new leadership in E.H. Harriman. Because the Union Pacific's Oregon Short Line held a substantial share of Oregon Railroad & Navigation Company stock, Hill and Harriman were in position to operate that line jointly. But Harriman rejected a cooperative effort, and by 1900, the Union Pacific had acquired the majority of stock in the Oregon Railroad & Navigation Company.[9] The Hill lines acquiesced, partly because of the obvious expenditure necessary to correct the poor locations and substandard construction of the Oregon Railroad & Navigation Company line with its unballasted light tracks.

Under the control of Harriman and the Union Pacific, the Oregon Railroad & Navigation Company reconstructed its old line and built new branch lines. The entire line from Portland to Pendleton was largely relocated and rebuilt according to the Harriman philosophy of straighter, well-built lines.[10] The old roadbed became the Columbia River Highway that opened in 1915. The Oregon Railroad & Navigation Company changed its name once again, incorporating in Oregon on November 23, 1910, as the Oregon-Washington Railroad & Navigation Company, with all of its stock owned by the Union Pacific's Oregon Short Line Railroad.

The Hill-Harriman Rivalry

Known as the last great railroad war, the Hill-Harriman struggle began in 1901 and did not end until Harriman died in 1909.[11] James J. Hill had established his investment resources, with the bulk of his financing from England. Hill's transcontinental line was placed under a new holding company, the Great Northern Railway, and the owners of the Manitoba road became the owners of the line from St. Paul to Seattle. Shrewd management that directed profits into the building of a better railroad that could deliver at cheaper rates had allowed it to survive the depression of the early 1890s. Hill then set out to acquire the Northern Pacific.

Henry Villard was a not a railroad man, and the Northern Pacific suffered for it. The Northern Pacific, narrowly controlled by Villard, had reached the West Coast, building a major tunnel through the Cascade Range and a direct line to Tacoma, Washington. Rather than improving the Northern Pacific, Villard returned profits to his German investors. The line was neglected, and the Northern Pacific was placed into receivership in mid-1893.

Hill traveled to London and convinced his English backers to acquire the Northern Pacific. The J.P.

Morgan company was involved with this reorganization, and cautioned Hill that bringing the Great Northern and Northern Pacific together would run contrary to Minnesota's laws that prevented a railroad from ownership in a parallel line.[12] Hill's lawyers believed this did not apply to the Great Northern because it had been chartered prior to the passage of the laws. The state courts ruled against Hill, leaving Morgan again responsible for the reorganization of the Northern Pacific. The management of the line was placed in a voting trust, but Morgan did not ignore Hill. An agreement was reached that the two lines (the Great Northern and the Northern Pacific) would not compete with each other, and both railroads would maintain the independence of the Oregon Railroad & Navigation Company, keeping it available for the use of all connecting lines.

At the time of the depression that began in 1893, Hill was in good fiscal condition. The Great Northern was financially sound. The Great Northern survived these times because it was well built, accommodating more frequent, longer, and bigger trains, and thus it could afford to unilaterally lower rates. The Great Northern could continue to make money while competitors were filing for bankruptcy. In fact, with the costs of labor and equipment dropping during the depression, Great Northern profits actually increased. Hill's net personal worth grew from $12 million in 1895 to $19.4 million in 1901.[13]

Competition among many lines created a state of limited cooperation, preventing the joint establishment of mutually beneficial rates. In addition, the funneling of money to investors left insufficient operating funds for railroads to pursue effective maintenance and modernization. This sorry state of affairs attracted public attention and soon Congress was acting to prevent cooperation and collusion by the railroads. The Interstate Commerce Act of 1887 outlawed the adjustment of rates by competing but colluding railroads. The only alternative remaining to achieve stabilization with competitive rates required the consolidation of competing lines into a few remaining railroads.

The poor physical and financial state of other railroads in the 1890s encouraged Hill to believe that these major lines would not continue to provide serious competition. He did not believe that the Union Pacific, in particular (and its northwest extensions the Oregon Short Line and the Oregon Railroad & Navigation Company), would challenge the Great Northern's dominance in the Pacific Northwest. The Great Northern, like most railroads, had close relationships with the lumber industry, not only hauling the lumber but consuming vast quantities of timber products for ties, bridges, and depots. James J. Hill's neighbor on Summit Street in St. Paul happened to be Frederick Weyerhaeuser, head of the largest lumber business in the country. In a deal with Weyerhaeuser involving unheard-of low rates, Hill used the Great Northern's surplus profits to improve the Northern Pacific line and arranged to have both lines haul lumber back to the East from the Pacific Northwest.

By 1895, the Union Pacific was bankrupt. The Oregon Railway & Navigation Company was facing foreclosure, and Hill had declined an offer from eastern financiers to stabilize the line and preserve a path to Portland. Arguably, Hill based his decision on a reluctance to jeopardize his friendship with Jacob Schiff, who had taken on the role of reorganizing the Union Pacific (which of course would soon be Harriman's major role in railroad history, a role that Hill had declined).[14]

Hill joined the Northern Pacific voting trust and by 1898, the financial reorganization of the Northern Pacific was complete. Hill could see that his competitor, Harriman, was also prospering, thereby threatening the independent status of the Oregon Railroad & Navigation Company. Hill wished to avoid building a line along the north bank of the Columbia, and therefore, a cooperative effort to maintain the neutrality of the Oregon Railroad & Navigation Company was to his benefit. Business was booming, and Hill continued his efforts to gain control of the Northern Pacific. Finally in November 1900 the voting trustees dissolved the cooperative trust, allowing Hill to have majority control in the Northern Pacific. Hill immediately increased the size of his investment and held control of the two lines without a formal unification, thus technically avoiding the Minnesota laws that made it illegal for one owner to have parallel and competing railroads.

The time around 1900 was a period of apparent cooperation, manifested by the creation of a Railroad Advisory Committee, incorporating the major financiers and railroad men, including Hill and Harriman.

But this soon changed with the direct competition between Hill and Harriman in the Pacific Northwest. Their competition was held in abeyance by the agreement to maintain the neutrality of the Oregon Railroad & Navigation Company, allowing all connecting lines (the Union Pacific, the Great Northern, and the Northern Pacific) to reach Portland along the south bank of the Columbia River. According to the agreement, the Union Pacific reached the West Coast by traveling north from Granger, Wyoming, via its Oregon Short Line and connecting to the Oregon Railroad & Navigation Company. The Northern Pacific linked with ocean transport in Portland by connecting to the Oregon Railroad & Navigation Company in Spokane, but soon the Northern Pacific built its own line to Tacoma. The Great Northern reached the West Coast on its own line to Seattle.

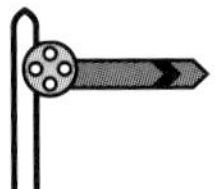

THERE WERE SEVERAL FORCES around 1900 influencing the visions of the competing railroads:

- The mountain forests and the fertile valleys of the lower Columbia River and the Willamette River were producing goods that demanded transportation.
- The direct route to San Francisco, the original combined Union Pacific and Central Pacific Railroad transcontinental line, failed to dominate the California market. Instead of using the first transcontinental route, the owners of the Central Pacific Railroad built the Southern Pacific Railroad and directed railroad traffic to and from California on this line. This was not difficult to do, charging high rates on the Central Pacific connection to the Union Pacific and lower rates on the Southern Pacific.[15] Because of the high rates on the Central Pacific, the Union Pacific valued its Oregon Short Line connection and path to the West Coast. Forced to follow this route, the Union Pacific had to compete with the Great Northern and the Northern Pacific.
- The formidable passage through the Cascade Mountains made the lines along the Columbia River a more affordable and practical route. The Oregon Railroad & Navigation Company already had this route, running from Portland along the south bank of the Columbia and to the south of the Snake River.

Suddenly, the Oregon Railroad & Navigation Company found itself a focal point of attention for the three major northern lines. The Great Northern and the Northern Pacific depended on the Oregon Railroad & Navigation Company to reach Portland. The Union Pacific also depended on the Oregon Railroad & Navigation tracks to reach Portland and a Northern Pacific line connecting Portland with Tacoma and Seattle. For these reasons Jacob Schiff had engineered in 1895 a neutral status for the Oregon Railway & Navigation Company. But after the depression, reorganization of the bankrupt lines, and the upturn in the economy, the Union Pacific and Harriman threatened the uneasy neutrality because the Union Pacific now had controlling interest in the Oregon Railroad & Navigation Company.[16]

Harriman acquired the Southern Pacific in 1901 and followed the Union Pacific business plan, pouring money into improving and extending the line, making it more efficient and ultimately more profitable. By 1909, the Southern Pacific stretched from Portland, Oregon, to the Gulf of California over 3,750 miles of track, adding to the wealth of Harriman and the Union Pacific.[17] Hill now began to seriously contemplate building his own line to Portland along the north bank of the Columbia River. Hill was tempted by the north bank route not only because of the threatened neutrality of the Oregon Railroad & Navigation Company but also because of the aging, inferior state of the Oregon Railroad & Navigation Company.

For the time being, the competition between Hill and Harriman in the Pacific Northwest was a stalemate, and Hill turned his attention to acquiring the Burlington Railroad. The name "Burlington" originated from a town on the west bank of the Mississippi River in Iowa, named by a settler from Vermont. The name was soon attached to the trail leading west across southern Iowa, and eventually to the railroad that followed this trail. A consolidation of several small lines leading to Chicago led to the formation of the Chicago, Burlington, and Quincy Railroad Company (known as the Burlington) in 1856, a poorly built (although standard for the time) short road using forty-six wood-burning locomotives.[18] By the time of the Civil War, the line owned a total of 400 miles of tracks in Illinois.[19] The first bridge across the Mississippi River at Rock Island, Illinois, opened in 1856, and railroad expansion to the West rapidly followed. The Chicago, Burlington, and Quincy reached Kansas City, where a bridge over the Missouri River in 1869 further opened the way west. In addition, the Chicago, Burlington, and Quincy reached across Iowa into Nebraska in 1870, securing land grants from Congress and profiting from advertising campaigns to recruit immigrants.

The railroad companies maintained large sales campaigns throughout America and Northern Europe.[20,21] The railroads circulated fancy pamphlets that emphasized testimonials from successful farmers, but also warned prospective buyers about how hard it was to be a pioneer. The railroads provided prospects cut-rate visits to home sites, and immigrants from Europe were guided by escorts. Once the buyers had settled the land, the railroads often had to wait patiently for farmers to make their deferred payments.

The Burlington line emerged from the post-Civil War years of economic expansion followed by a depression, with lines extending from Chicago into Colorado, Missouri, and Wyoming. By 1894, the Burlington connected with the Northern Pacific in Montana. When the Union Pacific went into bankruptcy, neither the Burlington nor James J. Hill elected to gain control of the Oregon Short Line and the Oregon Railway & Navigation Company, eventually allowing these lines to remain with the Union Pacific and Harriman. Instead, the Burlington, under the direction of its able president, Charles E. Perkins, expanded to the south into Texas and to St. Louis. Thus the Burlington lines serviced the rich western mine fields and forests, the agricultural heartland of the Midwest, and in the South, the cotton and livestock industry. Burlington's links to this valuable commerce and to Chicago attracted the interest of James J. Hill.

THE BURLINGTON extended from Nebraska to Chicago, but depended on a connection to the Northern Pacific and Hill's cooperation for business in the Pacific Northwest. Hill wanted the Burlington because it would give the Hill lines a route to Chicago. In addition, Hill would benefit because the line extended south to the Gulf of Mexico, providing a route for the transfer of wood to the southwest plains and meat and cotton to Chicago. Not surprisingly, Harriman and the Union Pacific also greedily viewed this traffic. The resulting battle for the Burlington is one of the best stories of the fierce Hill-Harriman competition.

Harriman acted first, and in 1900 when he learned that the Chicago, Burlington, and Quincy was not for sale, but would consider selling for the high cash price of $200 per share, he countered with offers of Union Pacific bonds and cash; but Perkins, the Burlington president, declined the offer.[22] Perkins favored an alliance with Hill, for good economic reasons such as the lumber market of the Pacific Northwest and the greater indebtedness of the Union Pacific.[23] Holding out for the high price, Perkins forced Hill to accept his terms. Rebuffed, Harriman turned to the stock market. This financial battle took place in the first week of May 1901.

Harriman began to buy Northern Pacific stock and eventually acquired 40 percent of Northern

Pacific shares. His activity precipitated a run on Northern Pacific stock, driving prices incredibly high. Ultimately, control of the Northern Pacific hinged on 40,000 shares of common stock. Hill, in New York City, met directly with Jacob H. Schiff in the offices of Kuhn, Loeb & Co. and became fully aware of the crisis. If Harriman acquired the 40,000 shares, he would control the voting common stock in the Northern Pacific.

Harriman called Kuhn, Loeb & Co. on Saturday morning, May 4, 1901 (the market closed at noon on Saturdays). He learned that Schiff was at synagogue, and he had to leave his purchase order with Heinsheimer, a junior partner. Seeking senior approval from Schiff, Heinsheimer personally went to the synagogue. In a decision never explained, Schiff elected to not make the purchase that Saturday morning. Meanwhile, Hill, by cable communication to J.P. Morgan, urged the purchase of $15 to $20 million of Northern Pacific common stock. Morgan, in Europe, immediately issued the order that reached New York on Sunday. Monday morning, in response to Morgan's purchase, Northern Pacific stock rose more than six-fold, but Hill had just enough to control the Northern Pacific. In the end, Hill had $42 million in stock, and Harriman had $37 million, leaving only $1 million of common stock held by others.[24] Forcing Harriman to negotiate, Hill solidified his control of the Northern Pacific, purchased the Burlington line, and acquired a right for traffic to Portland. Harriman received rights to Puget Sound. Out of this came the Northern Securities Company, a mammoth holding company with Hill as president.

The method Hill chose to unify his railroad lines was to create a new holding company, the Northern Securities Company. The investors in the separate lines turned their stock in, replacing it with shares in the new company. This was a large company, with a capitalization of $400 million, filed in New Jersey on November 12, 1901. Harriman held 23 percent of the stock, which meant little because Hill was president. The government soon viewed the new company as a monopoly designed to avoid competition, and President Theodore Roosevelt saw the opportunity for political capital by suing the new company, proclaiming its illegality under the Sherman Antitrust Act of 1890. A three-year struggle carried the battle to the U.S. Supreme Court, which ruled in March 1904, by a vote of five to four, to disband the Northern Securities Company, agreeing with a lower court that its purpose was to stifle if not eliminate competition.

The holding company was dissolved according to the wishes of the controlling interest, James J. Hill. Harriman filed suit, and it can be argued that this was the turning point from business competition to a bitter feud between Hill and Harriman. Harriman viewed Hill's control of the Burlington to be a major threat to the Union Pacific. Hill believed the lawsuit was unnecessary, and from this point on, cooperation between the two would be impossible. The suit was not settled until a ruling by the Supreme Court in March 1905 assured Hill of victory, and as a result the Burlington remained unavailable to the Union Pacific. However, the Union Pacific gained an enormous amount of wealth from the dissolution of the holding company (about $144 million). In addition, the Harriman lines were breaking profit records, and even though dividends reached new highs, there was a large amount of cash left over.

The Spokane, Portland & Seattle Railway

After seven years of these competitive financial shenanigans, the railroad picture in the Pacific Northwest remained unchanged, except for the emergence of a lack of trust between Hill and Harriman. Harriman controlled access to San Francisco and Portland, Hill to Seattle.

Until the Spokane, Portland & Seattle Railway, also called the North Bank Road, began operation, railroad service in Oregon was dominated by the Harriman lines. From the east, the Union Pacific entered the Northwest with the tracks of the Oregon Short Line connecting to the Oregon Railroad & Navigation Company at the Oregon-Idaho state border traveling to Portland along the Oregon bank of the Columbia River. From the south, Harriman's Southern Pacific came from California through the Willamette Valley. North of the Columbia River, the Hill lines dominated railroad business, but Oregon's wealth was not benefiting the Great Northern and the Northern Pacific.

The Columbia River is unique in that it provides the only travel route through the mountains of the

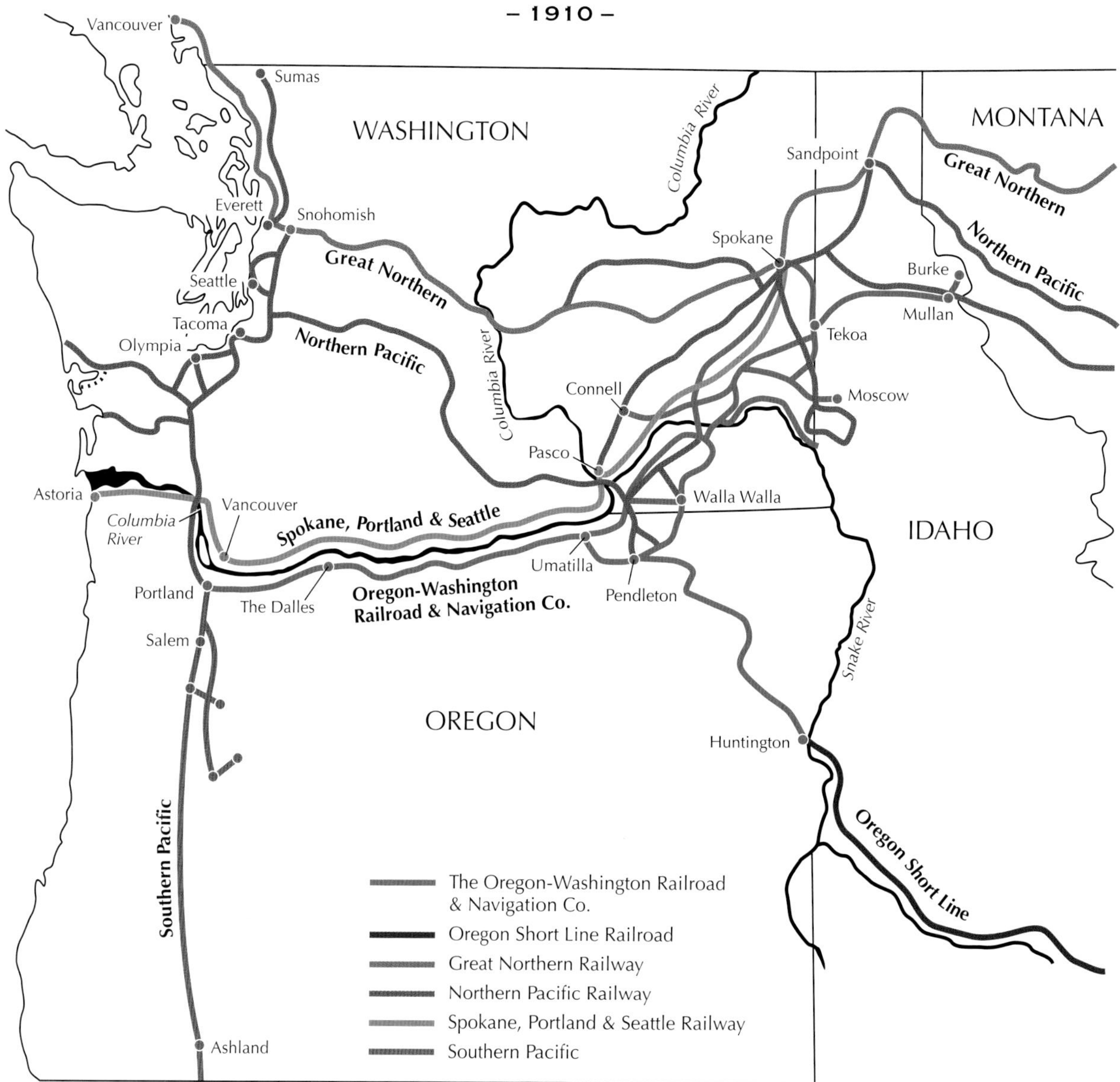

Pacific Northwest that is at water level. For this reason it attracted migrating Indians, explorers and traders, settlers, and railroad men. In 1905, Hill decided to compete for the Oregon market by building the North Bank Railroad along the Columbia River, a line that could serve branch lines into Oregon, such as the proposed railroad to Bend along the Deschutes River. The North Bank Railroad was initially the Portland & Seattle Railway (and the owners were kept secret until September 26, 1905), but the name was changed in 1908 to the Spokane, Portland & Seattle Railway.[25,26,27] However, an extension to Seattle was never realized, and it is possible that Hill deliberately identified this line as a Seattle-to-Portland route to mislead Harriman, keeping his intention to build from Spokane to Portland a secret as long as possible.

Hill intended to build his line from Spokane, along the north bank of the Columbia River in Washington, to Portland, and from there north to Tacoma and Seattle and west to the mouth of the Columbia

River. He first had to secure the right-of-way on the north bank of the Columbia River. In the spring of 1906, Hill's legal staff prevented possible Union Pacific blocking efforts by acquiring the right to build along the north bank. The Hill lines, the Northern Pacific and the Great Northern, would jointly own the new railroad. The extension from Portland to Seattle would use the old right-of-way purchased from the Northern Pacific. It was also planned to reach Astoria at the mouth of the Columbia River to connect with coastal steamships.

Hill visited Portland and the Lewis and Clark Exposition in October 1905, essentially throwing the gauntlet down to the Harriman lines. He was well received, and his speeches at various banquets widely reported. Hill construction camps on the north bank of the Columbia River were in place by the end of 1905, but work was delayed by difficulties in securing the entire 230 miles of right-of-way. One problem was that Harriman had articles of incorporation for a competing line, the Wallula Pacific Railroad Company, and his agents were buying land along the entry to Portland and at key points that had room for only one set of tracks. Hill and Harriman also engaged in a lawsuit over a considerable piece of land in Portland purchased by Hill for a terminal; the litigation between Hill and Harriman over this land was not resolved until 1920, when a contract was negotiated allowing all the railroads to use the Portland Union Station.[28]

Within a few months, Hill's north bank track construction had started, but the construction near Portland and a short segment at Cascade Locks posed a problem. At Cascade Locks, the line encountered the old portage railroad that extended downstream for about three miles, now owned by the Union Pacific. The Union Pacific refused right-of-way, an obstruction that required court action to resolve, resulting in a relocation of the Spokane, Portland & Seattle. On July 2, 1906, the court ruled in favor of the Hill line on all other points of contention, and the Spokane, Portland & Seattle was completed in February 1908, a distance of 246 miles at a cost of about $40 million.

In June 1909, John F. Stevens, by now Hill's dependable and intrepid friend, became president of the line. At the same time, he was put in charge of constructing the Oregon Trunk along the Deschutes River. Two years later, with the projects essentially completed, Stevens moved on, leaving his assistant Ralph Budd as chief engineer. Later Budd became president of the Great Northern and Burlington lines.

The Spokane, Portland & Seattle Railway did not produce substantial revenue until World War II, and was, therefore, a disappointment to Hill.[29,30] It was expensive to build, and its volume of traffic did not reach expectations. In fact, Hill had difficulty in financing the last leg of construction, even battling with those in charge of the Northern Pacific who objected to their share of the costs. Although the separate lines (the Great Northern and the Northern Pacific) were under the control of Hill, each functioned relatively independently, sometimes competing for business with each other. This is illustrated in the delightful story of their shared building.

In 1914 to 1915, Hill cleared a block in downtown St. Paul, Minnesota, and the fourteen-story Railroad and Bank Building was constructed to house the headquarters of the Great Northern and the Northern Pacific (the structure is now the Burlington Northern Building), as well as two banks controlled by Hill.[31] Each company had its own entrance on different streets, and the building was divided by a wall passing straight through the building's center. The only direct connection was a single passage on the tenth floor, connecting the presidential offices, a door that was kept locked with keys available to no more than a few. The Great Northern built a cafeteria on the thirteenth floor, and to get there, the Northern Pacific employees had to ride down their elevators to the street, go outside, enter the Great

Northern doors, and ride up the Great Northern elevators to the cafeteria.

SHORT, LOCAL BRANCH RAILROADS were important because they served local commerce, farming, and logging. This business was essential for the bigger lines, especially as they consolidated into a few large conglomerates. James J. Hill's railroad lines (Great Northern and Northern Pacific) acquired these feeder lines around Portland to serve the larger Spokane, Portland & Seattle Railway that ran along the north bank of the Columbia River. Two feeder lines that Hill acquired were the Oregon Electric and the United Railways.

The Oregon Electric Railway Company, incorporated on May 14, 1906, had electric trains connecting Salem to Portland by 1908, and by 1909, had trolleys running west from Portland to Forest Grove.[32,33] Hill purchased this largely passenger service in February 1910, and John Stevens added the operation of this line to his presidential duties as the Oregon Electric was assigned to the Spokane, Portland & Seattle Railway. In 1912, extensions were completed to Eugene and McMinnville, and connections were established with the United Railways that in turn joined the Spokane, Portland & Seattle Railway. Ultimately, automobiles, trucks, and buses forced the decline of the passenger service, but after the 1930s, a busy freight service provided the Hill main lines with good income.

The United Railways was a feeder line that attracted Hill because of its strategic location near potential income from logging.[34,35] On January 17, 1906, the United Railways Company was incorporated in Oregon, controlled by a group in California who had grandiose ideas of a line extending down the valley to San Francisco. Construction began in Portland in the summer of 1906, but no one wanted to buy the railroad's bonds, and the United ran out of money. C. E. Loss, a railroad contractor in San Francisco purchased the United for $500,000. Loss was able to sell his railroad bonds, but his company still went bankrupt, and he sold the railroad to Portland and Seattle investors, especially Wittenburg's Pacific Coast Biscuit Company in Portland, which was on the line's proposed route.

The increasing business of the United Railways attracted James J. Hill's interest in the summer of 1909. He arranged for an intermediary to negotiate the purchase of controlling interest for $300,000, while keeping his identity a secret. Hill's initial motivation was to obtain a line to connect the Spokane, Portland & Seattle with Tillamook Bay. Land for a terminal in Tillamook on Oregon's Pacific Coast was quietly purchased, with the objective of linking the railroad to steamship service out of Tillamook Bay, competing with the Southern Pacific train route to California. On May 4, 1910, James J. Hill admitted to purchasing the United and named John F. Stevens president (the same Stevens who was president of the Spokane, Portland & Seattle Railway and who soon would be building the Oregon Trunk line up the Deschutes River). Half of the stock was acquired by each of Hill's major lines, the Great Northern and the Northern Pacific, and then both companies granted their stock to the Spokane, Portland & Seattle Railway.

1906 was not a good year for Harriman. The wealth of the Union Pacific, easily visible because of remarkably high dividends, attracted the attention of President Theodore Roosevelt, journalists, and the public in general. Harriman became a symbol of unchecked power, climaxed by his appearance and testimony at the hearings of the Interstate Commerce Commission.

In 1908, the U.S. Attorney General announced a lawsuit (eventually unsuccessful) to force the Union Pacific to divest its holdings in the Southern Pacific, San Pedro, Sante Fe, and Oregon Short Line railroads.[36] The entire railroad industry and the financial community had a great interest in these proceedings, which ultimately would lead to the revision of the Sherman Antitrust Act. The Interstate Commerce Commission, established in response to perceived railroad abuses, had by 1940 gradually extended its jurisdiction to all surface transportation. Its functions were progressively transferred to other agencies, and it was terminated in 1995 and replaced by the Surface Transportation Board.

Harriman's health became problematic beginning in 1908. Chronic back pain forced him to endure long periods in bed, and he became progressively more frail. Digestive problems flared and left a lingering impact, leading to anorexia and weight loss. In June 1909, Harriman visited Europe, seeking medical experts. Cancer of the stomach was finally diagnosed by x-ray, but it had already become inoperable.[37] Harriman's family never admitted that he had cancer, and it is uncertain whether Harriman kept the information to himself.[38]

In 1886, Harriman had acquired 7,863 acres of land about forty-five miles north of Jersey City for $52,500, sold after foreclosure.[39] This forested land with a small lake near the Ramapo River became his country estate, given the name Arden (perhaps from the forest in *As You Like It*). Returning to this home in August, Harriman put his affairs in order, then died at age sixty-one on September 9, 1909. On Sunday, September 12, 1909, the day when Harriman was buried at his Arden estate, at exactly 3:30 P.M., every train and person on the Harriman lines stopped and observed a minute of silence.[40]

Hill issued a public statement:

> I have always regarded Mr. Harriman very highly. I have done a good deal of business with him in the last few years and some of it, as you know, has been of a rather strenuous character. So I think I ought to know him pretty well. He did the work of several men during his lifetime. He was one who never left anything undone and there are few men in this country whose place it will be harder to fill.[41]

Hill's son, Louis, succeeded him as the president of the Great Northern in 1907. In 1912, Hill resigned as chairman of the board of the Great Northern. He became a banker in St. Paul, active in charitable works. At age seventy-seven, after refusing surgery for a large hemorrhoid, Hill developed an abscess and spreading infection. He died on May 29, 1916. And as in Harriman's story, all trains on the Hill lines stopped at the hour of his funeral on May 31, 1916.[42]

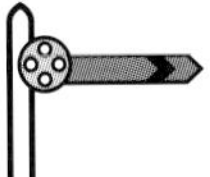

THE RAILROADS along the Deschutes River were built earlier and faster than they might otherwise have because of James J. Hill and Edward H. Harriman. It was their last competition, coming late in their lives, at a time when they had acquired the power and wealth required to support their small armies of workmen racing with each other in a rugged, formidable canyon. The Deschutes River Railroad War was a manifestation of each man's intense determination to avoid being bested by the other.

- CHAPTER SEVEN -

The Beginnings of a Railroad Along the Deschutes River

We Are Between the Devil and the Deep Blue Sea

In the chrysalis stage of railroad construction, mystery surrounds the movements of the representatives of the company actively engaged in the work of building for the reason that it is not infrequently the case that sudden change of policy and purpose are forced by circumstances that cannot be foreseen. The impression that railroads are legitimate prey for speculation and benefit makes it almost necessary that secrecy is maintained until all is in readiness for actual construction. Every resource of obstruction that can be drawn upon is employed by competitors and it's therefore incumbent upon the builder desirous of success to conceal from his left hand that which his right may be engaged in doing. ...It is a game in which the railroad officials themselves seem to be unprepared for each move until the position of the enemy is carefully determined, and even then it sometimes happens that like the Irishman's flea, it is impossible to land on the intended victim.

—*The Oregonian,* January 12, 1906

Railroad surveyors and engineers in the field were constantly hounded by local people and newspaper reporters. But these railroad men were taciturn and secretive, behavior imposed upon them by their superiors, the managers and owners who did not reveal their plans until they had to. It was left to reporters to speculate, "Even though they were about as talkative as oysters, they are the advance survey party for the line through Bend, apparently to Klamath Falls and California."[1]

Using the *nom de guerre* of John F. Sampson, the accomplished and famed engineer, John F. Stevens, went incognito. The guise he adopted was a familiar one for him, that of a fly fisherman, but this time a wealthy one.[2] Armed with a checking account well funded by James J. Hill, he traveled by automobile in 1909 along the Deschutes River, stopping at isolated sheep and cattle ranches, paying good money with personal checks for land options (each purportedly to serve as Sampson's entrée to the fly fishing on the river). He did fish for trout and was noted to curse his bad luck. He told one rancher he was going to start a fish hatchery at Trout Creek.[3,4]

With the completion in 1908 of the Spokane, Portland & Seattle along the north bank of the Columbia River, James J. Hill was now ready to tap into the agricultural and timber riches of central Oregon, and he was thinking ahead about a route to San Francisco. Harriman's Southern Pacific already ran through Eugene in western Oregon and controlled rail traffic between Portland and San Francisco. A new route to San Francisco by Hill's northern lines, therefore, would require an approach through central Oregon; this was Stevens' mission.

Oregon Frustration with Harriman

The farmers and ranchers of central Oregon were eager to have the services of a railroad. They and the business leaders of Oregon were exasperated with Harriman's failure to extend his tracks. In 1907, farmers had to pay 20¢ per bushel to haul their wheat by team to Shaniko. From Shaniko, the fee was 22¢ per bushel by train to Portland. This amounted to a total of more than $300,000 for transportation of the wheat from central Oregon to the markets.[5] Faced with this expense, the farmers attempted without success to haul one million bushels of wheat fifty miles from the Madras area to Shaniko using an engine pulling a train of wagons.[6] In 1909, Hill attended a banquet where the speaker said, "Oregon is bounded on the north by the Oregon Railway and Navigation Company, on the east by the Oregon Short Line, on the south by the Union Pacific, and on the west by the Pacific Ocean. Thus, Mr. Hill, you can see that we are between the devil and the deep blue sea."[7] Hill was viewed as welcome competition for the Harriman lines.

As early as 1903, Union Pacific surveyors were said to be in the field looking for new routes through central Oregon, prompting cynical editorials in the *Oregonian.*[8] "How long, how much longer, is the clash of interests or spirit of contention, among the great railroads, to hold back the development of the Pacific Northwest, and in particular the development of Oregon?"[9] Oregonians looked upon James J. Hill more favorably as "a railroad man who has always been short on promises and long on performances."[10] In contrast, Harriman was "the Union Pacific magnate who has been retarding the growth of Oregon for so many years."[11] "Our wagon is stuck in the mire and our prayers to Jupiter to haul it out are in vain."[12] The editorialists pulled no punches. "While promising extensions needed in Oregon—not for prospective but for actual, visible business—it [the Union Pacific] has failed to keep its word, but meanwhile has fostered roads building from California northwards into Oregon, intended to divert Oregon traffic into California pockets." The Harriman lines were making money, and the prevailing sentiment was: "No wonder that Mr. Harriman has fought shy of meddling with a machine which was coining money for its owners at this astounding rate."[13]

In August 1905, Harriman came to Portland to be feted at a banquet arranged by local Union Pacific officials. The banquet was attended by 255 invited guests, all prominent business men, including the president of the Chamber of Commerce and the governor of the state. "Socially, and from an epicurean standpoint, the event was one taking high rank among public functions in Portland."[13] Harriman announced at the banquet that an extension of his

Edward H. Harriman

Columbia Southern railroad into central Oregon was about to begin (the Columbia Southern had been built from Biggs on the south bank of the Columbia River to Shaniko in 1900). "I believe the railroad will be to the irrigation country about Bend before the settlers are there. There is not a place among our allied lines where we have not had track into new districts ahead of the settlers."[14] The front page article in the *Oregonian* featured a large drawing of Harriman's face, deliberately emphasizing his stern, squinting eyes.

The response was not what Harriman expected. "Oregon is ...not now and never was willing to accept accountability for the sloth and inertia which have marked all Harriman enterprises in this state for many years."[15]

> Mr. Harriman comes along and gives a banquet. The business community of Portland is invited. Its object is to place the great railroad president in more cordial personal relations with the constituency which his railroad lines serve. The railroad diplomats of Portland who arranged the affair desired to show the discontented public that Mr. Harriman was not a dreadful ogre. Likely enough they desired also to show Mr. Harriman a people in an admirable condition

> of docility. It was passed around that Mr. Harriman would very probably have something to say of highest importance. This was all very laudable and would have been a fine thing if it had been all carried out in accordance with the programme, or rather in accordance with general expectation. What really happened was that Mr. Harriman made a few observations on the railroad situation and subsided. His legal satellites delivered vehement homilies on the shortcomings of Oregon, and they subsided. If Mr. Harriman had said something a little more specific, and Mr. Cotton and Mr. Fenton had said nothing at all, the whole affair would have been a great success. The dinner was good, the wine abundant, and the society above reproach.[16]

Just two months later, James J. Hill was a visitor at Portland's Lewis & Clark Exposition, the centennial celebration of the Lewis & Clark Expedition, on October 3, 1905, a day officially named in his honor. His reception was considerably different than that of Harriman's. "Not since the late Henry Villard made his triumphal entry into Portland twenty-two years ago has the coming of a railroad magnate to this city been awaited with greater interest than that of President Hill, of the Great Northern. It is because of the entrance in Portland territory of a railroad man who is famed the world over for his policy of anticipating the future by building roads into new territory without waiting for the limit of development to be reached before commencing construction."[17] The *Oregonian* front page shouted the headline, "Mighty Ovation Greets J. Hill," and filled the page with three sketches of a smiling Hill drawn by the newspaper's artist, Harry Murphy. Hill's speech was printed verbatim, occupying five columns of dense print. And for the first time, Hill declared an interest in Oregon.

Just the previous month, the true owners of Hill's Spokane, Portland & Seattle Railway were revealed, and six months after Hill's speech, construction began on this Hill line from Spokane to Portland (Chapter 6). The cost of constructing the Spokane, Portland & Seattle Railway could only be regained by accessing Oregon's interior, and this required Hill to build branch or feeder lines. It was estimated that a line into central Oregon would make available about 16 billion board feet of pine.[18] Passengers, cattle, wool, and the farming products of the proposed irrigation systems would make up the rest of traffic.

In 1908 while vacationing in Oregon, Harriman promised again to build a railroad along the Deschutes River.[19] Harriman certainly had the resources to build an extension of the Oregon Railroad & Navigation line into Bend, but despite his promises, he was not inclined to do so. On the west side of the Deschutes River, the Great Southern, a line not owned by Harriman, connected Dufur with the Oregon Railroad & Navigation along the south bank of the Columbia River. Harriman had promised to extend the Great Southern into central Oregon, but when it became apparent that the grade was too great an obstacle, he abandoned his promise. On the east side, a Harriman line, the Columbia Southern, extended from the Oregon Railroad & Navigation at Biggs to Shaniko, but Harriman gave no indication that he wanted to extend the tracks further into central Oregon. Hill was building the Spokane, Portland & Seattle on the north bank of the Columbia River (completed in February 1908), and Harriman likely believed that the expense of a bridge over the Columbia River would keep Hill out of central Oregon.[20] There was no competing railroad driving Harriman to enter central Oregon. But forces were underway that would soon lead to the last direct confrontation between Hill and Harriman.

The First Surveys

The Oregon Trunk Line initiated the first survey along the Deschutes River, under the leadership of W.F. "Billy" Nelson of Seattle in January and February of 1905. Nelson was partnered with several Seattle bankers.[21] The survey was completed a year later in the winter of 1905–1906. Along most of the length of the lower Deschutes River there was room for two railroads, but construction would be difficult and expensive. In some places, sometimes on one bank and sometimes on the other, there was only room for one railroad. The Harriman camp jumped into action. In response to the early rustlings of the Oregon Trunk Line, Harriman incorporated the Des Chutes Railroad Company.

Three officials of the Oregon Railroad & Navigation Company, J.P. O'Brien, William Crook, and W.W. Cotton, filed Oregon perpetual incorporation papers for the Des Chutes Railroad Company on February 2, 1906, calling for a connection to the

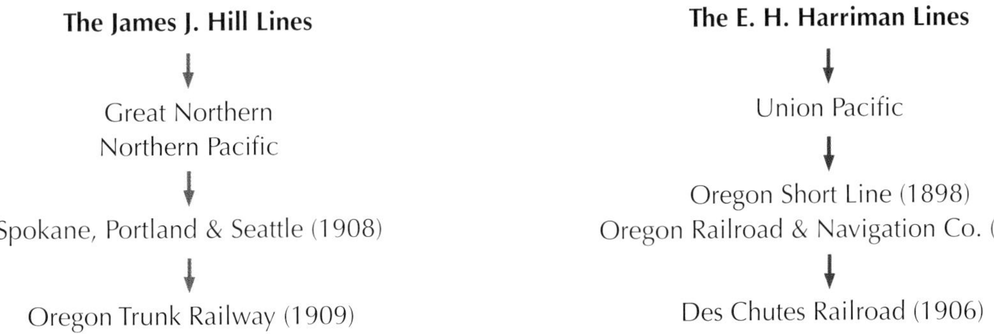

Oregon Railroad & Navigation line at or near the Deschutes Station on the south bank of the Columbia River.[22,23] In these early days, the Harriman line was called the "Des Chutes Railroad Company," the name under which incorporation papers were filed. Later, the more familiar "Deschutes" was popularly adopted, but it is more accurate to refer to this Harriman line as the Des Chutes Railroad.

Only ten days after incorporation, a Des Chutes Railroad survey crew began work, heading up the east bank of the Deschutes River. By March 16, 1906, they had completed the first twenty-mile survey. Because the line passed through public lands, the Des Chutes Railroad had to file its survey maps with the federal General Land Office. The documents for the first twenty miles were submitted on March 27. They completed their second twenty-mile survey on May 7, 1906, and filed their maps on May 17.[24]

The Oregon Trunk, under the supervision of F. S. Gordon, completed its surveys for 100 miles from The Dalles to Madras on April 3, 1906. Although the survey began in 1905, the maps filed on April 5, 1906, were all dated between February 24 and April 3, 1906.[25]

The Oregon Trunk also carried out a survey for an alternate route, extending the Great Southern Railway (the branch off the Oregon Railroad & Navigation at The Dalles to Dufur) through the Tygh Valley and following the White River to the Deschutes River. However, the surveyors made the same discovery encountered earlier by Harriman: following the Deschutes River would be fifteen miles shorter and a lesser grade. The grade on the alternate route was 2.4 percent for eight miles and 2.5 percent for two miles, compared with the 0.3 percent along the Deschutes River.[26,27]

"Peg" Anspach, Oregon Trunk surveyor

Oregon Trunk surveyors

The Seattle group had been slow to incorporate but, threatened with competition, the Oregon Trunk was formally incorporated in Nevada on February 24, 1906, as the Oregon Trunk Line, Inc.[28] Its three officials were W.F. Nelson, R.A. Ballinger (who would become secretary of the interior in 1909), and L.I. Gregory. The stated intent was to build and operate a railroad up the Deschutes River for about 250 miles. At the corporation's first meeting on March 1, 1906, Nelson, the major shareholder, was elected president. The company was mortgaged for $3.9 million of negotiable bonds.

Almost immediately Nelson began communicating with officials of the Great Northern Railway, trying to generate interest. By April 17, 1906, Nelson told the Great Northern that his company had practically secured the right-of-way for the entire distance to Bend, Oregon.[29] At this early date, Nelson's activity was referred to James J. Hill, who said, "We are not at present in a position to interest ourselves in matters along the lines suggested."[30]

Bend was at one of the few fordable points along the Deschutes River and was known by early settlers as "Farewell Bend," providing a last sight of the river as they traveled west over the mountains. Bend sits high and dry on a desert plateau, with an elevation of 3,628 feet that can bring hard frosts even on summer mornings. Today, there are about 70,000 people in Bend. In the early 1900s, there were only a few hundred, in an isolated location on the edge of forests and surrounded by irrigable land, a location that attracted the attention of the railroads. In 1881, John Sizemore from Kentucky purchased the Farewell Bend Ranch for $14,000 on a site that eventually became the Brooks-Scanlon lumber plant.[31] Sizemore filed for a post office in 1886, and post office officials shortened the name to Bend. In June 1900, Alexander M. Drake moved to Central Oregon from the midwest. A wealthy man and a fisherman, he formed the Pilot Butte Development Company, platted the town, and incorporated Bend with 258 people on December 19, 1904.

Even though its survey maps had not received approval, the Oregon Trunk began grading in the summer of 1906 on the west bank of the Deschutes River, a mile upriver from the Columbia River. This grading continued for 1.5 miles until the line ran out of money a few months later. Nelson was having no success in selling bonds, even attempting to interest English investors to no avail.[32]

On August 29, 1906, the General Land Office returned the survey maps to both lines, stating that the routes should be 100 feet above the river from the Columbia River to Sherar's Bridge to allow for the future construction of dams.[33] Indeed, papers had been filed with the government for three dams, at two, twenty, and forty miles upstream from the Columbia River.[34] The Des Chutes Railroad argued with the Land Office, promising that they would relocate to a higher line on ninety-days notice if necessary. The Reclamation Service backed off on its requirements for the proposed dams, but the

Des Chutes submitted a higher line survey on September 4, 1907. The Oregon Trunk chose to ignore the Land Office and made no effort to change its line, which is understandable because its line was above the water level at the proposed dams.[35]

There were good reasons to avoid building dams in the Deschutes Canyon. From the point of view of the railroads, tracks considerably higher than water level would require such an increase in costs that the engineers would likely have abandoned the Deschutes route. From the point of view of the Reclamation Service, building a dam in an area without roads or a railroad would be enormously expensive. The government and the railroads would eventually agree that only tracks near the river would be feasible in terms of ease of construction and costs.

Both lines had filed survey maps with the Interior Department requesting right-of-ways on government-owned land. The Oregon Trunk survey stopped about 100 miles south of the Columbia River, and the Des Chutes survey stopped at Sherar's Bridge (river mile 44). The government approved both surveys in April 1907. In the first surveys, the Oregon Trunk on the west bank crossed temporarily to the east side at Horseshoe Bend. The Oregon Trunk crossed again, permanently, to the east bank (river mile 73) at North Junction because of the hard rock from that point south on the west bank and also because of difficulties in obtaining approval to pass through the Warm Springs Indian Reservation. The Des Chutes officials grew in confidence, because at these two sites the Oregon Trunk was on the eastern route surveyed by the Des Chutes, and it was anticipated that this would block construction of the Oregon Trunk.

The Oregon Trunk had to pass through reservation land that was later organized in 1937 as the Confederated Tribes of the Warm Springs Reservation of Oregon. This land was home to three major groups of Indians: the Wasco, the Warm Springs, and the Paiute. The Wasco bands were principally fisherman on the Columbia River, the most eastern group of Indians who spoke the Chinook language (the Oregon Trunk used Chinook words for many of its stations). The Warm Springs bands (also known as the Walla Walla) lived along the rivers and included the Tygh, Tenino, and Wyam, but they spoke a different language and had different customs than the Wasco. In 1855, these bands were moved by treaties to the Warm Springs Reservation, to be joined later by the Paiute after 1879. The Paiute were a Shoshone Snake band, living in southeastern Oregon.

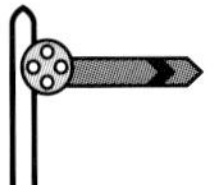

THE DESCHUTES RIVER POWER & DEVELOPMENT COMPANY, proposing to dam the Deschutes River, filed a protest against the maps of both railroads. But on March 25, 1908, the General Land Office rejected its proposal to build a dam at Sherar's Bridge, as well as the company's protest against the railroads.[36] At the same time, the commissioner of the General Land Office ruled that, where the two lines conflicted on their surveyed routes, the Des Chutes had prior rights. The Oregon Trunk appealed the ruling.

On June 18, 1908, a third railroad company, the Central Oregon Railroad Company, entered the picture, organized by local and Portland investors, who proposed to build from Shaniko to Madras and Bend.[37] The Central Oregon filed its maps from Madras to Bend in the summer of 1908, effectively tying up the best crossing site (in fact, the only reasonable one) over the deep Crooked River Canyon. Having this important site in its possession, the Central hoped for a takeover by Hill or Harriman, but neither man showed any interest.

The Department of the Interior ruled on the Oregon Trunk appeal July 18, 1908, defining the Deschutes Canyon as a "pass or defile," a definition that under federal law required that the maps of both railroads be approved.[38–40] Both lines appealed directly to Secretary of the Interior Garfield, who announced in March 1909 that he would approve the right-of-way maps before he left office within a week.[41] However, this didn't happen, and the controversy was left for the consideration of the new secretary of the interior, R.A. Ballinger (one of the Seattle bankers listed as an officer of the Oregon Trunk Line when it was incorporated in 1909).

During this interaction with the federal government, the ownership of the Oregon Trunk was changing. Unable to gain financing, Nelson acquired all the stock in the Oregon Trunk and sold out to V.D. Williamson of Spokane on August 6, 1908. Wlliamson, a millionaire whose father owned a large amount of real estate in Portland, then sold half interest for $39,342.50 to R. (Dick) B. Porter of the Porter Brothers & Welch construction company, the same company Hill used to build the Spokane, Portland & Seattle Railway.[42,43]

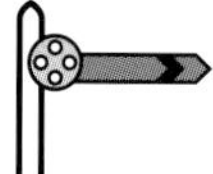

IN AUGUST 1908, the Porter Brothers and Nelson toured central Oregon by automobile, crossing the Cascades to Medford, and then by train to Portland. The men met with local banks and stated, "Work will commence in December, and it is understood that Porter Brothers will act as agents for the Hill interests."[44] In Portland they lunched with F.B. Clarke, president of the Spokane, Portland & Seattle, who learned that although Harriman had made a purchase offer for the Oregon Trunk, the owners preferred to deal with Hill. In August 1908, Dick Porter traveled to St. Paul to confer with Hill. This visit plus the comments the Porter brothers made on their trip through Oregon plus new surveying activity for the Oregon Trunk by N.W. Bethel (known to have worked for the Hill lines previously), stirred up talk about Hill's interest, which was rapidly and emphatically denied. A letter, from the St. Paul traffic department of the Great Northern to the assistant traffic manager in Seattle, reported a visit with John D. Porter. Porter indicated that the Porter Brothers had visited the Deschutes River, and that they had secured the charter of the Oregon Trunk, starting at Deschutes, twelve miles east of The Dalles, and running 127 miles upriver.[45]

But Johnson Porter said, "We are not fakers or holdup men. ...The rumor that the Hill system is behind our enterprise is entirely unfounded. There is absolutely no truth in the statement that we waited until the Harriman people began before we went on with our work. ...Within a week, we will have over 500 men at work. There is room for two railroads up the Deschutes if need be, but we selected this route first and do not mean to be crowded out."[46] Furthermore, according to Johnson Porter, Harriman tried to buy the Oregon Trunk (this was a month before John F. Stevens made Hill's ownership public). "The Harriman interests offered to give back all the money we had spent up to that time with a handsome profit thrown in and an interest in their contract besides if we would sell out to them. My reply both times was that we would not sell out for $5,000,000. ...Harriman hasn't a man in his employ who knows as much about Central Oregon as J. P Porter does. Why, it would take 700 cars a day for 30 years to pull the timber out of Central Oregon to say nothing about the wheat and other products."[47,48]

Prominent Hill officials claimed they had never even heard of the property. Nelson said emphatically, "Not only have there been no negotiations or purchase by the Hill people, but there is no understanding or intimation that the Hill people will purchase the line under any possible circumstances. The story is without any foundation whatever."[49] But by now, Hill had became more active, and it was getting harder to hide his involvement. In November 1908, he again invited Dick Porter to St. Paul. A representative of Siems and Shield, one of the contractors for the Spokane, Portland & Seattle, also participated in this meeting, as the subject of discussion was the cost of building the Oregon Trunk.[50] Porter told Hill that it was his desire to be the construction company for the first 100 miles, and if granted, he promised to sell his rights in the Oregon Trunk for what he paid. In anticipation, Porter obtained an option for the remaining shares owned by Williamson (the shares purchased six months later by John F. Stevens posing as John F. Sampson).

Both lines converged on privately held lands. Railroad lawyers were preparing condemnation actions against those private owners who refused to sell. Right-of-way agents were paying $25 per acre, and as much as $100 per acre for irrigated land.[51] By mid-November 1908, the Des Chutes Railroad filed its entire route to Bend with the Interior Department, and, immediately afterward, the Oregon Trunk filed its new plans. Remember that on November 10, 1908, the secretary of the interior had suspended all consideration of the survey maps, and a decision by the Interior Department was postponed pending a decision by the Bureau of Reclamation, which was considering a dam on the river. Not willing to wait, the Oregon Trunk started work on November 21, 1908, at the county bridge seven miles south of the

Columbia River.[52] It was said that Oregon Trunk working parties were also at Shaniko (for a possible extension to the Deschutes River) and at Sherar's Bridge, but this proved to be just a rumor.

Finally, the Interior Department discarded the private proposals for new dams, and in July 1909 Secretary of the Interior Ballinger ruled that both lines were entitled to the use of any locations where the narrow pass provided room for only one line. And thus both surveys were approved.[53,54]

Hill Turns Again to Stevens

In 1909, Hill called his trusted and good friend John F. Stevens to a meeting in New York City, with the specific purpose of persuading Stevens to take charge of the developments in Oregon.[55,56] Stevens was at first unwilling to resign as vice-president of the New York, New Haven and Hartford Railroad, but he reconsidered when Hill guaranteed him adequate financial support and appointed him president of the Spokane, Portland, & Seattle. Stevens accepted the job, believing that Hill viewed this as a first move to connect his northern lines through central Oregon to California.

Hill's first step was to provide Stevens with a bulging personal checking account and a mission to find a route through Oregon. Stevens immediately went to Portland, arriving on June 22, 1909. Sam Hill, son-in-law of James J. Hill, who lived at Maryhill near the Deschutes River although across the Columbia River, provided Stevens with two automobiles.

John F. Stevens — 1910

Stevens then embarked on his exploration of central Oregon as the fly fisherman, John F. Sampson.[57,58] It was apparent to Stevens that the only route with a reasonably low grade lay through the canyon of the Deschutes River, a route that would occupy the next two years of Stevens' life.

Later, the *Oregonian* remarked that "Stevens' incursion of extreme Southeastern Oregon is believed to confirm the suspicion that he has not invested in the Oregon Trunk without first having satisfied himself of a feasible outlet on the south," (to California).[59] Indeed, Stevens, accompanied by an unknown man who registered in hotels as H.P. Shannon (supposedly a Hill construction official), toured over a 10-day period, in addition to the Deschutes River, Shaniko, Madras, Bend, Prineville, Klamath Falls, and Burns.[60]

Reporters revealed Sampson's true identity when they tracked him to The Cornelius, a hotel in Portland, where the clerks identified him from a photograph.[60] Reporters were not the only ones on his trail; various representatives of the Harriman lines followed his path, holding extensive conversations with local people in an attempt to detect the true objectives of Stevens' trip. John F. Sampson didn't fool as many people as he thought.

It was a common practice among officials of the Great Northern to communicate in code when using a public method like a telegram. Stevens' code name was Proteus, a son of Poseidon who could assume various shapes and forms.[61] Proteus telegraphed R. Brown, James J. Hill's secretary, on July 4, 1909:

> WHEN WILL CHIME BENEFICIAL
> INDELIBLE SCARED GANYMEDE[62]

Stevens later sent Hill a handwritten letter that revealed the message in his coded telegram, "I have just completed a 600 mile trip thru Central & Southern Oregon. I am amazed at what I found. Oregon — in my opinion — is a greater state — by far than Washington. I have just wired Brown to find when you will be in St. Paul." [63]

Working as John F. Sampson and with the Hill attorneys in Portland, Carey & Kerr, Stevens learned (probably from Johnson Porter) that the Oregon Trunk held a railroad charter for a line, running along the Deschutes River and south to California.[64] The Great Northern traffic department in St. Paul reported a meeting with John Porter, indicating that the Porter Brothers had visited the Deschutes River, and that they had secured the charter of the Oregon Trunk.[65] Stevens also learned that the Oregon Trunk had done a little grading in 1906, but within three months, had halted the effort because of inexperience and lack of money.[66]

According to Stevens, Harriman had considered buying the line.[67] Harriman, in a visit to Oregon in summer 1908 publically declared his intention to build along the Deschutes River to Bend.[68] Indeed, Harriman offered to purchase the Oregon Trunk, but his attorneys reported that the charter was not legal (specifically that a charter filed in Nevada did not apply to Oregon, nor did it specify a southern terminus as was required by Oregon law). Harriman declined to pursue the purchase.

Avoiding publicity, Stevens clandestinely met the owner of the Oregon Trunk at midnight, August 15, 1909, on a rainy night in a Portland public park.[69] They reached a verbal agreement for transfer of the Oregon Trunk charter, and the next day Stevens delivered a check for $126,000, to be cashed a few days later. Many historians have indicated that Stevens met with W.F. "Billy" Nelson on that midnight in the park. Nelson, however, died at the end of 1908, and a controlling interest in the Oregon Trunk was acquired by V.D. Williamson.[70] Williamson was president of the company in 1909, and most assuredly he was the official meeting in the park with Stevens. Indeed, a day after the agreement on August 15, 1909, Williamson was quoted in the *Oregonian* saying, "A controlling interest in the Oregon Trunk railroad was sold to Mr. Stevens at a meeting last night."[71] The total purchase price for the Oregon Trunk was $165,342.50, including the stock Williamson sold to R.B. Porter. This does not seem like a lot of money until it is considered in historical context; today that amount of money would buy four nice automobiles, back then it would have bought 330.

The negotiations were a little complicated.[72] In September 1908, W.F. Nelson sold all of his stock in the Oregon Trunk to V.D. Williamson. Williamson sold half his total stock to R.B. Porter for $39,342.50. A holding company for the remaining stock was created, the Oregon and California Construction Company, owned equally by R.B. Porter and Williamson. Williamson assigned his half of the holding company to J.D. Porter for $126,000. The holding company was then purchased by Stevens and dissolved. R.B. Porter sold his share for the purchase price of $39,342.50. The Porter brothers did not profit from these deals because they knew that millions of dollars would come their way in the construction of the railroad.

The Great Northern Railway Company advanced the funds for the purchase and construction of the Oregon Trunk until 1910, when a half interest was acquired by the Northern Pacific; thereafter the companies jointly funded the project through the Spokane, Portland & Seattle Railway. The Oregon Trunk stock was transferred to the Spokane, Portland & Seattle, the value equaling the money thus far advanced to the Oregon Trunk, $10 million.[73] This final arrangement was not made public until all of the Oregon Trunk stock was secured. The last remaining stock in the Oregon Trunk not owned by the Hill lines was purchased in 1910 from Malcom Moody for $5,000.

Stevens immediately had engineers stake out the line on the west bank of the Deschutes River in the lower canyon near the Columbia River. The Harriman people first learned of this effort when grading began. Even at this early date, Stevens believed it was in the best interests of both Hill and Harriman to build and use a joint line. He traveled to Chicago to meet with a man close to Harriman, Julius Krutschnitt, director of overall maintenance and operations for the Harriman lines. Krutschnitt, however, offered no encouragement to Stevens' proposed cooperation. Indeed, he told Stevens, "The only way I could get up that valley would be to walk. That I was nothing but a penniless promoter and had no such backing as I boasted." Stevens replied, "Possibly so, Mr. Krutschnitt, I may be defeated, but if I am, you all will know that you have been in one hell of a fight."[74]

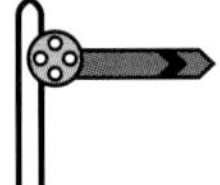

BEFORE HARRIMAN knew it, Hill had purchased the Oregon Trunk. Construction crews for both railroads entered the Deschutes Canyon in the last week of July 1909. Stevens argued with Hill that keeping the Hill involvement a secret was a hindrance. Stevens believed that making it public would reveal the seriousness of the effort; many in the Harriman camp believed the Porter Brothers were bluffing, that they were hoping to drive up the price for an eventual sale to the Des Chutes line.

Finally, on August 14, 1909, James J. Hill wrote to Stevens, "If you think best to come out and say that I am behind the enterprise you can do so at any time but be sure to uncover nothing west of Portland. ...As regards the DesChutes enterprise, so far I have not done anything with it in connection with either the North Bank Road or anyone else. So far it is my own enterprise and later I will dispose of it." [75]

Only two days later, Stevens announced to the press that the Hill lines intended to build along the Deschutes River to Bend, Oregon. "I have acquired a controlling interest in the project, have all necessary financial arrangements completed, and the road will be built as fast as it can be reasonably done with men and money."[35] Within a month, newspapers were saying, "This is going to be one of the hardest contested railroad fights that has ever been known in the West, with the Hill line on one side of the canyon and Harriman on the other."[76]

Stevens was a typical railroad man, saying only what he had to. "Mr. Stevens switched the conversation to a discussion of the series of championship baseball games between the Pittsburgh and Detroit teams. It is characteristic of Mr. Stevens, who is Hill's personal representative, that loquacity is not one of his traits. Further questioning as to the plans of the railroad of which he is the executive head was just as productive of results as could be expected from an equally persistent interrogating of a sphinx."[6]

In August 1909, V.D. Williamson purchased the Central Oregon Railroad for only $15,000.[78] Stevens acquired the Central Oregon Railroad when he purchased the Oregon Trunk. This was an incredibly important purchase. Both the Des Chutes Railroad and the Central Oregon had submitted survey maps for the line from Madras to Bend, but the date of submission by the Central Oregon, June 18, 1908, was a full four months earlier. The earlier submission date was significant because this part of the line went over flat land, and the Department of Interior could not enforce the principle of the "defile;" therefore

Central Oregon's possession of the only good site for a crossing of the Crooked River Canyon blocked the Des Chutes surveyed line.

Stevens was looking ahead. He sent his men to explore beyond Bend, south to California. In addition, Stevens considered an extension of the Burlington from Pocatello, Idaho, to Bend, and for this purpose, chartered a new railroad, the Boise & Western Railway on September 13, 1909, with the real owners kept secret. Over the next several months, he spent over $100,000, purchasing land and surveying a route through the Malheur Canyon in southeastern Oregon.[79] Stevens also purchased a twelve-mile line that ran northeast out of Medford, Oregon, the Pacific and Eastern Railway. This was major activity. Oregon Trunk officials admitted: "The railroad now has about twenty surveying parties in the field, each party composed of from five to eight men, that every surveyor in this part of the country seeking work had been offered a chance and that men have been brought from a distance."[80]

In August 1909, the Oregon Trunk officers occupied new quarters in the Henry Building in Portland. On September 6, 1909, Stevens, president of the Spokane, Portland & Seattle, took control of the Oregon Trunk, replacing Williamson as president. The Oregon Trunk was at that time incorporated in the State of Nevada, a state that held a dim view of dueling. Stevens' oath of office required him to say, " ...and I do further solemnly swear that I have not fought a duel, nor sent or accepted a challenge to fight a duel, nor been a second to either party, nor in any manner aided and assisted in such duel, nor been knowingly the bear of such challenge or acceptance since the adoption of the Constitution of the State of Nevada, and that I will not be so engaged or concerned directly or indirectly, in or about any such duel during my continuance in office."[81] Nevertheless, Stevens was already involved in a duel of a different sort, the Deschutes River Railroad War.

The Oregon Trunk filed new incorporation papers with the state of Washington on November 3, 1909, and changed its name from the Oregon Trunk Line to the Oregon Trunk Railway.[82,83] The aim was to overcome the possibility that the Nevada connection might prove to be an obstacle. At the same time, the filing empowered the line to build from the north bank of the Columbia River to Klamath Falls near California. The Oregon Trunk Railway took over the 104.1 miles of the Oregon Trunk Line and the 11.7 miles of surveyed line of the Central Oregon Railroad.[83]

In the fall of 1909, the Oregon Trunk submitted updated and revised survey maps to the federal government. At Moody, the line would be built 160 feet above the water line to avoid potential future conflict with a private dam proposed by Malcolm Moody. The line was seventy feet above water line at Sherar's Bridge, another potential private dam site, and 100 feet above water line at the site where dams were subsequently built. The Oregon Trunk lawyers tried repeatedly to get revisions approved without stipulations that might put the railroad at risk for future relocations. But the government failed to respond, and the Oregon Trunk finally acquiesced, recognizing the fact that it was extremely unlikely that some future activity would force a relocation of its tracks.[84]

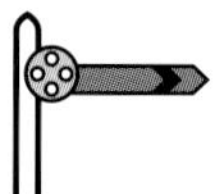

THE HARRIMAN LINES had already planned a route to Bend on the east bank of the Deschutes Canyon connecting to the Oregon Railroad & Navigation, but as it headed south it traversed land that Stevens had acquired. As soon as they were aware of the Hill effort, the Harriman lines hurried men and supplies into the canyon (having the benefit of the nearby tracks of the Oregon Railroad & Navigation) and there followed a few hectic weeks of confrontation (see Chapter 8). The general manager of the Oregon Railroad & Navigation Co., James P. O'Brien, said in November 1908 that surveying of the Harriman line will be finished in two weeks, and then "the dirt will fly."[85] A few months later, O'Brien ordered Chief Engineer George Boschke to start construction. The Oregon Trunk contractor, Porter Brothers, immediately began to move their workers and equipment into the river canyon. Each railroad was in the hands of individuals, George Boschke and John Stevens, judged by many to be the two of the most competent railroad engineers in the country.[86]

Initiation of Construction

On February 15, 1909, Hill secretly approved construction of the Oregon Trunk, but he could not begin building because his maps had not been approved. The estimate was for 130 miles at a cost of $4,773,000 over a year-and-a-half.[87] Just two days later, General Manager O'Brien of the Harriman system in the Pacific Northwest, announced that he had been authorized to begin construction of a railroad in central Oregon. He said: "The opposition of the Oregon Trunk line which is accused of placing obstacles in the way of the Harriman project can hardly prove serious."[88]

The Hill lines, the Great Northern and the Northern Pacific, competed with each other for business. At this early stage of construction along the Deschutes River, management officials in St. Paul were exhorting local offices in Seattle and Portland to influence the purchase of supplies and materials.[89] They further closely watched the purchases of the Porter Brothers to make sure they used the parent railroad's good customers, such as Closset & Devers, wholesale coffee and tea merchants, who imported entire railroad cars of goods to Portland.

ON JULY 15, 1909, Harriman gave the go ahead for the Twohy Brothers Construction Company of Spokane to begin the extension up the Deschutes River.[90] One week later, Stevens ordered the Porter Brothers to begin work. Construction material immediately began to be transferred from steamboat at The Dalles by wagon to the Porter camps. On July 28, 1909, the *Bend Bulletin* headlined, "The Fight is On."

Steamers at The Dalles unloaded sixty horses and mules, forty wagons, twelve new Studebaker wagons, camping gear, and construction tools for the Porter Brothers. Horse-drawn wagons carried the supplies from The Dalles to Sherar's Bridge, across the river to Grass Valley, and then down into the Deschutes Canyon to camps forty and seventy-five miles upstream. Johnson Porter was supervising the unloading at The Dalles, not admitting that he worked for Hill, but there were so many former Hill men now working for the Oregon Trunk, that most observers were not fooled.[91] The editorialist for the *Bend Bulletin* said, "It looks like war. And we hope it is."[92]

- CHAPTER EIGHT -

Railroad Construction and Competition Along the Deschutes River

We Are Not Building a Turkey Track up the River

Two stretches along the Deschutes River became areas of contention between the two railroads, both on the river banks and in the courts. The two sites were on the east bank of the Deschutes River, locations at forty-one and seventy miles upstream where the Oregon Trunk on the west bank wanted to cross the river.

The Des Chutes Railroad was the first to begin construction along the river, early in July 1909, laying track from its junction with the Oregon Railroad & Navigation Company line on the south bank of the Columbia River. The junction site went through a confusing progression of name changes, from Deschutes Junction to Sherman, to its present day name of Ainsworth. The Oregon Trunk was not laying track, but had created a large supply yard at Moody, bringing equipment and material across the Columbia River by ferry from the Spokane, Portland & Seattle tracks. Further upstream, both companies began construction in the Deschutes Canyon at midnight, July 27, 1909, the date designated by the Department of the Interior when the approved survey lines went into effect. In mid-July the Department of the Interior approved the Des Chutes survey. Thirty miles were in conflict with the surveys of the Oregon Trunk. In two segments, the Oregon Trunk crossed to the east bank, and the two railroads both planned to lay track in the exact same sites on the east bank. The first confrontation emerged on the supply road to Horseshoe Bend.

In July 1909, Harriman's Oregon Railroad & Navigation Company shipped twenty-six railroad cars of equipment, supplies, and laborers to The Dalles for movement into the Deschutes River Canyon, and they began grading the first forty miles.[1] The Des Chutes contractor, the Twohy Brothers, had allegedly received verbal approval from local ranchers for construction roads into the canyon. In three weeks, a long supply road was built at a cost of $8,000, down Harris Canyon, dropping 2,000 feet to the east bank of the river, and proceeding upstream to river mile 41.[1–3] River mile 41 marks the location of Horseshoe Bend, a curve in the river where both railroads intended to build a short-cut tunnel 800 feet long. This large horseshoe-shaped bend is also known as Twin Crossings. This is because the engineers for the Oregon Trunk decided it was significantly shorter to cross the river and build alongside of the Des Chutes through its own tunnel, and then return to the west side—two bridges, Twin Crossings.

The Conflict at Horseshoe Bend

By the time he was thirty years old, Harry E. Carleton was a respected construction contractor and tunnel builder who faithfully used Italian immigrants as his workers (they called him "Carletoni"). Quinn, Quinn, and King, in writing their *Handbook to the Deschutes River Canyon,* included facts and stories from conversations with Carleton's widow living in Dufur, Oregon. Mrs. Carleton also made available Carleton's journal.[4]

The Oregon Trunk's surveyed line was along the west bank of the river, except for the two locations where it moved to the east bank, the first being Horseshoe Bend. When the Des Chutes began

Harry E. Carleton — 1921

construction on the east bank, The Oregon Trunk crew, under the direction of Harry Carleton, promptly invaded the east bank to work at Horseshoe Bend. Johnson Porter told Carleton, "We're going to have to organize an army and go in there and take the Union Pacific bunch out."[5]

Carleton recruited about 100 of his usual Italian workers in Portland and took them up the Columbia River by sternwheeler to The Dalles. While camping on the shore, Carleton's force grew to about 150 men. They set out in four-horse wagons to cross the Deschutes River to the small town of Grass Valley. Unwittingly, the men took the wrong road and went south, arriving in Boyd late at night. In 1909, Boyd was the home of the Boyd Rolling Mills, which produced Rolling Pin flour.[6] The Boyd townspeople were perplexed and alarmed by this invading force of foreigners, who camped in a vacant space across from the general store. Carousing around bonfires, the young men did nothing to quell the town's anxiety. The next morning, the outfit quietly left as the men of Boyd, holding loaded shotguns, watched from behind locked doors.

Crossing the Deschutes River at Free Bridge, seven miles upstream from the Columbia River, the men and their wagons climbed to the east plateau. At the top of Harris Canyon, they encountered armed men guarding the road the Twohy Brothers had built. Carleton offered no resistance and quietly retreated. After darkness fell, Carleton's army of Italians descended the road into the canyon, where they were met by gunfire. Immediately, both sides were firing their guns, fortunately poorly aimed. No one was harmed and Carleton was able to set up camp at the river's edge. For the next three weeks, the two groups mingled with each other, on the verge of violence. Each day, Sheriff Jay C. Freeman of Sherman County visited the site with several deputies, preserving order in the two camps. Freeman's deputies did not carry firearms, but prevailed by virtue of their legal authority.

John F. Stevens had allegedly purchased three ranches along the canyon, including the 320-acre Fred Gurtz (sometimes referred to as "Girt" in the old newspapers) ranch, which contained the new Twohy Brothers' wagon road.[1] Stevens ordered Porter Brothers to erect a gate with "no trespassing" signs. The major water supply for Twohy Brothers was a spring located on one of the other ranches, sixteen-acres owned by L.R. French and H.F. Downing.[7] At this site, Porter Brothers posted a sign reading, "No water to spare. Porter Brothers."[1,8]

Sherman County records revealed that Stevens and Porter Brothers had not purchased the ranches, but had merely secured sixty-day options for them: $200 cash for the Gurtz ranch and $100 to French and Downing.[9] At the end of sixty days the ranches could be purchased, not for the $30,000 Porter Brothers publicly stated, but $4,600 for Gurtz and only $1,200 for French and Downing.

Erecting a wooden gate on the river side of the wagon road and a padlocked wire gate at the side toward Grass Valley, Harry Carleton and seventy-five of his armed Italian workers blocked the road. They intended to cause dwindling supplies, forcing the Twohy men to leave.[10] Supply wagons backed up, single file, along the road. Within several days, on Sunday, August 1, 1909, Sheriff Freeman arrived at the gate, accompanied by newspaper reporters, Judge Littlefield from Moro, and several deputies, carrying a Moro court order granting passage for the wagons.[9] George Palmer Putnam was the on-site reporter for the *Oregonian* and would go on to own the newspaper in Bend, and much later become Amelia Earhart's publicist and husband.

G. P. Putnam in Deschutes Canyon — 1909

Johnson Porter

Littlefield: Who is in charge?

Carleton: I guess I am.

Littlefield: I am going to open this gate.

Carleton: I have orders from headquarters not to let anyone go through.

Littlefield: I'm ordering you that they will go through. I have an order from the court. I'm going to open that gate. (And he did.)

Littlefield: What are you going to do about that?

Carleton: I'm not going to do anything while you open the gate but you're still not going through. I've got to obey orders, same as anybody else.[11]

Littlefield signaled the first wagon to proceed. Carleton described what happened next: "I gave orders to my men to stop the team, and right then I lost control of the whole layout. Not being the army, why the next I knew, the Italians had piled all over everything. They pulled Freeman and his deputies off their horses; the judge was bounced around in the dust and was just completely wild-eyed; and the Italians, instead of just stopping the team from going through the gate, unhitched the horses and pulled the harnesses off. There were horses running wild all through the sagebrush. After a while things quieted down and the judge walked up to me and shook his hand and said, 'I'm going to see that you're indicted for inciting a riot!' and then, besides that, Sheriff Freeman walked up and placed me under arrest. I said, 'Well, I guess I have to obey the law, but still nobody's going through the gate.'"[12]

In the midst of this mêlée, a message from Johnson Porter arrived, ordering his men to allow passage. Ten wagons with 200 Twohy workers, including the Sheriff and twenty deputies, passed through the Italians lining the road.[1,9] Afterward, Sheriff Freeman arrested Carleton and two of his men, A. "Tony" Scapelli (the boss of the Italian workers) and Sam Sappano; they were released on $750 bail by Justice of the Peace R. I. Westerfield in Grass Valley.[9,13] From then on, the Italian workers hailed Tony Scapelli as the "Italian hero of the gate."[14] When Scapelli's pet bulldog, the "Dago King," arrived from Spokane, the Italian workers offered an ovation so enthusiastic that it threatened to temporarily stop their work.

Tony Scapelli

Perhaps it was Porter's intention to start an altercation that would motivate the U. S. District Court to move promptly in this stalemate. Meanwhile, the confrontation was the talk of the town in The Dalles and tiny Grass Valley:

> The railroad scrap on the Deschutes River was compared with a difference of opinion by two men on the streets of this city [The Dalles] Monday. One man, a short heavy set fellow, who appeared as though he might be able to hand out a pretty stiff fight, publicly announced that he was open for a scrap and as is usual with the fistic element before the fight, announced that he could whip all comers. ...He was rather surprised to have his challenge immediately taken up by a tall slim fellow who looked like one good stiff one would break him in two ... without waiting he turned loose a regular Kid McCoy corkscrew stemwinder which ended with a sharp crack on the point of the champion's jaw and which put him to the mat like a sack of wheat dropped out of a second story window. He recovered quickly however and came up gamely but another blow, a twin to the first, floored him again. He came again and clinched and they rolled over and over on the sidewalk until just as this critical moment Night Watchman John Crate came around the corner and the embrace of the couple at once became friendly.
>
> "I'll buy you a drink," said the short heavy fellow.
>
> "I'll be d---d if I won't do the same," said the tall one and they walked away into a thirst parlor with their arms lovingly around each other's shoulders.
>
> Some people have gone so far as to say that the fight for the right-of-way up the Deschutes is like the one Monday in this city, saying that both roads will hand each other some stiff ones until the public comes around the corner, expecting to be able to say that at last the people have been able to get a railroad into Interior Oregon and then suddenly there will be a change to the other extreme and there will be a love feast and one opinion and one road will be the result. The only thing to do, however, is to wait.[7]
>
> A person might as well try to talk in some foreign language unknown to the residents of Grass Valley as to speak of anything except railroads and the fight that is being waged on the Deschutes with Grass Valley as the central point of interests, for this subject is the only thing people in that thriving little town think about or have any time for. This place is bustling from the wee small hours of the morning until late hours at night, and it sometimes occurs that there are things doing there every minute of the 24 hours. ...That trouble is a contingency and might break out at some stage of the game, on the other hand, is evidence among the men along the camps on the river by the fact that many of them are armed. About 50 Italians were sent out from Grass Valley Friday by Porter Brothers to establish their own camp above Horse Shoe bend. Several of the foreigners carried rifles across their backs, while others wear armed revolvers which may be seen sticking out from the hip pockets on nearly every man who travels between Grass Valley and the river. The rattlesnakes are very numerous on the sides of the Deschutes canyon and it is possible that the weapons are carried as a protection from these reptiles.[9]

In Federal Court

Johnson Porter arrived in Grass Valley on August 4, 1909, accompanied by his attorney, Charles H. Carey, to be personally served with the complaint and restraining order the Harriman forces obtained in the local court.

> I came here on purpose that they might serve me with any papers they want. I am not going to evade service in any way. The reason we closed the wagon road was because when I first came up ahead of my teams I was informed by the Harriman people that we could not go down to the river over their road unless we forced our way. I thought it's a pretty good way of using force to buy the ranch and cut off their wagon road. The other road has had a big advantage over us, also, by having a month's head start and by shipping over the railroad. We wanted to offset that advantage, and I think we did it.
>
> It was our intention to open the wagon road last Saturday but they boasted about how they were going to send their teams through the next day, and so we kept the road closed just for the sight of seeing their teams turn back.
>
> Yesterday we sent a messenger from The Dalles with instructions to our men to open the gates. Yes, we expect to contest the injunctions in the courts; that is the proper way to settle the matter. I believe we will win, but I don't know that we shall lock the gates again. It will depend on whether they try to shut us off the wagon road down the canyon.
>
> We are not building a turkey track up the river.[13]

Charles H. Carey, the attorney representing the Porter Brothers, issued a statement that there would be no further disregard of the court's orders; the controversy would be thrashed out in the courts.[13] In response to the involvement of the local court and Judge Littlefield on the road to Horseshoe Bend, the Oregon Trunk obtained an injunction on August 9, 1909, from U.S. District Court Judge Wolverton, ordering the Des Chutes line to cease work on the southern sixty miles of their surveyed route. In a forty-two-page typewritten complaint, the Oregon Trunk charged the Des Chutes with trespassing, blowing up part of the Oregon Trunk right-of-way, removing grade markers, and concluded that violence was threatened unless Des Chutes work ceased.[15] Carey declared that he had the affidavits of all the ranch owners who gave options to John Stevens, and that they had not entered into verbal agreements with the Harriman people permitting the latter to cross their lands.[13] The Des Chutes attorneys welcomed the opportunity for a hearing in court, where they planned to attack the legality of the Oregon Trunk.

Twohy Brothers retaliated with a restraining order issued in the Sherman County Circuit Court of the State of Oregon against Porter Brothers operations in the 7.5 miles around Horseshoe Bend.[16,17] However, Judge Butler in Moro, Oregon, dissolved this temporary injunction.[18,19] Butler ruled that Carey was correct, and that Twohy Brothers could not prove that they had secured a right to cross the Gurtz ranch. Thus Stevens' option to purchase the ranch gave Porter Brothers the right to close the road. The armed guards at the road across the Gurtz ranch resumed their posts, and for a month forced Twohy Brothers' supplies and men to follow other routes. The road was reopened on September 22, 1909, after the hearings in the U.S. District Court.[20]

James J. Hill had some advice for John Stevens, "I see by the newspapers that the Union Pacific people are making all the opposition in their power. Naturally, this is to be expected, and I think it safe to assume that you may look for all the opposition and delay they can give you. However, your lawyers will have to put up a steady contest until everything is settled. Of course, you understand the question of grades is a very important one and that every water power company will hold you up wherever they can and for as much as they can. I hope you have a good right-of-way man who will button up all trades as promptly as possible. The right-of-way experience on the North Bank Line was terrific because they [Union Pacific] did not act with sufficient promptness."[21]

WHILE THE TWO CAMPS waited for the district court decision, they continued to work in the same

Construction camp at Beavertail, river mile 31.5

general area at Horseshoe Bend, each building their own tunnel, 100 yards apart. The tunnels were sufficiently close to each other that blasting would fling rocks into each other's workers and camps.

The two construction companies didn't begin work at the mouth of the river and move progressively upstream. Instead, both companies opened work camps at multiple sites along the river and worked at these sites simultaneously. At a hillside opposite the mouth of the Warm Springs River, two opposing crews of fifty men each were grading at a point on the east bank where the surveys overlapped.[14] The Porter men were about four feet higher than the Twohy men. As quickly as the Porter men shoveled the hillside down to the Twohy line, the Twohy men working below shoveled the dirt even further downward. This cooperative effort may have continued but the upper gang soon began loosening large boulders that rolled down on the lower gang. Leaving their surveyed route, the Twohy men climbed the hillside and began rolling boulders down on the Porter men. Both construction crews believed they had priority and that the other would have to give way.

Forty-one miles upstream from the Columbia River, Harry Carleton encountered surveyors working for the Des Chutes at Horseshoe Bend. One surveyor, named Craven, yelled at Carleton, "All you are is a mercenary, and a hired gunman brought in here to cause trouble." A short fist fight ensued as Carleton's friend, Albert Hill, restrained the other surveyors by brandishing his gun.[22]

A few days before court proceedings began, Johnson Porter acquired a right-of-way for $3,000 through W.W. Brown's ranch, adjoining Willow Creek 105 miles upstream. Although they already owned a right-of-way on the Brown Ranch, the Harriman line had further attempted to buy this one as well (which sat on 0.3 acres of land between their own existing right-of-way and the river), a deliberate effort to keep the Oregon Trunk off the ranch. But, Brown refused to sell to Harriman and sold the second right-of-way to Porter for the same price, saying he wanted to see both lines built.[23] He did enjoy the profit from selling two right-of-ways.[14] "If you see a man in Shaniko," said an Oregon Trunk right-of-way agent, "who is particularly well dressed and exhibits lots of dog and has money to spend, you can be sure he owned land in the Deschutes Canyon. We know."[14]

The Des Chutes Railroad had acquired the Dean Ranch and posted "no trespassing" signs, controlling access to a Porter Brothers camp at Whitehorse Rapids.[24] James B. Eddy, a right-of-way agent for the Oregon Railroad & Navigation Company, was the man who acquired the ranch, but to keep it a secret he used his married daughter's name in drawing up the deed.

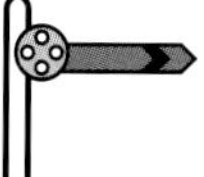

THE CONTEST moved to the federal courtroom in Portland, presided over by Judge Robert S. Bean. The Harriman side attacked aggressively, with attorney W.W. Cotton assailing the legality of the Oregon Trunk and charging the line with perjury and fraud. He made these claims in an opening statement on August 18, 1909, which lasted three hours, and in a closing argument three days later, which required over four hours.[25,26] Specifically, the Harriman attorney claimed that the Oregon Trunk survey was made long ago by another company, subsequently purchased by the Oregon Trunk and filed illegally with the Department of the Interior as its own survey. He further argued that it was unfair to enforce an injunction solely against Twohy Brothers, thereby preventing their work, and that instead the injunction should apply to both railroads.

Cotton emphasized that the Des Chutes Railroad had incorporated on February 2, 1906, and filed its papers with the Department of the Interior in March and May of 1906, giving it priority. Cotton further argued that Oregon Trunk's Nevada incorporation actually did not give the Oregon Trunk permission to build a railroad, let alone a railroad in Oregon, and thus it had no right to build.

> I know it will be heralded abroad that I have tried to have railroad building in the Deschutes stopped altogether, when really my only interest is to prevent the spending of needless money, with the great injury that may be done to the side which is restrained from working; and to prevent fighting and bloodshed, which is likely to follow otherwise. It is absurd, expensive, and unnecessary for one side to hire a bunch of Dagoes under a man with a reputation as a fighter to drive off our men. And it is absurd for us to employ a counter-gang of Austrians or Irishmen to lick the Dagoes.[25]

No one bothered to point out that "Dago," the slang name for an Italian or a Spaniard (corrupted from the Spanish name, Diego), was used only when the intention was clearly to be derogatory and offensive.

The Oregon Trunk took its turn on the second day in court. The Oregon Trunk lawyers argued that its surveys were made earlier, between February 24 and April 3, 1906, and that it had filed for incorporation on February 24, 1906 and filed its survey on April 16, 1906. Indeed, the case hinged on the Oregon Trunk's argument that the Harriman survey was filed three months after the Oregon Trunk survey had been approved. Attorneys C. H. Carey and J. B. Kerr further claimed that the Harriman forces did not really want to build a railroad; they just wanted to block the Hill line. Johnson Porter testified that the construction engineer for the Des Chutes, H.A. Brandon, told him that the Des Chutes was not doing any serious building, just enough to challenge the Oregon Trunk's right-of-way.

Judge Bean ruled in favor of the Oregon Trunk. On the same day the ruling was announced, August 25, 1909, a front-page article of the *Oregonian* reported Harriman's return home from Germany. He was said to be with an alert mind but rumored to have a serious illness (his terminal cancer was still a secret). The front page featured a large cartoon of a representative Wall Street tycoon reading details of Harriman's health, "Mr. Harriman's temperature has risen slightly. Suppose that certain information received from Central Oregon had something to do with this?"[27]

Judge Bean ruled that the Des Chutes Railroad was enjoined from obstructing the work of the Oregon Trunk and from trespassing on its property.[27] His ruling pointed out that the Des Chutes maps, filed in March and May 1906, were returned to address objections regarding future dams. It was not until June 21, 1906, that new maps were filed and approved. The problem was that these Des Chute maps covered only the first forty miles up the river. The Des Chutes had made no survey beyond the forty-mile mark before the Oregon Trunk's approval by the Department of the Interior on July 21, 1908.

Remember also that the Oregon Trunk had purchased the Central Oregon Railroad with its approved surveyed line from Madras to Bend in August 1909. The Central Oregon Railroad was formed in 1908 by local people in and around Bend, but its principal owners were Portland men and their company, the Deschutes Irrigation & Power Company.[28] The Central Oregon Railroad owned two key pieces of right-of-way: a line through Davidson's Ranch at North Junction and a line from Madras to Bend with the only reasonable crossing site over the deep Crooked River Canyon.

Des Chutes surveys beyond the forty-mile mark began on August 29 and were completed October 9 of 1908. Judge Bean concluded that the Oregon Trunk already had an approved map of a line over the disputed territory. But the Des Chutes Railroad raised three important questions: Did the Oregon Trunk Nevada incorporation invalidate their maps? Did the Oregon Trunk actually carry out their survey as they claimed? Did the Oregon Trunk act falsely and illegally?

Judge Bean said that the Des Chutes was powerless to raise these questions because it was not interested in the Deschutes property at the time of Oregon Trunk's incorporation in 1906. "It was a stranger to the proceedings and the title."[27] Furthermore, because the secretary of the interior had the right to dispose of public lands, his action could only be challenged by someone in the government or someone who had acquired a right to the land before he had approved ownership.

The outcome of the case was determined by the fact that the Des Chutes had not performed a survey in the disputed area before the approval of the Oregon Trunk's maps. Bean concluded, "Each of the parties is now actually engaged, apparently in good faith, in building its road from the mouth of the Deschutes to Eastern Oregon, and neither should be permitted to obstruct the work of the other. The plaintiff's [Oregon Trunk] ownership and right to occupy the disputed territory does not prevent the defendant [Des Chutes] from proceeding with its road. If the plaintiff's road as delineated on its approved map is through a canyon, pass or defile, it cannot, on account of any priority it secured by reason of such approval, prevent the defendant from using or occupying the same upon such terms as may be adjudged most equitable."[27]

The Hill lawyers said that the Hill interests would not oppose the building of a line by the Des Chutes Railroad, and that they wished to compromise to avoid further litigation. A few days later, on September 9, 1909, E.H. Harriman died. The front-page headline in the next day's *Oregonian* said, "Victor in Battles of Finance Loses to Grim Reaper."[29] Harriman's replacement as president of the Union Pacific, Judge Robert Scott Lovett, had several meetings with Hill in February 1910. Lovett was never enthusiastic over the Des Chutes line and was responsive to Hill's overture to share track rights from the Columbia River to Madras. Hill denied having a wish to enter California, saying that he only wanted to tap the timber in Oregon around Klamath Falls and Medford. The two men agreed to have the chief engineers, George Kyle for the Oregon Trunk and George.W. Boschke for the Des Chutes, meet to discuss details.

The negotiations did not go well. The Harriman men wanted to use the Oregon Trunk tracks in two places, over the eleven miles opposite the Warm Springs Reservation and over the Crooked River Bridge. Stevens proposed joint usage all the way from the Columbia River. Lovett would agree if Hill would absorb the $2 million already spent by the Des Chutes line, something Hill would not do. In Stevens' opinion, pride was in the way; the Harriman men were angry over the thought of using Hill tracks.[30]

Back to Work

Within days after the decision in federal court, Porter Brothers had five camps established. Johnson Porter said, "We are not watching the Harriman forces. We are just sawing wood and going ahead ourselves and don't care what they do. They have 120 miles of river to go ahead on if they mean business and we did not stop their operations by buying their wagon road. ...On the other hand they watch us like hawks. When we want to know where to locate one of our teams, where it spent the night etc., all we have to do is ask some of the Harriman men and they can tell us in a minute without any expense to us. ...While they watch us work, we go ahead and do things."[1]

Oregon Trunk north portal, Horseshoe Bend

Mustachioed Harry Carleton at north portal, Horseshoe Bend

Harry Carleton at Horseshoe Bend

Oregon Trunk north crossing, Horseshoe Bend

Construction stations, south side, Horseshoe Bend

South crossing, Horseshoe Bend, Des Chutes Tunnel in background

Twin Crossings, Horseshoe Bend

North crossing, Horseshoe Bend — 2005

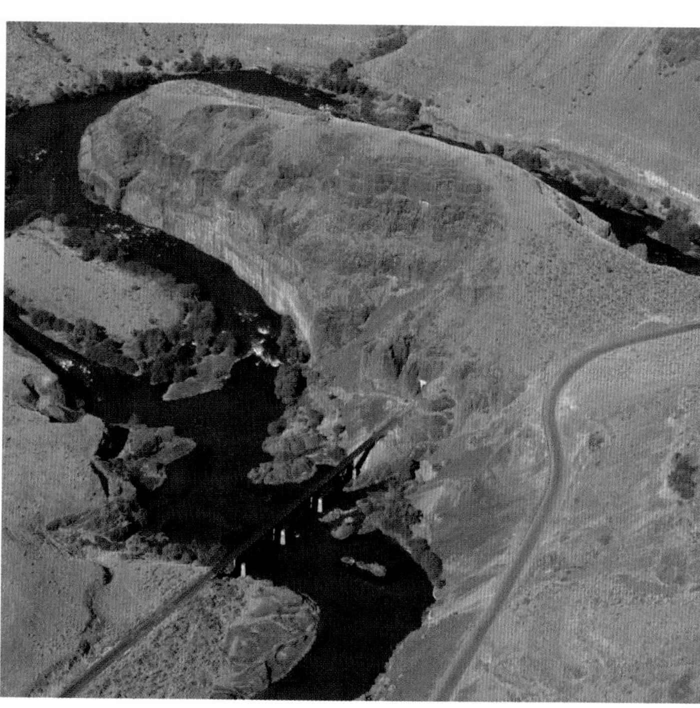

South crossing, Horseshoe Bend — 2005

Horseshoe Bend — 2005

In September 1909, the owners of the Deschutes Irrigation & Power Company sent a telegram to their engineer in Bend, giving him permission to publicly announce the purchase of the Central Oregon Railroad by the Oregon Trunk.[31] Within a few days, the Oregon Trunk had 180 men working at the Crooked River crossing. The work crew left Shaniko, traveled forty miles over rough roads, arrived at 2:00 in the morning, and went to work at daylight.[31]

RAILROAD CONSTRUCTION in the Deschutes Canyon was the last major railroad project to not use large machinery. The Des Chutes Railroad attempted to use a large steam shovel, dismantling it and lowering the pieces over the canyon walls twenty miles upstream near Macks Canyon, and reassembling it. But the steam shovel was of no use because the rock was too hard for the power equipment of that day. Instead, the basaltic rock had to be blasted. Even the ties and rails were laid by hand, although the men were assisted by the track-laying machines described in Chapter 3; usually about 1.5 miles of track were laid per day.[32] The only machine power was the steam engine: a steam shovel digging ballast for the Des Chutes at Warm Springs, steam shovels on the Washington side of the Columbia River digging ballast for the Oregon Trunk,[33] a steam shovel excavating the Oregon Trunk roadbed for the two-mile stretch along the Columbia River, the donkey steam engines used to hoist timbers and steel on the bridges, and the small donkey engines helping to move ties and rails with the Harris and McCoy track-laying machines.

Railroad construction in the Deschutes Canyon was also the last major blasting job that did not use dynamite; the cost of dynamite and the isolated location dictated the use of hand power and black powder. The men blasted the rock by hand, mucking with picks, shovels, wheelbarrows, and small rail cars running over light, twenty-pound temporary rails. Hammers and hand-held drills were used to excavate blasting holes. In really hard rock, the hand-drilled holes would be about two inches in diameter and twelve to eighteen inches deep. In softer rock, the men created coyote holes. A "coyote hole" is a term borrowed from mining, an almost man-sized hole excavated and filled with black powder for blasting. On the Deschutes River, coyote holes were about two feet in diameter and three to four feet deep.[33] Packed with black powder, the force of the blasts threw debris that would cover newly laid track on the other side of the river.[4] Reporters from the *Oregon Journal* personally observed that blasting hurled rocks eight to twelve feet in diameter as far as seventy-five to 100 feet.[34]

Oregon Trunk steam shovel at mouth of Deschutes River, ORNC track & bridge

Coyote blast

After a coyote blast

River Mile 57–58, upstream of Maupin, Oregon Trunk on right

River Mile 66, Oregon Trunk fill

Mucking a cut

Large fill on Oregon Trunk

Grading upstream of Sherar's Bridge

Ballast gang, Oregon Trunk

Getting equipment and supplies into the canyon was a formidable task. There were only three wagon crossings over the lower Deschutes River in 1909:

1. *A county bridge located seven miles upstream from the Columbia River at Free Bridge.* Harris Canyon eleven miles upstream on the east bank of the Deschutes River is named for John E. Harris, a homesteader, who in 1873 built a toll road up Rattlesnake Canyon, connecting The Dalles and Moro, with a toll bridge crossing the Deschutes River seven miles upstream.[35] In 1887, Wasco County bought the Pratt truss bridge, deliberately making it a free bridge to avoid the toll bridge at Moody, and it came to be known as Free Bridge. The Des Chutes Railroad camp near the bridge was called Freebridge, and a small town (a population of 100 even today) named Freebridge was settled in 1908 on the Great Southern tracks, eleven miles southeast of The Dalles. In 1905, the Free Bridge was replaced by a steel and concrete bridge that lasted until one day in November 1912, when the crew of a northbound Oregon Trunk train noticed that the bridge had collapsed.[36] The cause of the collapse remains a mystery although some have suggested that this was the last event in the Deschutes River Railroad War.

2. *The toll bridge operated by Malcolm Moody at his town, Moody.* This was the preferred crossing because it was only one mile upstream from the Columbia River and the road to Free Bridge was steep and perilous.

3. *An old toll road and bridge in place forty-four miles upstream.* John Y. Todd built the first toll bridge here in 1860 at the site of an old Indian trail and bridge. Todd sold the bridge site to Ezra Hemingway and Robert Mays, who in turn sold it to Benjamin O'Brien, who sold it in 1871 to Joseph Sherar, a cattle rancher in Tygh Valley, for $7,040.[37–39] Sherar charged high tolls collected in buckets hanging at each end: 25¢ per person, $3.75 for a team and wagon with an extra $1 for the driver. He built a three-story tavern and hotel on the west bank and roads extending thirty miles on each side of his bridge; the road was called

Free Bridge, looking upstream

the Tilkenny Toll Road. In 1912, Wasco County purchased the bridge for $3,000. After passing through six owners, the inn burned in 1940.[40] Joseph Sherar also operated a very successful sheep ranch on the eastern plateau at Finnegan, and he built the first flour mill in the area at the White River falls; his estate was valued at $54,209 when he died in 1908.[41]

Sherar's Bridge & Hotel on west bank

Sherar's Bridge & Hotel

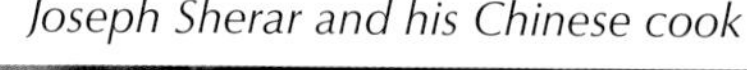

Joseph Sherar and his Chinese cook

Sherar's Bridge — 2005

Sherar competed with Howard Maupin, who in 1880 began operating a ferry eight miles upstream from Sherar's bridge, near Bakeoven Creek. Maupin sold the ferry a few years later to W. E. Hunt, and it came to be known as Hunt's Ferry. Howard Maupin and his family are buried along the edge of Trout Creek.[4] Maupin is best known for tracking and killing Paulina, a Walapi Snake Indian who was the leader of a notorious marauding band of renegades.[42] For years, Howard Maupin had Paulina's scalp nailed over a door of his ranch house. W. H. Staats bought the site, anticipating the coming of railroads, and named it Maupin's Ferry (a name shortened by the post office to Maupin in 1909). A concrete bridge, built across the Deschutes River at Maupin in 1912, was replaced by the current bridge in 1921.

The existing railroad lines near the Deschutes River were the thirty-mile-long Great Southern from The Dalles to Dufur, that was used by the Oregon Trunk to ship equipment and supplies, and the Columbia Southern from Biggs to Shaniko, used exclusively by the Des Chutes Railroad and by the Oregon Trunk for constructing the northern forty miles of its line. Using the Union Pacific-owned Columbia Southern for supplies was not without problems for the Oregon Trunk. "...It is stated a favorite method of the Harriman road for harassing the Oregon Trunk is that when a carload of freight is shipped to Porter Bros. the car is taken a short distance, then side-tracked and marked 'car damaged.' There the car remains until Porter Bros. look it up. Then the car is again 'started' for its destination which it reaches, maybe."[43]

The Wasco County Court eventually sold the Great Southern for junk because of unpaid taxes and loans.[44] The Columbia Southern to Shaniko was dismantled bit by bit until it was completely gone by 1966.[45] Shaniko, once a major shipping point for wool and grain, is now nearly a ghost town (current population, 25), although the Shaniko Hotel has been restored to attract travelers passing by on the highway.

The Columbia Southern. During its existence, the Columbia Southern transported virtually all of the grain produced in central Oregon east of the Deschutes River and west of the John Day River. The plateau grassland attracted livestock ranchers in the early days. The shift from livestock to farming occurred slowly, and by 1885 about one million bushels of wheat were being harvested, using the fallow system of growing wheat on a piece of land every other year.[46]

Construction of the Columbia Southern began in June 1897 and reached Shaniko in May 1900.[47] The town of Shaniko was created by the railroad to receive trade from the surrounding area, but unfortunately it was a flat, treeless, unattractive site. The town got its name from an early settler, August Scherneckau, whose name was pronounced by local Indians as Shaniko.[48] Central Oregon was also a large sheep range, and wool equaled wheat for Columbia Southern revenue. For a time, Shaniko may have been the largest shipping point for wool in the U.S.

The completed Columbia Southern line "was a masterpiece of sophomore-level engineering."[49] It was built cheaply, with scrap rails, and with no cuts or fills, it made its way over sixty-two bridges and trestles and through 198 curves that would have totaled nineteen complete circles. It had only six miles of level tracks; grades ranged from 1.68 percent to 3.47 percent. The grain-laden northbound trains struggled up a ruling grade of 2 percent, and it took about 3.5 hours to travel the seventy miles between Shaniko and Biggs northbound and four hours southbound. The Columbia Southern was slow, but the farmers no longer had to spend long days on the difficult roads transporting their goods, and the cost of transportation was about 60 percent cheaper.[50]

The farmers delivered their grain in four- and six-horse wagons to warehouses. These quotes come from Giles French who for thirty-two years was editor of the *Sherman County Journal.*

> From July till late Fall the wheat was piled in the warehouses. The floors of these warehouses were constructed to be level with the floors of freight cars, seldom a difference of more than an inch or two. Wheat was handled in such warehouses on iron wheeled hand trucks. Each owner had his own pile duly marked in lamp black and oil with his name. In years when the crop was good the sacks were piled high, sometimes clear to the rafters by crews of burly men, usually of more than average size, or at least more than average durability.
>
> When a farmer sold his wheat these men tore into his pile no matter how high and trucked the sacks, five to a truck load, to the railroad car that had been spotted at the door. Inside the little freight cars—for years, forty tons was the capacity—the first sacks were dumped five high right off the truck and then with one man as booster two men took the sacks off the trucks and threw them toward the roof. This was manful endeavor at a time when hard labor was expected of every working man.[51]

The Columbia Southern operated independently in its early years, although it received support from the Oregon Railroad & Navigation Company. In 1905, the Union Pacific took over the Columbia Southern, and in 1911, absorbed it into the Oregon-Washington Railroad & Navigation.[52] In June 1942, the Union Pacific abandoned the Columbia Southern line, perhaps because a federal agency wanted the rails to fulfill needs for the war effort.[53] In response to local and national protests to this policy, only the tracks south of Kent were confiscated. The floods accompanying the severe storm in December 1964 washed out 8.5 miles of tracks and twenty-four of twenty-six bridges.[54] The Union Pacific decided not to rebuild, and the Columbia Southern ceased to exist.

The Great Southern. The land west of the Deschutes River is higher and wetter than the eastern plateau. The land closest to the Deschutes River is rough land with steep slopes. Creeks do not run dry in the summer, flowing swiftly from elevations of 4,000 to 5,000 feet within the short distance of twenty to twenty-five miles. The Tygh Ridge extends in an east-west direction south of Dufur, creating an obstacle to travel and excessive grades for railroad building. The town of Dufur, established in 1872 by A.J. and E.B. Dufur, sits where the Barlow Road (Chapter 9) crossed Fifteenmile Creek.[55] By 1900, people had settled the area south of The Dalles and were growing wheat.

Dufur — 1910

The Great Southern was the result of the dedication of a wealthy Seattle businessman, John Heimrich, whose interest was stimulated by W. F. Nelson, the first president of the Oregon Trunk. It was incorporated in Washington on March 16, 1904.[56] Nelson left the managing board to concentrate on the Oregon Trunk. His place was taken by Julius Meier, a lawyer who developed the premier department store in Oregon, Meier and Frank. The building of the railroad was supervised by Heimrich's son, John G. Heimrich. Construction ended in September 1905, connecting to the Oregon Railroad & Navigation tracks in The Dalles. There were thirty-eight bridges and 143 curves in the thirty-mile length, with an overall 0.8 percent grade.[57] Northbound, a free boxcar could have rolled gently to The Dalles. Later, the tracks were extended about twenty miles to Friend, Oregon. The goal of the Great Southern was to reach Bend, but the building of the Oregon Trunk and the Des Chutes along the Deschutes River put an end to that dream.

The thirty-mile trip between Dufur and The Dalles required two hours. Traffic consisted mainly of wheat; in 1910 Dufur had only 523 people (current population, 625). Automobiles and trucks stole the rail business, however, and after years of struggle highlighted by a family quarrel that resulted in a lawsuit in 1931, John G. Heimrich was forced to give up his share in the railroad.[58] The family failed to resurrect the railroad, and in 1935 the line was abandoned, and the tracks sold for scrap to pay money owed to the county.

THE BUILDING of the railroads in the Deschutes Canyon provided the last boom for the Columbia Southern and the Great Southern lines. All of the Twohy Brothers traffic used the Columbia Southern, but the Porter Brothers used both railroads, especially the Columbia Southern for the construction near Sherar's bridge. The Columbia Southern was running four freight trains daily into Shaniko, each train loaded to capacity, and the one passenger train had no trouble filling all of its seats.[59]

> Shaniko boomed as never before. This was not the slow pace of stockmen delivering the produce of a year's work; this was a celebration of death, a monumental wake for the death of a town. The bars were full of construction men coming and going, of teamsters with expressive oaths and tremendous thirsts; the brothels were busy with pianos tinkling all night and the money rolled in as never before. It was all over in less than two years. ...Shaniko became a dreary, dusty spot with little but an eventful decade of history to sustain it.[60]

ONLY ONE ATTEMPT was made to transport goods downstream by rafting the river, when a gang of six Greeks tried to transport a raft-load of camp utensils, hand-lined by ropes along the shore. In less than half a mile, the raft capsized and one man drowned.[61] Supplies had to be transported from the railroad terminals in Dufur and Shaniko by horse-drawn wagons. Both railroads used horses and mules in large numbers. Dwyer & Company, a subcontractor working for the Des Chutes Railroad between Trout Creek and Madras, had a large tent, about fifty x fifty feet, which served as a stable for its mules. Dwyer called his mules "the menagerie" and always invited visitors to "see this part of the show."[62]

Hauling trestle timbers

Supply wagon

Porter Brothers

Eventually, the railroad companies built about sixty-five miles of wagon roads, and contractors another eighty-five miles.[63] Some zigzags down the canyon walls had grades of 20 percent.[64] At age nineteen, James F. Morrell came to Oregon from Colorado. He spent his last two dollars for river transportation to reach the Porter Brothers office in The Dalles.[65] He was hired as a "bubble skinner," the name for an automobile driver taken from a popular song about an Oldsmobile and "automobubbling,"[66] to drive the roads in and out of the Deschutes Canyon.

After getting a Studebaker-Garford in shape to travel, Morrell made his first trip to the Porter & Clarkson Camp at the head of Willow Creek (at Madras). Morrell carried Johnson Porter and "Doc Dutton," a physician contracted for medical care by the construction company. Driving up the grade from The Dalles to Dufur, they took an old freight road to Sherar's toll road. At that point, they had to drop into the canyon. Descending in second gear, Morrell would periodically short the magneto to add engine compression to the braking. Demonstrating their confidence in the driver and their regard for the road, the two passengers stood on the running boards, prepared to abandon ship if necessary.[67]

At the bottom, they had dinner at the Sherar House, the three-story inn built in 1893. After dinner, they crossed Sherar's bridge, and climbed the east bank, noted for a sharp bend called Chinaman's Bend, the site of an overturned wagon and the demise of its Chinese driver. The turn was so sharp, Morrell had to take two turns, running his front wheels up the bank of the road. Porter exclaimed, "Good work, kid. I guess you know how to skin a bubble."[68] They turned right on an old wagon road to the camp. The next morning, Morrell observed early Madras—a general store, livery stable, a hotel with a stage station. A house of prostitution had opened but was forcibly closed by the contractors.[69] However a "tent city" of prostitutes could soon be found on the edge of the small town.

THE OREGON TRUNK was challenged by a need to transport equipment and supplies from the Spokane, Portland & Seattle north bank line across the Columbia River. Congress approved on March 2, 1910, the Oregon Trunk request to build a bridge across the river at Celilo Falls. In the meantime, Stevens solved the transportation problem by buying and restoring a 488-ton, 165-feet-long, 32-feet-wide sternwheeler, the *Norma.* Built in 1891 in Huntington, Idaho, *Norma* made its way through the rapids of the Snake River (one of only two steamers to ever come through the rapids in Hells Canyon[70]) to carry wheat between Lewiston and Celilo. It was wrecked and beached in 1908 near the Deschutes River, and thus, it was available for the Oregon Trunk. Beginning in September 1910, the Oregon Trunk organized a system whereby the restored *Norma,* captained by George F. Hayward, pushed loaded barges across the river, one 182-foot barge holding eight railroad cars and one 142-foot barge holding six cars on double tracks.[1] On the north bank of the Columbia River, the Oregon Trunk built a small temporary facility two miles east of Fallbridge (now Wishram) at Clarke, with 500 feet of track connecting to the Spokane, Portland & Seattle. On the Oregon side, a temporary line 2.8 miles long climbed a 3 percent grade to reach the Oregon Trunk at Moody, crossing over the Oregon Railroad & Navigation line on a trestle a mile west of the Deschutes River.[1,71] Double-tracked inclines at each end provided access to the *Norma,* allowing for a twenty-two-foot variation in water level. The cost of this temporary operation totaled $123,000.[72] When the Oregon Trunk began operations in March 1911, the *Norma* carried both passengers (capacity of 150 people) and freight until the bridge over the Columbia River at Celilo Falls was finished on January 7, 1912.

"Norma"

Unloading "Norma"

Loading ramp for "Norma" in Washington, connecting to the SP&S

The ferry began operating in September 1910, transporting eighty to 100 railroad cars per day. Even at this rate, it took two months to acquire enough supplies at Moody to begin the laying of track (the grade was already complete to Madras). The Oregon Trunk transported material across the Columbia River, including enormous amounts of rails, ties, bridge materials, and ballast, without a single accident. This was a noteworthy feat considering the high winds in the summer and the storms and ice in the winter. These conditions occur because the passage of the river through a narrow corridor between high cliffs produces a wind-tunnel effect: the rising hot air in the desert drawing the wind from the west in the summer and a cold wind blowing from the east in the winter.

By March 1910, the Des Chutes Railroad had 3,600 men at work, and the Oregon Trunk had 3,800.[73] The Des Chutes had graded twenty miles south of the Columbia River on the east bank of the Deschutes River, and a crew of 350 men had laid six miles of seventy-five-pound track. The Oregon Trunk had graded twenty-five miles along the west bank, but had laid no rails.

THE LAST CONFLICT

The Oregon Trunk entered the Warm Springs Indian Reservation about seventy miles upstream from the Columbia River. The originally surveyed line stayed on Indian land for five miles before it crossed the river to avoid blasting in difficult terrain and hard rock. In addition to the blasting, for the Oregon Trunk to stay on the west bank would require more surveying, more filing of papers with the government, and prolonged negotiations to use Indian land. Fortunately for the Oregon Trunk, their

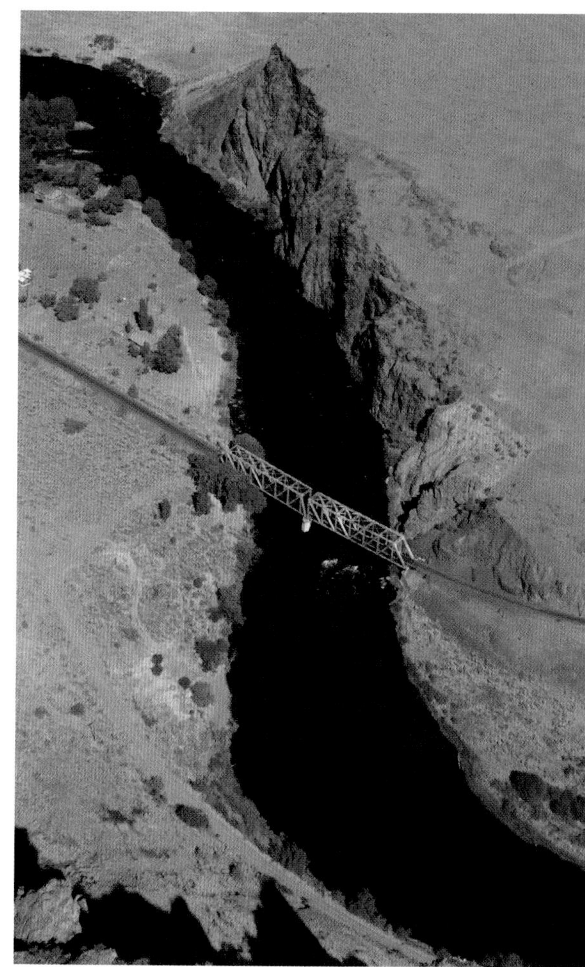

North Junction bridge — 2005

original survey and filing maps from the crossing at North Junction to Trout Creek on the east bank antedated those of the Des Chutes.

At the current site of North Junction (so named in 1910 because it was the site of the northern junction of the two railroads), the Mutton Mountains reach the river on the west bank. The size of the cliffs on the west bank would have required a lengthy tunnel or massive blasting. But the hardness of this rock, the jumbled, harder composite from the volcanic explosions that produced the John Day and Clarno Formations, was a major reason for the original routing of the Oregon Trunk from the west bank to the east bank. In contrast, the rock from the Columbia River up to North Junction is largely the softer, fissured columns of the Columbia Basalt Flows. Thus the two railroads were building parallel tracks on the east bank at North Junction.

At North Junction, a telegram arrived for George W. Boschke, the Des Chutes chief engineer, asking him to come at once to Galveston, Texas. The telegram said that the Galveston seawall had broken in a severe storm on July 21, 1909. Nine years earlier, a hurricane had struck Galveston Island on September 8, 1900, with winds greater than 120 miles per hour, generating a tidal surge that killed over 6,000 people on the island and thousands more on the mainland, destroying one-third of the city.[74] The city built a seawall to prevent another such catastrophe. By 1962, it was seven miles long and seventeen feet high, fronting a new city on a raised foundation. George Boschke was an engineer for the initial construction, completing a length of three miles by 1904. Confident in his engineering, Boschke immediately concluded that the telegram was a fake, and he discarded the message.[73]

Tunnel No. 4 at end of Whitehorse Rapids

The two railroads both tried to obtain the property of R.F. Smith, a rancher twelve miles upstream of North Junction, near the current location of Tunnel No. 4 at the end of Whitehorse Rapids. Smith secured his homestead after the Oregon Trunk had its maps approved, but he filed his homestead deed while the Oregon Trunk approval was pending, giving him entitlement.[75] Johnson Porter offered Smith $2,500, but the Des Chutes bought the ranch for $3,050.[15] Posting armed guards on this land, the Des Chutes had the Oregon Trunk stymied. The right-of-way was too narrow just south of North Junction to allow side-by-side railroads. While the federal government pondered the problem, the Oregon Trunk carried its equipment beyond the Smith Ranch and resumed building. This confrontation at the Smith ranch was a major motivation for the Oregon Trunk to file new articles of incorporation in the state of Washington.[76] Believing that this conflict would have to be settled in court, the Oregon Trunk officials wanted to avoid having the legality of the original Nevada incorporation challenged again.

The federal government finally decided that the problem fell under the federal law that stated, "Any railroad company whose right-of-way, or whose track or roadbed upon such right-of-way, passes through any canyon, pass, or defile shall not prevent any other railroad company from the use and occupancy of said canyon, pass, or defile for the purposes of its road. …And that where the space is limited the United States district court shall require the road first constructed to allow any other railroad or tramway to pass over its track or tracks through such canyon, pass, or defile on such equitable basis as the said court may prescribe. …"[77]

A federally forced agreement on May 17, 1910, produced a 999-year cease fire and joint track usage at North Junction for the next 10.41 miles. At the end of the 10.41 miles, the Des Chutes Railroad left the joint track and built its line out of the canyon at Trout Creek. After leaving the canyon, this segment of the Des Chutes had extreme curves, a tunnel, and a long steel trestle crossing the Oregon Trunk line. The Oregon Trunk continued along the

Willow Creek Canyon near Madras

Louis W. Hill, William Hanley, and E.C. Leedy

east bank of the river for another ten miles, climbing out at Willow Creek, just upstream of Warm Springs. Mecca Flat, ninety-six miles upstream from the Columbia River, was the last campsite of the Oregon Trunk, receiving its name because when the rails reached Mecca the men knew the hardest work was over.

The Agreement

Louis W. Hill, who succeeded his father as president of the Great Northern Railway in 1907, visited Bend in May 1910, together with E.C. Leedy, the immigration agent for the Great Northern.[78,79] The small town turned out for a royal welcome, complete with flags, bunting, and lines of school children along the road. At the courthouse yard, Hill stood in his automobile and addressed the crowd, conveying the certainty that the Great Northern would reach Bend and sharing his plans to advertise the region. He predicted a huge increase in the region's population.

Hill's visit to Bend was part of a 1,500-mile journey through the state, accompanied by Oregon's millionaire stockman, William Hanley. Louis Hill promised growth for Oregon. "The Great Northern is going to open up Oregon whether the people want us to or not, but I feel the people are with us."[79] That same month, less than a year after construction was started, the Oregon Trunk established a headquarters for engineering and construction in Bend, leasing Lara's Hall (owned by A.M. Lara).[80] In addition, two local physicians, Urling Coe and Barney Ferrell, erected a small hospital in Bend and were awarded a medical contract with the Oregon Trunk.

Louis Hill's visit to Oregon was not all pleasant depending on one's point of view. In the Klamath Falls area, Hill attacked government policies that were aimed at conservation and preservation of public lands, not a surprising attitude for a businessman who depended on immigrants and growth of the population.[81] The next day, the *Oregon Journal*, in a disagreement with its competing newspaper, said, "He should be told that the people of Oregon have not the slightest idea of turning over their public resources to be exploited in the interest of a few people, but that this state has in view the interests and opportunities of the many. … it is well known that the Oregonian in no sense voices or represents the purposes of the people of this state. …"[82]

In the midst of Louis Hill's visit, it was announced that peace had been declared between the Hill and the Harriman forces throughout the Deschutes Canyon.[83] The agreement was the result of long, almost daily, conferences between attorney C. H. Carey acting for John Stevens and the Oregon Trunk and W.W. Cotton, chief attorney in Oregon for the Harriman lines. This agreement was probably linked with another agreement allowing the Southern Pacific a right-of-way over the Northern Pacific line into Seattle.

After Harriman died, James J. Hill found the new president of the Union Pacific to be more cooperative. After a visit to New York, Hill wrote to Stevens, "I have had a very pleasant interview with Judge Lovett, the President of the Union Pacific, in which he gave me to understand that they did not favor their Company building any road in the DesChutes [sic] Valley. I told him if he wanted to come down the valley from Madras to the Columbia that we would arrange fair trackage to enable them to do this, which was very satisfactory to him."[84] Nevertheless, Hill wired a stern message to Stevens:

> WITHHOLD NEOPHYTE HIGH
> EVACUATE PARODY ORPHAN
> PUBLISHING OVERTHREW
> OBSTRUCTING WITHHOLD CARROT
> OCCULTATION HIGH PENNYS
>
> (We must have entire ownership of property or none. We can not have partners.)[85]

But the negotiations at the local level were at an impasse. Stevens described the problem to Hill, who bluntly incorporated Stevens' letter into his own letter to Judge Lovett, a letter that finally got things moving:

> I am today in receipt of a letter from Mr. Stevens writing as follows:
>
> Mr. O'Brien just from New York seems to have very vague ideas regarding the nature of the proposed contract; in fact, until I explained to him our understanding of the matter, apparently had very little conception of what is proposed, as I understand it.
>
> I understand that the Oregon Trunk was to construct its line through to a point near Madras, or somewhere south, on its present located line, and that it was to use, wherever practicable, such parts of the work which have been done by the other company, paying the latter the cost of the same; that the DesChutes [sic] Company was to be given equal rights as far as operation and the transaction of business was concerned with the Oregon Trunk; that the ownership and control of the line was to remain entirely with the Oregon Trunk and that the other company was to pay rental based on interest on one-half of the cost of our line for that part of the road to be used by the other company, and that of course the maintenance and similar expenses were to be divided on a wheelage basis. …
>
> In other words, I understood they were to connect with us at Celilo, or as near that point as practicable, and thence use our line to a point as far south as Madras, or perhaps further south, in its entirety. Mr. O'Brien's idea is that the engineers of the two roads should go on the ground and pick out a joint line, and for us to construct the same.
>
> Now this is not at all I believe what we should agree to. They claim they have their line 75% completed. I do not believe for a moment that this is true. In any case the line they are building is one we could hardly adopt as a gift. They claim they have spent upwards of two million dollars thus far in their work. It may be they have but I do not believe it, and I do not understand that this factor was to enter at all in the negotiations, but that they consider it would be cheaper to abandon their line completely and to pay interest on one-half the cost of ours.
>
> One suggestion that they make is that we should enter into an agreement covering only the twelve miles in the upper DesChutes [sic] where we have had conflict,

and also from Madras south to Crooked River. I do not see advantages enough for us to even consider this proposition. ...They also suggest that we could use their line from the DesChutes [sic] up around Trout Creek to Madras. While this line is four or five miles shorter than ours, it is not nearly as good a line, and if we undertook to revise their present line to the same standard of construction we are using elsewhere, even after allowing for the work they have done, it would cost us nearly, or quite, as much as to complete our present line from Willow Creek to Madras.

...the fact remains that these people here are completely at sea, as far as I can ascertain, as to what is proposed. ...I have always found their local officials here very bullheaded and always trying to obstruct any movement looking towards peace. ...

Now my suggestion is that if you take up the matter again with Judge Lovett that he find out exactly the situation, how much money they have spent, and consequently what amount of extra capitalization, on account of any work he might abandon, that he may have to take care of.

(Hill closes the letter):

While there is nothing urgent as far as we are concerned, I think it will be better so far as it can be done to close up the DesChutes [sic] matter as early as convenient.[86]

A month later, in another coded telegram, Hill told Stevens, "I see no objection arranging for use of our line from point twenty-five miles south of Columbia River for sixty miles or to any convenient point of separation to include crossing of Crooked River but in not any case should we allow them any pay for work done which was not a part of our line or which could not be made a part of our line without increasing our cost or reducing operating value of our line."[87] And finally, due in no small part to James J. Hill's intervention, one month later on May 17, 1910, the Oregon Trunk and the Union Pacific signed an agreement that included the following:

To avoid further conflict in the Deschutes canyon, an agreement has been perfected whereby the Des Chutes Railroad [Harriman] shall have running rights in perpetuity over the Oregon Trunk [Hill] for a total distance of 37 miles. In this distance the 10.41 miles of conflict in the Deschutes canyon are included, as are also the bridge across the Crooked River and the line into Redmond.

The Oregon Trunk would own the line between North Junction and South Junction, but would allow joint use by the Des Chutes. Thus the Des Chutes Railroad preserved its running rights on the 10.41 miles north of Trout Creek on the east bank where the Trunk had filed its surveys first. In return the Des Chutes conveyed its interest to the Trunk at cost the right-of-way through the Smith ranch at mile 75 which had been purchased by the Harriman line, as well as all lands the Des Chutes Railroad obtained between the Smith Ranch and Trout Creek. The Des Chutes company is granted permission for the overhead crossing of Trunk tracks at Celilo, and sells to the Hill line the right-of-way between Celilo and the mouth of the Deschutes River.

The Oregon Trunk retains sole ownership of its entire line. The Trunk relinquishes its claim to right-of-way on the east back from the Columbia River to mile point 50. The Des Chutes relinquishes its claims to right-of-way on the west side. From Trout Creek southward to 6 miles south of Madras each line will construct it own road. From 6 miles south of Madras, the Deschutes will again use the tracks of the Trunk for 42.7 miles to the Bend Station. For use of the lines the Deschutes will pay rent. The Trunk will supervise and control the joint operations.[88,89]

HILL announced that in the future there would be no "pulling of faces by the workmen employed in the rival camps across the river." That meant no more pummeling of the camp kitchen with rocks as they sat down for dinner. Even before the agreement, the Trunk had signed a contract for about $4 million with the C. K. Henry Company of Seattle for the stretch south of Madras.[90] The Henry Company had just completed a three-year project, extending the Milwaukee system from Butte, Montana, to Puget Sound.

Although Stevens still wanted to keep going to California, Hill established the terminus at Bend (forcing the abandonment of preliminary work), basing his decision to do so on the slow market conditions in 1910. Nevertheless, the Oregon Trunk amended its articles of incorporation on August 15, 1910, allowing a line to Klamath Falls and Medford, and another line east to Burns.[91]

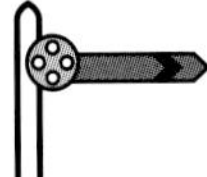

BY 1910, thousands of laborers on the two railroads were working in peace along each bank of the Deschutes River. Did they wonder: Why two railroads? It would take years before the Hill and Harriman lines would use one set of tracks from the Columbia River to Bend.

- CHAPTER NINE -

Working on the Deschutes River Railroads

The Railroad Laborer Is a Peculiar Genius

The Deschutes railroads recruited their workers largely in Portland and Spokane and subsequently transported them to The Dalles. The work crews included "a legion of Greeks and Italians" for Porter Brothers and Austrians, Swedes, and Italians for Twohy Brothers.[1,2] "Several times a day their representatives make the rounds of the various resorts of the unemployed here at The Dalles. The saloons and shady corners are crowded with those who are 'blowing in,' and all of these that the Porter agents are able to procure are shipped out to the camps in one of the 50-odd teams that are constantly freighting supplies to the canyon camps."[3] The workers made their way to the camps in wagons or they walked single file down the trails. A recruiter in The Dalles for Porter Brothers said, "The railroad laborer is a peculiar genius. He is here one week and somewhere else the next. It is easy enough to get men but the trouble is to keep them after they have a few dollars ahead. It is often said that when a railroad contractor has 100 men working that there are in reality 300 men on the job, that is, there are 100 men coming, 100 men working and 100 men going."[4]

A major reason for this constant motion of laborers was the nature of the work. It was hard work, living conditions were harsh, and the pay was low—as soon as a worker could, he sought other jobs. The railroad industry had a long history of seeking an inexpensive work force, knowing that work in scattered and desolate areas of the West made it hard for laborers to organize in protest. It is not surprising that unskilled migrant laborers were recruited for this purpose. Prior to 1894, western railroads employed thousands of Chinese workers. White, organized workers actively agitated against the practice of hiring less expensive Asian laborers. By the early 1900s, the railroads turned to southern and eastern European workers.[5] They were paid slightly more than Asian workers, but not as much as American-born white workers. These European immigrants were recruited by labor contractors. The Western Employment Company, owned by H.W. Osborn, had offices in Saint Paul, Sioux City, Grand Forks, Fargo, Seattle, Spokane, and Portland.[6] Until late in 1910, this company supplied the Hill lines with Greek, Italian, Bulgarian, and Austrian immigrants. American-born workers regarded these men as competition, treating them nearly as cruelly as they had the Chinese and Japanese laborers that preceded them. It wasn't until World War I, in response to federal pressure to avoid strikes and slowdowns that would impair the war effort, that wages and working conditions began to improve.

The Deschutes railroads paid their immigrant workers with weekly checks. Most would make the hard trip on foot to a nearby town, usually Grass Valley, to cash their checks and obtain money orders at the post office, sending most of their pay back to the "old country." With their remaining money, the workers purchased work clothes and boots—and a substantial amount of alcohol.

By March 1910, the Deschutes Canyon contained approximately 20 subcontractors with 9,000 men working on both railroads, living in about 100 camps.[7] Common laborers received 20¢ to 30¢ per hour, carpenters and concrete men 35¢ to 40¢, steel workers 50¢, well drillers $7 per day, teamsters $6. The men did not have to pay for camp lodging, but the men had to pay 25¢ to 30¢ for each meal. [8,9]

The Dalles

Workers and supplies were funneled through the town of The Dalles. "Dalles" was the name given by the French Canadian traders of the Hudson Bay Company to confined river passages through rocks, and specifically to the rapids in the narrow, rocky section of the Columbia River just east of the town of The Dalles.[10] The Dalles was the first settlement east of the Cascade Mountains, established at the point where emigrants following the Oregon Trail came by land around the falls at Celilo and reached the end of overland travel. Once there, they faced a float through stiff winds and turbulent water hemmed in by steep cliffs of hard rock. Their only choice was a dangerous and expensive passage by boats and rafts until the Barlow Road around Mount Hood was opened in 1846.

Sam Barlow, age fifty-three, arrived in The Dalles in 1845. Running out of money and food, he tried to pass around the south side of Mount Hood, but he had to abandon his wagons and follow a narrow Indian trail on the north side of the mountain. This experience motivated him to obtain permission to build a toll road, called the Barlow Road, the following year around the south side of Mount Hood, a distance of 150 miles from The Dalles to Oregon City.[11] The toll of $5 per wagon and 10¢ per head of livestock stirred an angry response in emigrant travelers, especially since the road was a very rough road (a crude path at best), going over slopes so steep that downhill travel was possible only with roping of the wagons to trees. Nevertheless, the road operated with toll gates until 1915. The state took ownership of the road in 1919. The road was so difficult that nearly one of every four emigrants still preferred to risk their lives on the river. The safety of the option around Mount Hood was so attractive, however, that within one year a cutoff from the Oregon Trail provided a more direct route. The cutoff from the Oregon Trail to the Barlow Road began just west of the John Day River, went through Grass Valley, crossed the Deschutes River at the bridge that Joseph Sherar bought in 1871 or by using the ferry at Maupin, and continued up the Tygh Valley (the valley was the home of the Tygh, a small band of Indians who eventually joined the Confederated Tribes of the Warm Springs) to connect with the Barlow Road.

The federal government established a military post at The Dalles in 1850 (visited by Lieutenant Abbott in 1855—Chapter 4) and abandoned it in 1861. By 1856, 252 people lived in The Dalles, and only two years later, The Dalles had three hotels, two grocery stores, two saloons, a general store,

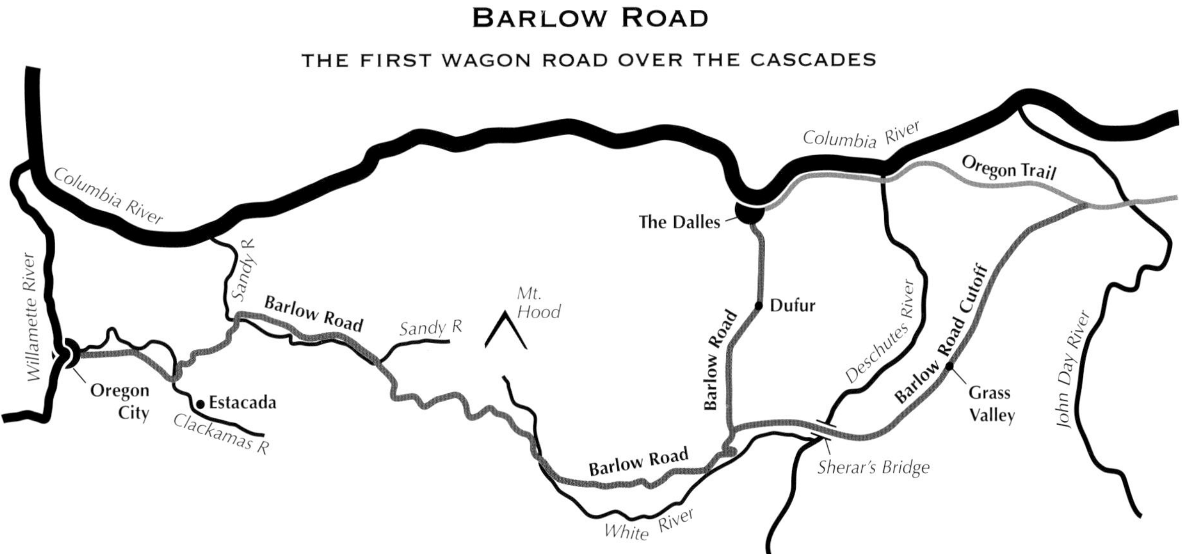

a drug store, a cigar store, and a bakery—all along the river.[12] The Dalles became a major shipping and trading center for the livestock and wool produced by ranchers to the south. The town was hard hit by multiple fires and floods, but by the time railroad construction came to the Deschutes River, there were many businesses including a brewery, a sarsaparilla-producing company, salmon-canning plants, a flour mill, and even an undertaker.

The Oregon Steam Navigation Company began steamer operations on the Columbia River in 1860, using the portage railroads to pass freight and passengers around the six-mile-long Cascades, the rapids forty miles west of The Dalles, and around the several miles of turbulent water and two sets of rapids east of The Dalles (Chapter 6). City business in The Dalles increased when, after fifteen years of construction, the Cascade Locks began operating in November 1896. With the opening of the locks, sternwheeler passenger fare from Portland to The Dalles dropped from $2 to $1.[13] In 1910, both steamers and the Union Pacific's Oregon Railroad & Navigation tracks served The Dalles. With local stops, a sternwheeler trip lasted ten to twelve hours. The sternwheelers eventually yielded to the railroads—their very last trip left The Dalles in 1923.

The Porter Brothers Construction Company, with offices in Spokane and Portland, had long been allied with the Hill railroads. For the Deschutes project, Johnson Porter, the younger brother, was in charge, and George A. Kyle was the engineer in the field. For the construction of the Oregon Trunk, Porter Brothers established their main office in The Dalles.

The Twohy Brothers Company was hired by the Des Chutes Railroad, with George W. Boschke in charge of construction and H. A. Brandon, the engineer in the field. The Twohy Brothers Company was founded in 1900 in Spokane by the three sons of Irish immigrants, John Jr., James, and Dennis Twohy.[2] In 1910, the original company was incorporated

Porter Brothers headquarters at The Dalles

in Oregon with John Jr. and his three sons, John D., James, and Robert, as the owners. The Twohy family liked to stay in the Umatilla House, a fine hotel that catered to steamboat and railroad passengers in The Dalles. Even after burning down several times, the Umatilla House in the late 1800s was the city's major building, a square structure three stories tall with 141 rooms, each with a wood-burning stove.[14,15] The hotel linked to the sternwheelers with a boat landing in the back and to the portage railway with tracks running next to the building in the front. Later, the Oregon Railroad & Navigation Company established its station and baggage room in the hotel, near the highly acclaimed restaurant and bar. Meals were 25¢; meals and a room cost $1 per day.[14] Business waned with aging and railroad traffic that no longer stopped in The Dalles, and the building was demolished in 1929. John D. Twohy began a courtship with Genevieve Fish, the teenage daughter of one of the hotel owners, and finally married her on October 6, 1909, while he was in the midst of construction along the Deschutes River on October 6, 1909.[14]

SHANIKO

By 1910, over 4,000 people lived on the plateau east of the Deschutes River: 378 in Moro (current population, 310), 342 in Grass Valley (current population, 160), and 495 in Shaniko (current population, 25).[16] The first decade of the 1900s was a boom time for these small towns, a time of prosperity soon lost after the completion of the railroads in the Deschutes River Canyon. During the building of the Des Chutes Railroad, the Twohy Brothers maintained a major headquarters in Grass Valley, receiving supplies on the Columbia Southern Railroad to be transported by wagon teams to the river canyon.

> Shaniko filled an economic need by caring for the shipping of livestock and wool and it grew until a thousand people lived on the greasewood prairie around the town and the railway terminus. Men were needed to handle the wool, take care of the stockyards, drive stages, carry on the extensive business. Shaniko also filled a social need. The men who brought the sheep or the wool to the railroad wanted entertainment, for many of them had been out of sight of another human for most of a year. The same applied to the riders who brought cattle to the stockyards. None of them had much money but all of it was for spending.
>
> The business for Shaniko's bars and brothels came in small bunches. The town never had conventions, never did all shippers bring bands or herds at one time. There was time for Shaniko's inhabitants who lived on what was called sin to take care of all the business. It was on that the town earned its reputation, not because thousands of dollars worth of livestock were sold there—the actual sale and exchange of money often

Shaniko — 1910

occurred elsewhere—or thousands of pounds of wool were auctioned at the sales. The incidental business of billing railroad cars, of making out stage tickets, of teaching the village school, of selling supplies went on every day; the business that made Shaniko best known went on after dark.

The rainfall was and is insufficient for agriculture and promises—hopes really—of eventual irrigation never materialized. There was not enough water, almost none from the blue sky and not near enough from the eastern slopes of the Cascades that flowed away to the sea in deep gorges. For a decade Shaniko offered the only transportation into or out of this inviting expanse of desert and Shaniko profited from this ghoulish business. Shaniko was not a place to look for moral judgments, nor for advice; a man was supposed to look out for himself.[17]

Working on the Railroad

Appreciating what it was like to work at hard labor on the Deschutes railroads requires some thought to the weather. Summer nights along the Deschutes River are very pleasant; a drop in temperature of 30° to 40° is common. This makes for good sleeping and a pleasant morning the next day. Summer mornings are beautiful: a comfortable temperature, clear air, and a cloudless, rich blue sky. But by afternoon, the temperature is certainly in the 90s, often over 100°. The highest temperature recorded at Madras is 112°F.[18] On the river, it can be pleasant, even though the daily, upriver wind is hot; however, a few feet inland from the river bank, the heat is so intense that it creates a physical pressure, the rocks are hot, and energy is sapped. It is arid country, but the pleasure of low humidity is overcome by a hot sun that can be appropriately called brutal. Thankfully, the low humidity allows palpable relief for those sitting in the shade; however, there was scant shade on the canyon cliffs and river banks for the railroad workers. In the morning, the sun rising over a canyon cliff is welcome for its warmth, but in the evening the sun sinking below the western canyon edge is a relief, an escape from the scorching rays.

The heat brings out the snakes. "It is reported that the heat and the rattlesnakes in the Deschutes canyon give the railroad workmen all kinds of grief. In one camp a den of 38 rattlesnakes was encountered and the canyon is reported to be alive with them. A rattlesnake is not a very agreeable bedfellow and it is known that they have a penchant for a comfortable berth if it happens to be a cool night. But snakes and hot weather will not stop the railroad."[3]

The Deschutes Canyon is home to the western rattlesnake, *Crotalus viridis.* More specifically, it is the Northern Pacific rattlesnake, a subspecies, *Crotalus viridis oreganos,* Oregon's only venomous snake.[19] Deschutes rattlesnakes are not large; their circumference is at most equivalent to an average forearm, and the length is about two to three feet. Their predominant color is brown with a greenish tinge. If lucky, a rattlesnake can live twenty years. Rattlesnakes hibernate in the winter. Body temperature must reach about 61°F before they leave their dens, usually sometime in April or May. During the heat of the day in the summer, rattlesnakes seek shade, especially in rocks or tall grass. But in the mornings and evenings, they seek warmth. In spring and fall, rattlesnakes are active throughout the day.

A rattlesnake adds a new rattle to the end of its body each time it sheds its skin (one to three times per year). Contrary to popular belief, the buzzing rattle of a rattlesnake coiled in a defensive position is usually not the first evidence of an encounter. In fact, the rattle is rather subdued and can't be counted on for a warning. The first sign of a rattlesnake's presence is most often perceived as illogical movement in one's peripheral vision.

The Deschutes rattlesnakes do not strike unless provoked. Fortunately rattlesnakes sense vibrations. Physical disturbances, even just walking, usually cause a rattlesnake to seek safety. Snakes and men react to their encounters in a similar fashion, a polite retreat in opposite directions. The noise and vibrations from a large number of men, the grading of a roadbed, and the blasting of rock surely must have driven most, if not all, rattlesnakes away from the railroad workers. And even though a bite from a small rattler can cause pain and tissue damage, it is rarely fatal. Many rattlesnake bites are "dry" bites with no venom injected.

Many Deschutes railroad stories are part of an oral history, making their way into books and conversations even though they cannot be documented.

One such story tells of a powder blast that revealed hundreds of hibernating rattlesnakes balled together in their den. The workers decided to row across the river to the Oregon Trunk camp with burlap sacks of snakes and place them next to the sleeping men's wood stoves in hopes the heat would awaken the snakes.[20,21] It is said that many of Carleton's Italian workers were sufficiently frightened that they quit their jobs.

Central Oregon is dry country. Bend receives an average of eleven inches of rain per year (compared with forty-six inches in Eugene and thirty-six inches in Portland).[22] Most of this rain falls from November to June. It can be a cold rain, and the winter occasionally sees snow. Nighttime temperatures below freezing are not uncommon in the winter; the record low temperature at Madras is an incredible 40° below zero in December 1924.[23] A winter rain with gusty winds makes for cold and muddy working conditions. But there are many days when the cold night is replaced with sunshine despite rain on the western side of the mountains. In the summer, protection from the burning sun could only be achieved with

Harris track-laying machine work gang

Oregon Trunk work gang

Working by hand on the Oregon Trunk

long pants (overalls were common), long-sleeved shirts, and a hat. The same clothes that would be hot in the sun would be wet, heavy, and cold in the rain. Even in the summer, a windy, rainy day can be a chilling contrast to the usual sunshine and heat.

Flash floods occur in central Oregon. In November 1909, the heaviest rainfall recorded up to that time caused the Deschutes River to rise ten feet in twenty-four hours, washing away two Des Chutes construction camps and one Porter Brothers camp.[24]

Winter and spring rains bring a light green color to the land, but by August the ground is dry and brown, except for the river banks. The banks of the Deschutes River form the riparian zone, thin strips of vegetation that are vital for the life cycles of the animals and insects. This zone is fragile, but it has been treated with respect by the railroad workers in the past and by the fishermen of the present. Some of this respect is due to the widespread presence of poison oak.

The Deschutes River smells good. In early summer the air is filled with the scent of the blooming Mock Orange flowers. Beyond the riparian zone, the arid land is filled with sagebrush and juniper, providing the prevalent and characteristic aromas of the Deschutes area.

A summer day on the Deschutes River

Blooming Mock Orange

Oregon Trunk construction camp at Sinamox

Sinamox — 2005

The railroad construction camps were semi-permanent, small tent towns near the banks of the river. The men reinforced their tents with wood and used stoves for heat. Edward "Rufe" Armstrong was twenty-three years old when he spent a year as a surveyor for the Des Chutes Railroad from June 28, 1909, to July 18, 1910. He recorded his experience in a diary with very curt sentences and comments.[25] As one of his jobs was to complete a daily census of the foreign workers, Armstrong displayed the attitudes of the time, calling the Italians "Dagoes," and the Slavic Europeans, "Bohunks." The construction companies maintained an impressive mail service; Armstrong received and sent mail almost every day.

Some of the workers maintained vegetable gardens. The better paid workers, such as surveyor Armstrong, supplemented their diet by buying pigs and used coal for heating. Baking ovens in the camps, measuring about six feet wide and four feet high, were solidly built of rocks. The rocks were heated by a fire inside the structure; after either removing the fire or allowing it to die down, baking pans were inserted through the door on the side. Several have withstood weather and storms over the years, such as the one at Sinamox.

U'Rens Flat was an area owned by Charley U'Rens and used as a construction camp in 1910, two miles north of South Junction. Named Jersey by the Oregon Trunk, this site was the location of the wye used for helper engines. The entire herd of cattle on the U'Rens Ranch was purchased for the commissaries of the Porter Brothers.[26] The men consumed 15,000 pounds of beef daily, obtained from herds that grazed above the canyon.[21] It has been said that the workers enjoyed crossing the river and stampeding the other railroad's cattle. Twohy Brothers butchered eight cattle every day in four separate locations along the river. When local supplies proved inadequate, the construction company transported cattle by train from Montana (800 in one recorded shipment).[27] The stealing of cattle and horses was common enough to keep Sheriff Jay Freeman of Sherman County busy tracking down the thieves.[28]

Baking oven at Sinamox

Accidents and Injuries

Despite claims to the contrary in numerous melodramatic newspaper stories over the years, no evidence can be found for a fatality or serious injury resulting from a conflict or confrontation between workers of the two railroads. But serious accidents and injuries were common.

Rock slides were a constant danger, causing at least two recorded fatalities. At South Junction, a rock slide injured several Oregon Trunk workers. It was presumed Des Chutes workers caused the slide. Almost immediately, both sides had armed men guarding the workers, but after several days, nothing further happened.[29] A. Rowson, a thirty-seven-year-old English immigrant, was sleeping peacefully at 11 P.M. when a rock crashed into his tent, fracturing his left leg and causing internal injuries. He died the next morning.[30] John Legin, a thirty-year-old Austrian laborer, died when a falling rock struck him during construction near Madras.[31,32] A blast from a coyote hole threw a twelve-pound rock into the skull of a man named Nelson, killing him instantly, and a premature explosion was responsible for two more deaths.[33,34] One recently married man, A.A. Paine from Seattle, died when the derrick used to hoist steel for the Des Chutes viaduct across Willow Creek fell over and a 4,500-pound piece of steel crushed him.[35] Premature blasts were a common cause of injury; one Italian worker lost both eyes and both legs, surviving only a few weeks.[26]

Blasting was a risky business, not only for the workers but for anyone within range. Mr. and Mrs. William Williams lived near Hunt's Ferry in Maupin.[36] Porter Brothers workmen on the west bank had prepared a coyote hole blast and warned the Williams family, living across the river 600 feet away, to move from their house to avoid the possibility of falling rocks. Mrs. Williams told the men that her husband was sick, could not be moved, and she would use her husband's rifle to shoot the first man who attempted to fire the blast. The next day, when the husband was feeling better and after the family moved out of their house, Porter Brothers fired the blast, hurling a rock across the river, into the Williams' home, smashing the sick man's recently vacated bed. Porter Brothers men immediately repaired the house.

Coyote blasts were spectacular. The largest was witnessed by many spectators on March 24, 1910, in the Willow Creek Canyon.[37] The coyote holes for this blast were fifty feet deep and required five tons of black powder. The resulting debris at the bottom of the canyon reached a height of twenty feet.

Coyote blast

Powder Cave across from Macks Canyon — 2005

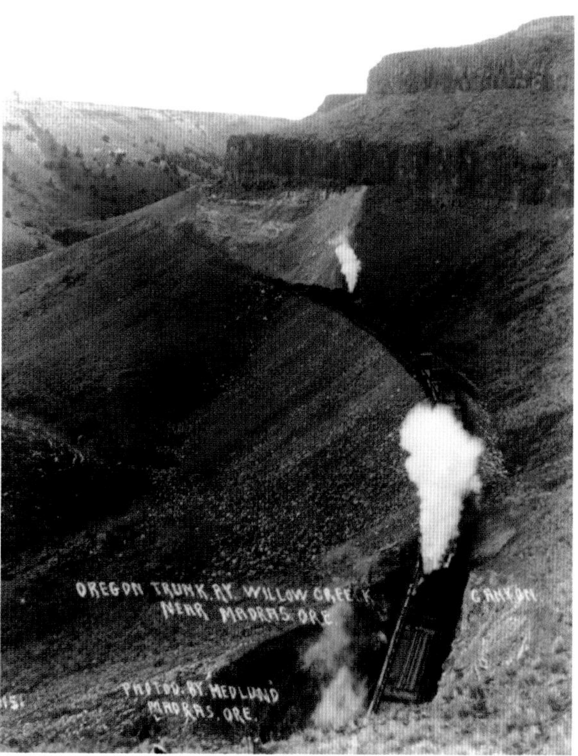

Oregon Trunk in Willow Creek Canyon

Oregon Trunk approach to the Warm Springs Tunnel

Almost every supply train returning to the Columbia River carried one or two injured workers to be treated at the hospital in The Dalles. While the work itself was hazardous, it was not an uncommon event for the workers to entertain themselves after supper by rowing across the river for a little scrap with knuckles, pick handles, and rocks.[8] Eventually the Oregon Trunk contracted with physicians, who opened twenty-five-bed hospitals to care for the workers, one in Bend and the other in an out-of-the-way location near Freebridge.[38] The Des Chutes Railroad had hospitals in Grass Valley and Nebeck (a station on the Great Southern tracks near the Free Bridge).

Urling C. Coe came to Bend in 1905, and for five years he was the only practicing physician in the new town. In 1940, Coe published the stories of his early years in a book entitled *Frontier Doctor.*[39] Barney Ferrell joined Coe's practice, and the two physicians opened a hospital in a large house in the center of Bend on the Deschutes River. When the Oregon Trunk awarded the contract to the H.C. Henry Company of Seattle for the homestretch into Bend, Coe promptly drove to The Dalles, where he caught a train that had him in Seattle the next day. The Henry Company agreed to a contract with Coe and Ferrell to provide medical and hospital care for the construction workers. To pay for this service, the company deducted a dollar per month from each laborer's wages.[40] In each construction camp, the two physicians placed a medical box, containing dressings, bandages, antiseptics, aspirin, quinine, cathartic pills, cough remedies, medications for rheumatism, dysentery, and colds. Typhoid fever was a recurring problem, a consequence of polluted water from the improper handling of human waste. Occasionally workers feigned illness to avoid bad weather or to obtain free meals in the hospital. Malingerers were cured by a treatment of a light diet combined with a strong cathartic; this proved to be effective preventive medicine.

To immobilize injured limbs, the physicians used porous plaster casts. Coe discovered that large quantities of his porous plasters were disappearing. Investigating, he learned that the men used the plasters to patch their overalls and to make pads for their pick and shovel handles. Coe and Ferrell solved the problem by buying plasters from Boston for $5 per gross, making them affordable for the men to use the plasters however they wished.

The Des Chutes hospital in Grass Valley closed after one year, having treated 528 patients, and burying eighteen workers, most in graves without markers, lost to sickness and accidents.[27] Because both railroads employed about the same number of workers, it is likely that the Oregon Trunk experienced a similar rate of morbidity and mortality.

Blind Pig Booze

Memorable stories have made their way into the Deschutes River oral history. Whether these episodes really happened is now impossible to document. It has been said that when occasionally the camps left the edge of the river, the opposing gang would ignite the grass below their camp. Others have reported that sniper fire from across the river punctuated the nighttime. "Spotters" were said to climb the canyon walls during the day to discover where the other side stored their powder, a target for nighttime forays.[8] This sporting exercise had a specific objective: delay in progress because of insufficient black powder. One night, a Des Chutes Railroad watchman allegedly discovered a lit fuse in the middle of camp. After extinguishing the fuse, he discovered that it led to a keg full of black powder. This scare was sufficient to cause many workers to leave the next day, producing a desired delay in construction.[42]

When the conflicts were resolved by legal agreements, workers on the two sides became amicable. "One of the interesting features of the rival railroad building now is that where the early invasion of Central Oregon was attended by 'military operations,' as Judge Twohy expressed it, the competing construction gangs are peacefully blasting out the canyon cliffs, side by side, with only the narrow river gorge between them. There hasn't been the semblance of trouble of any sort for months."[42]

Some of the altercations were probably fueled by alcohol because the men working on the Deschutes River had no difficulty in obtaining moonshine. Sheriff Levi Chrisman of Wasco County nabbed two bootleggers in the camps near Sherar's bridge.[43] He arrested Albert Knight and George Gardner with thirty bottles of whiskey in their possession, which

Mostly moonshine

Italian musician

they intended to sell for $2 per bottle. Their whiskey was homemade, in quart beer bottles labeled "Beer."

Illegal saloons were known as "blind pigs."[44] Joe Schnere of Henry & Schnere, a subcontractor, complained to the Porter Brothers about the presence of a new blind pig in camp. Off to investigate the complaint, Johnson Porter climbed into the driver's seat of his automobile, and his usual driver, James Morrell, cranked the engine. This was the first time Porter had attempted to drive. Following Morrell's instructions one step at a time, he drove the car across a field and promptly hit a rock. Porter decided it would be prudent to turn the car over to Morrell. Stopping just above Joe Schnere's camp, they spied the three tents that made up the blind pig. Porter tied three sticks of dynamite together with a blasting cap and a short fuse. They turned the car around for a quick getaway, tossed the dynamite, and after

Workers hiking a roadbed

an agonizing delay, were rewarded with a satisfying explosion. They didn't see the results, making their hasty exit up the road. Back at the office in their camp, they saw the blind pig operators carrying their bags and blankets, heading for the stage station.

Despite the vigilance of the construction company managers, illegal liquor was easy to find. Bootleggers drove to the work sites, offering a choice among the bottles arranged in the back compartments of their vehicles. A fully stocked liquor store in a cave was called a "gallon hill" or a rural blind pig. In a lonely spot along the road from The Dalles to Maupin, such a cave was hidden from sight by a camouflaged door.[45] A secret knock opened the door revealing the liquor. The workers made their payments on the honor system, according to a displayed price card. The *Madras Pioneer* informed its readers that "The liquor obtained at a 'gallon hill' is said to taste something like a concoction of sheep dip and alcohol."[45]

"Rufe" Armstrong's diary reveals that the surveyors liked to party. They often made the hard three-hour hike to Grass Valley to drink beer, play baseball, and go to dances.[25] Female companionship was not hard to find.

THE RAILROAD TODAY stands silent about the past. The Deschutes stories have faded into history. The workers and managers who built the Deschutes railroads reflected late nineteenth- and early twentieth-century American history: competing moguls striving for profits, providing work for immigrants, and opening new lands for settlers. Today, the railroad along the Deschutes River reminds us of the entrepreneurial conflicts and the harsh working conditions endured by thousands of immigrants determined to make a new start: an historical struggle among men and with earth's geology.

- CHAPTER TEN -

BRIDGES

THE FALLS! WE DON'T HEAR IT ANYMORE

All bridges have a story, especially the two major bridges on the Oregon Trunk Railway. The Crooked River Bridge is an inspirational structure because of its height and grace. It is a symbol of human achievement that evokes awe and some trepidation in the crew of crossing trains. The bridge over the Columbia River is forever linked with Celilo Falls, a traditional site used for thousands of years by Indians for salmon fishing. Today, the bridge stands over the submerged falls in the impounded water behind the dam at The Dalles, like a commemorative marker in a cemetery.

An efficient railroad, in limiting its grade and miles of track, cannot avoid building bridges. Wooden truss bridges, being relatively simple to build, provided a level deck, and by their design, transmitted the load vertically to the ground. Wooden bridges most often used the Howe truss, developed by William Howe of Massachusetts in 1838.[1] Iron bridges adapted the Howe truss or other truss designs, and by the middle of the nineteenth century, bridge designs evolved to reflect scientific advances and stress analysis. Nevertheless, between the years 1870 to 1880, about forty railroad and highway bridges collapsed every year.[2] By 1900, the combination of steel and technological development allowed the construction of larger, safer bridges.

RALPH MODJESKI designed and supervised the building of the Oregon Trunk bridges. Born Rudolf Modrzejewski near Krakow, Poland, in 1861, at age fifteen, he immigrated to America, along with his mother, Helen Modjeska, a famous Shakespearean actress.[3] Modjeski, an accomplished classical pianist, returned to Europe to receive his education in civil engineering in Paris. On returning to the U.S., he became a famous designer and builder of American bridges. His first bridge was a combined railway and highway bridge (the first highway bridge over the Mississippi River) at Rock Island, Illinois. It led to a series of standard bridge designs for the Northern Pacific Railroad. Modjeski also designed major suspension bridges, such as the Ambassador Bridge in Detroit and the San Francisco-Oakland Bay Bridge. He built the Spokane, Portland & Seattle railroad bridges over the Columbia and Willamette Rivers connecting Portland to Vancouver, Washington. He died at age eighty in 1940, and his surviving firm is active today, with offices in many American cities. John Stevens called on Modjeski to design and supervise the construction of the Columbia River Bridge at Celilo and the Crooked River Bridge for the Oregon Trunk Railway.

Bridges Along the Deschutes River

The first confrontation between the two railroads building along the Deschutes River took place at Horseshoe Bend, where the Oregon Trunk crossed to the east side of the river. To avoid following the river around the large curve, the line crossed the river, passed through an 800-foot tunnel and immediately crossed back over the river. The first crossing went over a channel only 120 feet wide. The force of the current in this narrow channel was so strong that it proved impossible to measure the depth of the water with a 125-pound anvil lowered from a cable spanning the river.[4]

North Crossing, Horseshoe Bend

South Crossing, Horseshoe Bend

Twin Crossings

The first bridges at Horseshoe Bend were wooden trestles that were rapidly replaced in 1912 with steel structures. The bridge at the first crossing, 70 feet over the water, was a Howe truss with a 120-foot span, erected on a suspension span swung across the river; the steel for the twin crossings was from the Pennsylvania Steel Company. This bridge was seated on a crib on the east bank, built with riprap using stones larger than one cubic yard in volume, transported across the river on a traveler running on a 1.5-inch cable. On the west side, the crib sat directly on rock bottom in about ten feet of water. The crib was built to fit the site, floated into position, and sunk by filling it with riprap. These cribs supported the towers of the suspension span. Both bridges at Horseshoe Bend are placed on four concrete piers. The second bridge on the south side is about 600 feet long; its concrete piers were constructed using cofferdams to divert the stream. Underwater footings were built using the technique of bucket and tremie.[5] The concrete was delivered by a bucket to a tube (the tremie) that funneled the concrete underwater to the bottom of a cofferdam, building the concrete pier from the bottom up. As the structure filled with concrete, the water was displaced.

Des Chutes Railroad Trout Creek Viaduct

The Union Pacific steel viaducts crossing Trout Creek and Willow Creek are also notable. The Union Pacific Trout Creek viaduct is 550 feet long and 100 feet high sitting on four 40-foot towers placed on concrete pedestals. The bridge includes three intermediate spans, one 100-foot, one 60-foot, and one 40-foot span; two 50-foot spans at the northern approach; and two 40-foot spans at the southern approach.

Trout Creek Viaduct — 2005

The Union Pacific Willow Creek viaduct that crossed the Oregon Trunk line along Willow Creek is 1,050 feet long, 275 feet high, and took six months to complete.[6] The bridge sits on eight 40-foot towers and includes five 100-foot intermediate spans, one 50-foot approach span at the northern end, and two 60-foot spans at the southern end.

The rest of the bridges along the Deschutes River were lightly constructed wood trestles, covered with galvanized iron for protection against fires. The timber for them came from nearby mills, hauled into the canyon over the new construction roads. All stringers, ties, and guard rails were of Oregon or Washington fir; all other components were of central Oregon pine or fir.[4]

Des Chutes Railroad Willow Creek Bridge

Willow Creek Bridge — 2005

Oregon Trunk trestle near South Junction

Oregon Trunk trestle in Willow Creek Canyon

Oregon Trunk trestle in Willow Creek Canyon

The Bridge Over the Crooked River

The location of the Crooked River Bridge was the only reasonable crossing of the deep canyon, which the river slowly carved out over four million years. Here, the canyon walls were closer to each other than at any other place along the Crooked River. Despite its narrowness, the canyon's depth provided a formidable challenge for the bridge engineers.

The Crooked River Bridge is high enough, and the air is so dry, that a kitchen match dropped from the top ignites spontaneously from the friction of the air. Oregon Trunk officials verified this doubtful statement, and it was featured in Ripley's *Believe It or Not.*[7] The bridge is a two-hinge arch span with a total length of 460 feet, crossing Crooked River Canyon 320 feet above the river below. At the time it was built, the Crooked River Bridge was the second highest bridge in the U.S.; the Southern Pacific viaduct over the Pecos River was just one foot higher.[4,8]

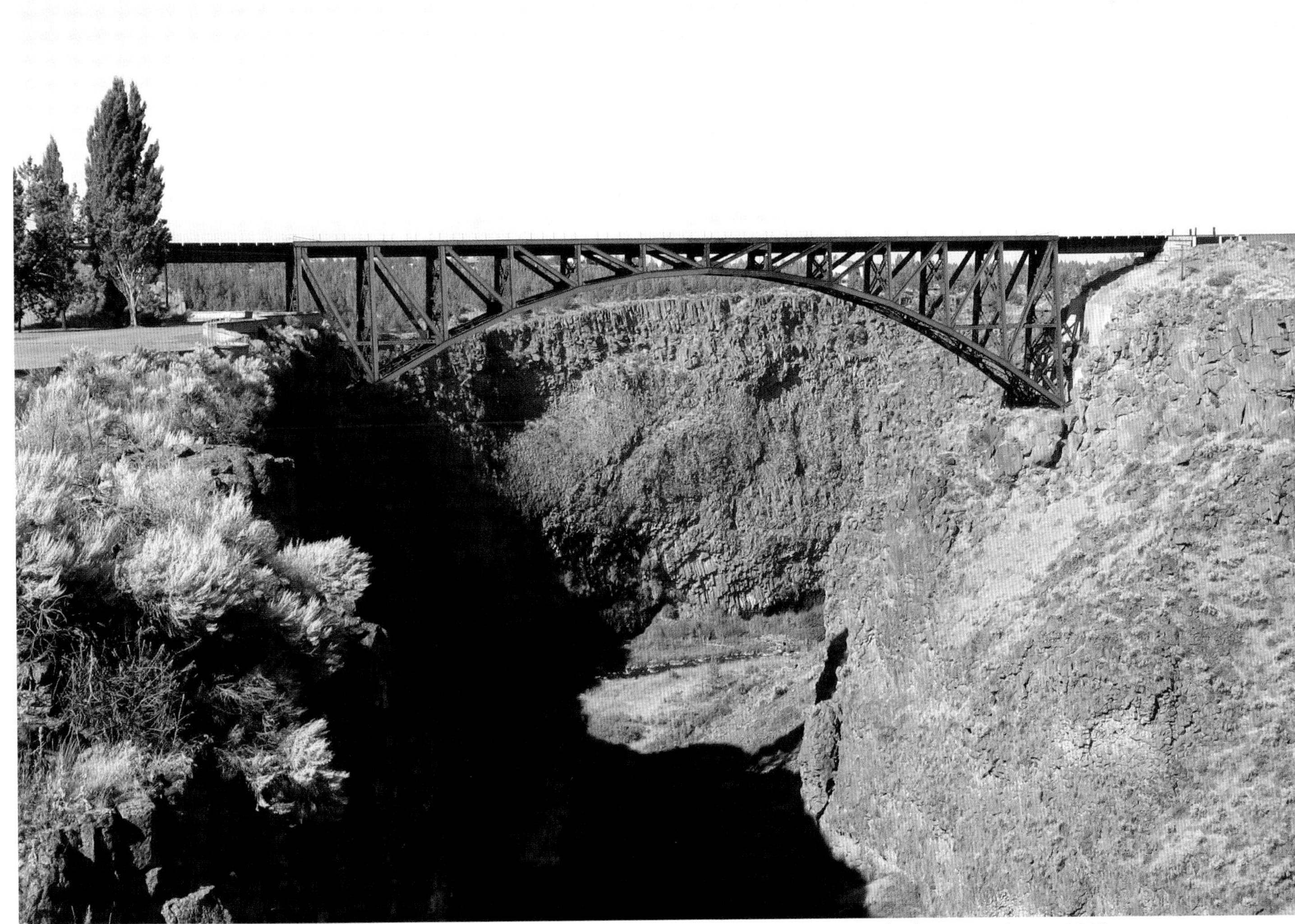

Crooked River Bridge — 2005

The span of the Crooked River Bridge's steel arch is 340 feet long with a 60-foot deck girder approach at each end. The Missouri Valley Bridge and Iron Company of Leavenworth, Kansas, built the bridge by cantilevering it out from the hard, solid basalt walls on each side of the canyon. When construction of the bridge began, the Oregon Trunk was building south from the Columbia River, and thus access was at the north side of the canyon. So that construction could proceed simultaneously from each end, workers installed a cable across the canyon to carry materials to the other side. Steam engines mounted on each cantilevered projection provided the power for hoisting and placement of the steel.

Crooked River Bridge

Crooked River Bridge donkey engine

Crooked River Bridge final span

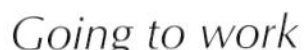
Going to work

Walking the plank

A surprisingly small crew of forty workers camped on the canyon floor. To work on the bridge, they climbed up and down a rope ladder.[9] When the two sides were close enough, workers crossed back and forth by walking on planks!

The Crooked River Bridge is 122 miles from the Columbia River, four miles south of Opal City, a busy tent town during construction. But construction was delayed, while workers awaited the shipment of steel. The delay motivated one of the engineers to spread a story explaining the slow rate of construction.[10] He pointed out that the steel, when put together, would miss the prepared site by two to four inches, either due to shrinkage of the steel or more likely because the canyon walls were moving. One gullible, local resident urged the engineer to rig a heavy bolt to each canyon wall to restrain the movement. The engineer said not to worry, the heat of the sun will expand the steel, and when it reaches the proper length, workers will quickly rivet it in place, thus preventing the canyon walls from further spreading.

Bridge steel workers are a hardy lot. One day, the foreman of the steelworker's camp summoned Dr. Urling Coe of Bend to extract a painful tooth.[11] But the man with the toothache couldn't stand the pain. As Coe made his way to the bridge, the man made his way to the dentist in Redmond. He had the tooth extracted after consuming sufficient whiskey to provide anesthesia. He walked back to the Crooked River, where he faced the choice of crossing the cable

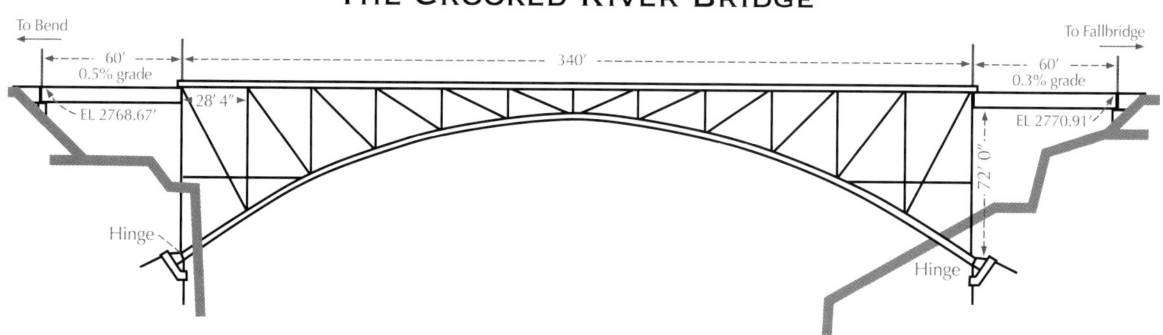

First train over the Crooked River Bridge

across the canyon or walking many miles around. The steelworker chose the cable, crossing the canyon in the dark, going hand over hand, hanging on the cable. The doctor and the worker arrived in the camp at the same time.

The first steel shipment filled eleven railroad cars and arrived in Opal City on May 18, 1911.[9] Only four months later, the first train crossed the bridge on September 17, 1911, with only half the rivets in place![4]

The Columbia River Bridge at Celilo

The original plans of the Oregon Trunk called for its connection to the Union Pacific tracks of the Oregon Railroad & Navigation Company on the south bank of the Columbia River. But once the Hill forces acquired the Oregon Trunk, a connection to Union Pacific tracks was no longer a possibility nor was it desired. The Hill strategy called for a connection to the Spokane, Portland & Seattle on the north bank of the Columbia River, completing a network that would reach west to Portland and Seattle, east to Chicago, and eventually south to California. This connection required a bridge.

Congress authorized the Oregon Trunk bridge across the Columbia River at Celilo Falls on March 2, 1910. The Missouri Valley Bridge and Iron Company of Leavenworth, Kansas, built the bridge, with seven spans of steel from the Pennsylvania Steel Company, resting on concrete bases footed on exposed rock islands at a cost of $1 million.[12] Although he was near the end of his business career, James J. Hill, still a hands-on manager, personally negotiated with competing steel companies for the best price.[13]

In the summer of 1910, construction crews built inclines on each bank of the Columbia four miles upriver from the bridge site to service the large ferry that would carry railroad cars across the river until the bridge was open. These inclines were at Clarke on the north side and Moody on the south side, about three miles upstream from Celilo Falls. A half-mile-long spur connected the north incline to the Spokane, Portland & Seattle mainline. At Moody, a 2.8-mile track,

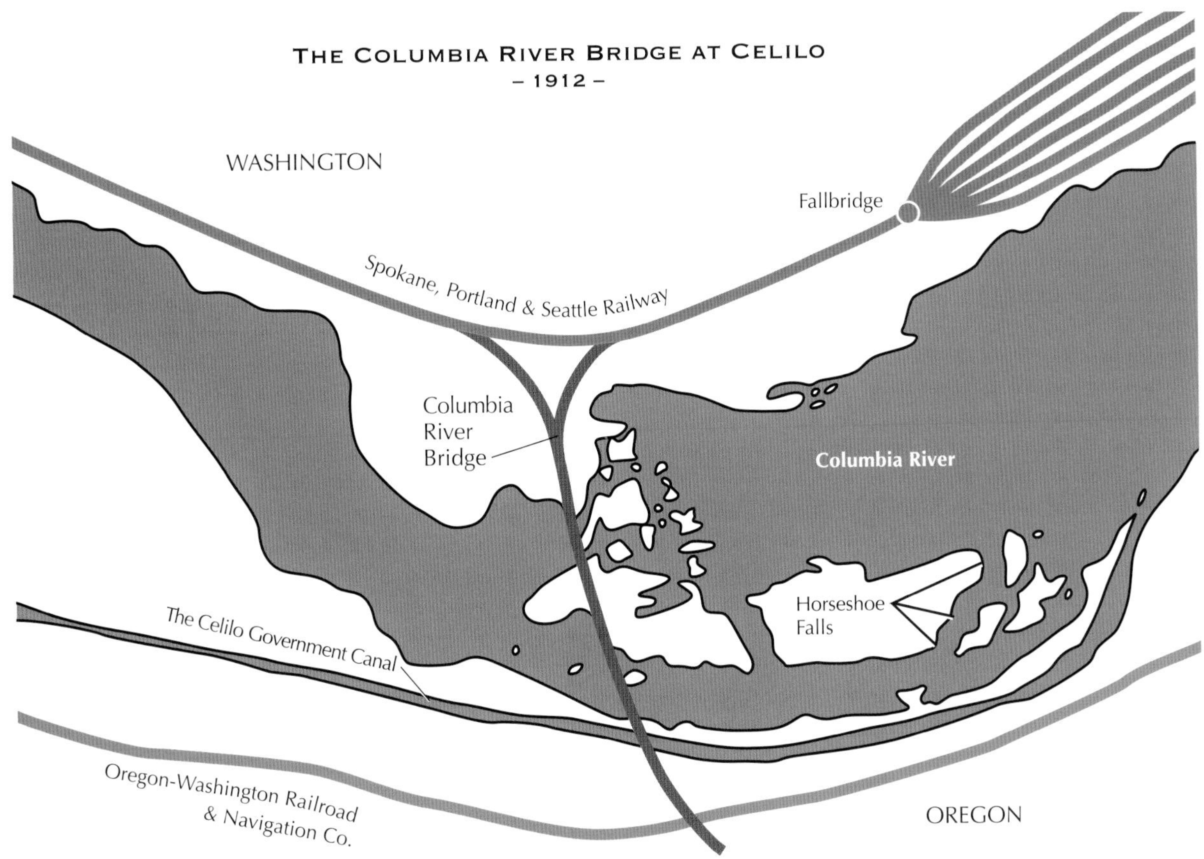

mostly on a trestle, connected with the line along the Deschutes River. In September 1910, the ferry began operating, providing a link to the Spokane, Portland & Seattle tracks on the Washington side of the Columbia River until the Celilo Bridge was completed.

The bridge was built immediately over the lower part of Celilo Falls. The major fishing site, known as Horseshoe Falls, was about one-half mile upstream, near the Oregon bank. Another location, about five miles downstream, was considered but abandoned because of greater difficulty and cost. The advantage of the site at Celilo Falls was the narrowing of the river to a width of 2,700 feet. Celilo Falls was not a single waterfall. It consisted of multiple channels through the low points in the basaltic rock riverbed. At low water, the basaltic base of the river was exposed as a series of islands. The main channel was only 300 feet wide, near the south bank. When The Dalles Dam was completed, the islands upon which the Celilo Bridge was footed disappeared under the impounded water. Because these islands dictated the positioning of the bridge piers (made of concrete, with granite facings), the bridge itself does not cross the river at an exact right angle.[4]

To carry out the survey work for the bridge at Celilo, surveyors reached one of the islands using an aerial tramway they constructed just for this purpose. Two of the islands were reached by rowboat, but the island in the midst of turbulent water required a tramway on a heavy cable strung between the two islands reached by boat. The small car running on the cable was seventy-five feet above the water. "Three days of hard work were spent in getting the light wire from one island to the other. Carrying a telegraph wire from the first island reached, a rowboat made a score of attempts to gain the third island with the end of the wire, and after numerous breakages of the light wire it was finally strung across, and the heavy cable was then drawn into place"[14]

THE COLUMBIA RIVER BRIDGE[4]

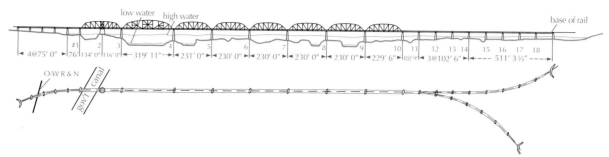

low water
high water
base of rail
#1 2 3 4 5 6 7 8 9 10 11 12 13 14 15 16 17 18
4@75′ 0″ 76′ 134′ 0″ 116′ 0″ 319′ 11″ 231′ 0″ 230′ 0″ 230′ 0″ 230′ 0″ 230′ 0″ 229′ 6″ 102′ 9″ 3@102′ 6″ 511′ 3¾″
O-W R & N
gov't canal

Columbia River Bridge swing span over Government Canal

Columbia River Bridge, Indian Village on north bank, Celilo Village across the river on left

The high winds through the gorge along the Columbia River made it difficult for the men to work on the bridge. For this reason, the spans were pre-assembled and erected by cantilevering them out over the channels until the bridge reached the falsework used at the north end.[4] The swing span extended over the canal built around the rapids. The swing span had unequal legs because the center and north piers had to be situated on the island bases. The north approach was a wye, connecting to the Spokane, Portland & Seattle.

The Celilo Bridge over the Columbia River sits on twenty-nine piers and three abutments. The 4,197-foot steel structure consisted of sixteen deck girder spans 102 feet long, six through-truss spans each 230 feet long, one swing span 250 feet long over the

Columbia River Bridge, low water

Columbia River Bridge north bank wye

Celilo Government Canal, one 320 foot span, one deck girder 76 feet long, and one deck girder 75 feet long.[4] Construction began July 9, 1910, and the first train crossed on January 4, 1912. Work was essentially impossible during high water, so surveyors had to work from September 1909 to March 1910. Major construction took place between summer 1910 and spring 1911, and again in summer 1911, until completion in January 1912. The worst injury occurred when a man fell fifty feet from the deck of the Celilo Bridge into a pool of water that was only two feet deep. The water saved his life, and he quickly returned to work.[15] After completing the Celilo Bridge, the steel crews then moved to the Deschutes and replaced wooden trestles at several crossings, including the twin crossings at Horseshoe Bend and the bridge at North Junction.

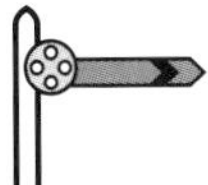

THE INDIAN FISHING VILLAGE on the Columbia River ninety miles east of Portland was called Wyam, meaning the sound of water on the rocks. Celilo Falls just downstream from this site provided fish for major trading among many widespread Indian tribes. Using wooden platforms on the banks and islands, the Indians used dip nets to nab salmon and steelhead ascending the falls. The arid climate allowed the fish to be air dried. The origin of the name "Celilo" is unknown, although some believe it to be a name derived from the "Si-le-lah" tribe.[16] Celilo Village, built by the federal government, replaced Indian facilities at their traditional fishing grounds; but most of the Indian land was lost to the canal in 1913, railroad and highway easements, and finally the impounded water behind The Dalles Dam in 1957.

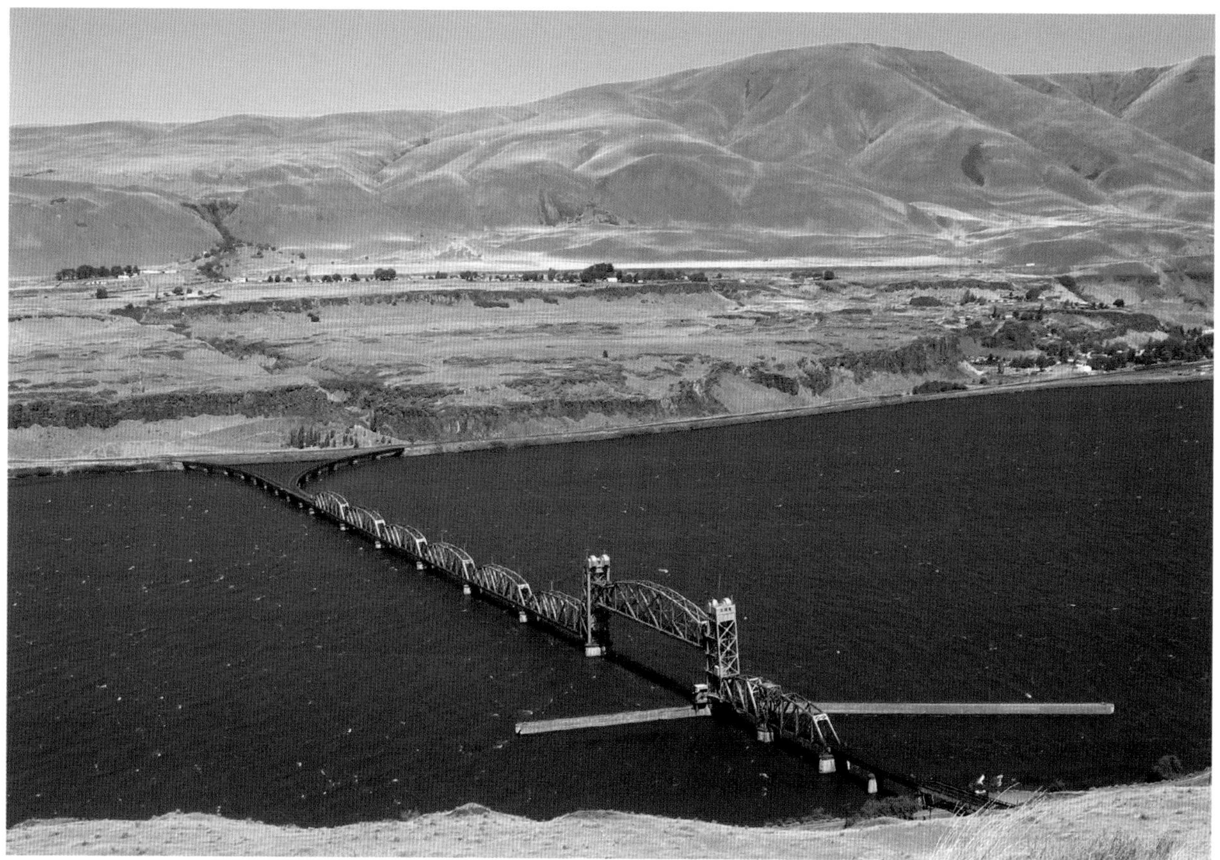

Columbia River Bridge — 2005

Columbia River Bridge — 2005

When The Dalles Dam was completed, the rising water covered Celilo Falls and the rocky islands. No longer needed, the government canal was closed and a new vertical lift span was added to accommodate the river traffic. The steel structure of the entire bridge had to be raised several feet. The old swing span (the span on the Oregon side of the lift span) was left in place, but the operating engine was removed in 1974. Prior to the dam, the railroad men in Wishram could hear the roar of the water over Celilo Falls around the clock. On March 9, 1957, the newly completed dam at The Dalles began to stop the flow of the Columbia River. Kenny Prager and his fireman, Tom Craine, walked down to the bridge to watch the water rise.[17] They were surprised to find themselves enormously saddened upon seeing something with such a long history disappear. When they returned to Wishram and prepared their steam locomotive to leave, both men simultaneously sensed something was wrong. Craine said, "What's that funny noise?" Then together they exclaimed, "The falls! We don't hear it anymore."

- CHAPTER ELEVEN -

Completion of Two Railroads to Bend

I Don't See Any Golden Spike, *Durnit!*

The Oregon Trunk's Harris track-laying machine entered Bend on Saturday, September 30, 1911. The line was completed the next afternoon despite a steady rain.[1] A temporary depot was already in place, and nearby stood the foundation of a stone depot to be completed in 1913, using pink volcanic rock quarried locally and paid for by the city of Bend.[2] Later, a similar depot made of the same rock would be built in Redmond. James J. Hill's special train backed into Bend after turning around on the wye in Opal City. Hill was accompanied by his son, Louis, president of the Great Northern, and Carl Gray, president of the Spokane, Portland & Seattle and the Oregon Trunk. William McMurray, General Passenger Agent for the Oregon-Washington Railroad & Navigation Company, represented the Union Pacific.

The celebration of the last spike on October 5, 1911, drew a crowd of 1,500 to 2,000 people, an impressive gathering given that Bend had only 536 people (although ten years later the population was 5,415).[3] The town celebrated for two days, enjoying the bright and clear weather that followed the rain. The local people and visitors participated in the many festivities that included bronco busting, log rolling, football, boxing, horse and canoe races, pillow fights, climbing a greased pole, a parade, and a baby show.[4,5]

At the edge of the depot grounds, a welcome arch crossed over Fir Avenue. A large cornerstone, inscribed with "1911," was laid at the stone depot foundation by William "Bill" Hanley of Burns, who was honored in recognition of his efforts that stirred James J. Hill's interest in central Oregon.[6] Just in front of the speaker's platform, where an iron spike was removed from the track, seventy-three-year-old James J. Hill drove a golden spike home with two blows. Afterwards, Hill rose to speak and emphasized the economic need for immigration to central Oregon. "You could not build a prosperous community in the Garden of Eden and we could not run a railroad there if there was nobody but Adam and Eve to use it."[7] Hill directly addressed the conflict with the Union Pacific, "... We have here our railroad neighbor of the Union Pacific and we are like Daniel in the lions' den. Now we mean to get along with them. When they get in a tight place we are going to extend the helping hand of fellowship and if we get into a tight place we will call on them. We won't make faces at each other across the fence."[6]

W.E. Coman, traffic manager for the Spokane, Portland & Seattle, took the golden spike to Portland to be displayed. The plan was to return it to the Commercial Club in Bend.[8] However, the golden spike is now missing. In 1999, the Oregon Trunk Depot in Bend was dismantled and relocated as the Art Station, a center for creative arts. The workers were surprised to find a time capsule hidden in a cavity chiseled into the cornerstone. Hoping to find the missing golden spike, a small crowd gathered at the Des Chutes Historical Center during a light snowfall on April 27, 1999, to open the capsule, a small tin box. The crowd was disappointed. The box contained three Bend newspapers from 1911, some railroad posters, and a 5-cent metal token to the Carmody Brothers Pool Hall.[9] Barry Slaughter, chairman of the historical society, said, "I don't see any golden spike, durnit!"[9] A plastic time capsule was placed in the cornerstone of the reconstructed and relocated depot on June 7, 1999. In keeping with the tradition of the 1911 tin box, the capsule's contents included a gift certificate from the D&D Bar and Grill in Bend.

William Hanley laying 1911 cornerstone

Bend Railroad Day Parade

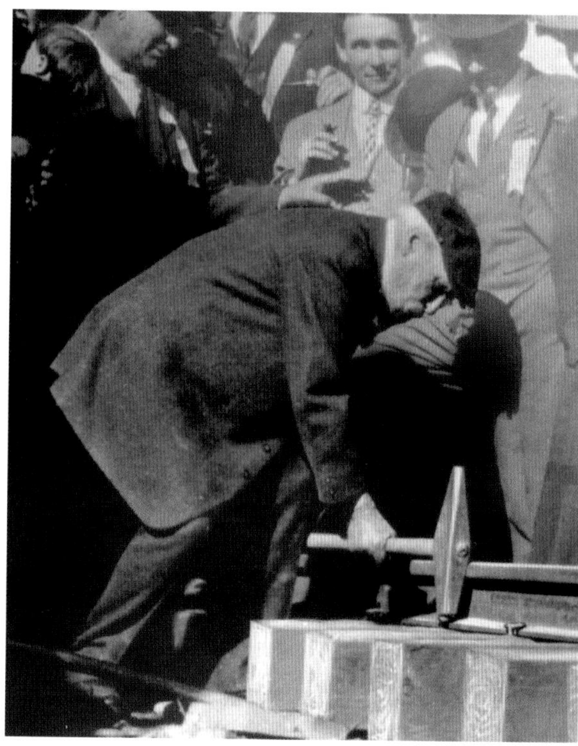

James J. Hill and golden spike

James J. Hill in Bend

Poster in 1911 cornerstone

Building the Home Stretch

The Oregon Trunk track-laying crew reached Madras on February 15, 1911. As the line advanced, the Oregon Trunk used locomotives from the Great Northern and railroad cars from the Northern Pacific. The first train passed under a celebration archway on a day formally declared by the town as "Railroad Day," billed as the greatest event in the history of Madras.[10] The Bend Band joined a group of people from Bend who traveled to Madras to celebrate the arrival of the first Oregon Trunk train, an engine and two coaches from Portland with John F. Stevens and prominent businessmen. People cheered as they watched the last 400 feet of track laid in twenty-two minutes.[11] Led by the Bend Band, the crowd marched through the town to a barbecue of two "monstrous" steers.[10] The crowd gave Stevens a rousing ovation as he recounted his famous incognito trip as John F. Sampson. The Des Chutes tracks reached Madras three months later, its first train carrying a circus to add to the celebration.[12]

The first Oregon Trunk train leaving Madras for Portland consisted of six cars, four with 980 head of sheep, one box car with about twenty central Oregon people along for the ride, and a caboose. For the first fifty miles, the train had to travel at eight miles per hour over unballasted track.[13] The first passenger train to arrive in Madras carried 135 people, a number that far exceeded the capacity of its lone hotel.[14] These passengers included railroad and express company officials, merchants, traveling salesmen, real estate agents, stock buyers, land speculators, financiers, and prospective settlers.[15]

The Oregon Trunk reached Metolius only six days after entering Madras, and on March 1, 1911, daily train service in each direction began running between Fallbridge and Metolius, taking 8.5 hours to make a one-way trip. To reach Fallbridge, passengers had to cross the Columbia River onboard the sternwheeling steamer, *Norma,* to make the connection between the Oregon Trunk and the Spokane, Portland & Seattle.

Madras, "redlight" tent city in foreground on right

Madras welcome arch

The Crooked River was at track mile 126, which the Oregon Trunk reached in April 1911. A wye was installed at Opal City, and trains began running to this point on April 18. Work on the Crooked River Bridge was stalled while workers awaited the delivery of steel, which did not begin to arrive at the canyon until June 14.

At this point, John Stevens left the Hill lines (resigning on May 1, 1911) to open a private practice as a consulting engineer in New York. A measure of the respect, trust, and confidence James J. Hill placed in John F. Stevens is the fact that all of the millions of dollars spent in building the Oregon Trunk and extending the Oregon Electric and United Railways passed through Stevens' personal hands, with no accounting until the completion of the work.[16] The Oregon Trunk books carried millions of dollars under a line that read, "John F. Stevens—Special."[17] Stevens' chief engineer, Ralph Budd, remained, and Carl Gray was installed as the new president of the Spokane, Portland & Seattle and the Oregon Trunk. Budd later became president of the Great Northern from 1919 to 1931.

The first serious train accident on the Oregon Trunk occurred even before the line was complete on July 10, 1911.[18] Trunk Train 102 with a mail and baggage car and two passenger cars, with conductor Fred Cass and Engineer John Myles, was running thirty-five minutes late, approaching the north end of a temporary curve around the Frieda (later known as Dant) tunnel site, twenty-two miles south of Sherars. The track was not fully ballasted and tamped, and the 11° curve had a ten miles per hour speed limit, but it was rarely observed. Number 102 hit the curve doing thirty-five miles per hour. The engine rocked and then tipped over, landing twenty-five feet down the bank of the river. All the cars passed by, except the last, which fell on the engine. Steam from the locomotive entered the broken windows of the car killing eight people.

A tragedy was narrowly averted in January 1912, when a train crossing the river on the temporary bridge at North Junction had to stop because the bridge began to give way. The passengers crawled across the quivering bridge to the bank.[19] Wrecks have given their names to rapids. Wreck Rapids, at river mile 39.5 just before Horseshoe Bend/Twin Crossings, immortalizes the three crewmen who died in a head-to-head train collision on September 22, 1949. Only one of the many horses in the freight cars survived unharmed, acquiring the name "Oregon Trunk" and living for the rest of his life at the station-master's house in Maupin.[20] Boxcar Rapids at river mile 54, just two miles upstream from Maupin, immortalizes a derailment caused by a rock slide in March 1954. The engineer and fireman drowned when the locomotive and one boxcar fell into the river, which was high from spring rains and snowmelt.

Passenger service between Portland and Madras started in May 1911. Leaving Madras in the morning, it took 11.5 hours to get to Union Station in Portland (crossing the Columbia River required boarding the sternwheeler *Norma* until January 1912).[21] Shipping freight over the Oregon Trunk to Portland was $1 to $4 per 100 pounds less expensive and eight to ten days faster compared with shipping it over the Union Pacific route from Shaniko.

When the Oregon Trunk tracks reached Redmond at mile point 135, the small community rose to the occasion. They erected a welcome arch, perhaps the only one ever constructed of alfalfa! The honor of driving a commemorative spike was given to Laura Jones, the daughter of Mayor Howard Jones.

Redmond Railroad Day, alfalfa welcome arch

Redmond Spike Ceremony, Laura Jones in center

Oregon Trunk Harris track-laying machine entering Bend

The Oregon Trunk reached Bend on September 30, 1911, with 150 men laying two miles of track per day.[2] On the next day, they extended the tracks one mile south of the depot to the train yard. The first regular passenger train arrived in the evening of October 31, 1911; only twenty minutes late, it was greeted by several hundred people.[22] The Des Chutes crew was still lagging behind. The Des Chutes finally reached Metolius on September 23, 1911, and the next day began service to Opal City. It cost about 20¢ to 25¢ to ride the train for two miles in 1911. A one-way trip from Bend to Portland cost $7.45.

Beginning Dates for Train Service

November 17, 1910	to Maupin
February 1, 1911	to North Junction
March 20, 1911	to South Junction
April 30, 1911	to Gateway
July 14, 1911	to Madras
March 2, 1911	to Opal City
November 1, 1911	to Bend

A Comparison of the Two Railroads

The Oregon Trunk Railway was longer and better built than the Des Chutes Railroad. It had seven tunnels, ten steel bridges, and seventy-nine trestles on the mainline and one steel bridge and ten trestles on sidings and spurs.[23] The cost of the Oregon Trunk eventually reached $16.6 million, compared with the $9 million spent by the Harriman forces.[24] The large Oregon Trunk bridges over the Columbia and Crooked Rivers added to the cost, but the biggest cost difference between the two railroads was due to the Oregon Trunk's superior quality.

Oregon Trunk Expenditures[25]

Road	
Grading	$7,626,427
Bridges	$2,089,428
Rails	$1,582,094
Engineering	$577,294
Tunnels	$572,073
Ties	$368,752
Ballast	$350,907
Equipment	$911,116
General Expenses	$1,027,115
Legal Expenses	$35,962
TOTAL	**$15,141,168**
	as of June 30, 1912

The Oregon Trunk tracks covered 151.5 miles from the junction with the Spokane, Portland & Seattle Railway on the Washington side of the Columbia River to Bend.[26] Yard track and sidings accounted for another 39.6 miles of tracks. The final Des Chutes Railroad was 95.3 miles long, including 71.3 miles from the Oregon-Washington Railroad & Navigation tracks to North Junction and 24 miles from South Junction to Metolius. Track rights over the Des Chutes and Oregon Trunk shared line added 10.41 miles between North Junction and South Junction and 42.7 miles from Metolius to Bend, giving a total distance of 148.41 miles.[27,28]

The Oregon Trunk Railway

John F. Stevens	President
Ralph Budd	Chief Engineer
J. C. Baxter	Division Engineer
Porter Brothers of Portland and Spokane	Grading from the Columbia River to Madras, all track laying, and the concrete work for the Columbia River Bridge.
H.C. Henry of Seattle	Grading from Madras to Bend
Bates & Rogers	Concrete work south of the Columbia River

The grading on the Oregon Trunk was heavy, about 55,000 cubic yards per mile for a total of about 9 million cubic yards—68.8 percent solid rock, 15.1 percent loose rock.[25] All of the material was blasted and moved by hand except for about 200,000 cubic yards near the mouth of the Deschutes River moved by steam shovel. Small cars, 1,140 of them, each with a 1.5 cubic yard capacity, moved rock and dirt over 62.5 miles of lightweight, twenty-pound rails. There were sixty miles of wagon roads that kept 600 horses occupied.

The Oregon Trunk Grading and Excavation[29]

	Cubic Yards	Percentage of Total
Solid Rock	5,944,146	68.8%
Loose Rock	1,301,363	15.1%
Hard Pan	783,122	9.1%
Earth	598,823	7.0%

The Oregon Trunk Grading and Excavation for Bridges and Culverts[29]

	Cubic Yards	Percentage of Total
Solid Rock	81,228	53.3%
Loose Rock	47,204	30.9%
Hard Pan	17,651	11.6%
Earth	6,266	4.2%

The Oregon Trunk had seven tunnels when it first began service, ranging from 515 feet to 800 feet long.[23,29] The tunnels were lined with timber and relined later with concrete. The roadbed was graded eighteen feet wide on earth and sixteen feet wide on rock fills. Cuts in dirt were twenty-four feet wide; cuts in rock were twenty feet wide.

Tunnel at Whitehorse Rapids

An Oregon law required railroads to be fenced within three months after initiating operations. The Oregon legislature revised this law to permit the omission of fencing when the railroad was protected by natural barriers (like steep cliffs or water). Except for ten miles without fencing in the canyon, the rest of the Oregon Trunk was fenced with cedar posts every twenty-four feet holding four barbed wires.

The railroads obtained timber for ties and bridge construction from nearby trees. For example, the Oregon Trunk purchased a timber claim on upper Willow Creek and signed a contract with Lou Hamilton for logging and delivering the timber to a mill constructed on the site.[30] A steam engine, delivered from Shaniko, powered the large mill.

The Oregon Trunk track consisted of ninety-pound steel rails, 133 miles of which came from the Open Hearth Company, twenty-three miles from Bessemer.[29] One mile of eighty-five-pound rail near the bridge over the Columbia River was the exception. Today the rails range from 112 to 133 pounds. The Oregon Trunk built a total of 3,000 feet of passing track about every seven miles, laid with seventy-pound rails.

Ties, 3,200 per mile, were untreated and laid over ten inches of ballast that was partly gravel and partly burnt clay. A natural, bright red burnt clay was discovered in a cut two miles south of Opal City. Material from this site was used to ballast the line from Metolius to Bend. The Oregon Trunk used tie plates only on curves and short tangents, in other words, when first built, spikes directly in the ties held most of the rails in place.[29] The gravel on the northern fifty miles of track came from the Avery pit (and some from the Dean pit) on the Washington side of the Columbia River.

Oregon Trunk's water stations, constructed by the Auto Gas Engine Company of Chicago, were of two types: tubs placed on side hills or water tanks on posts.[31] The tanks had a capacity of 50,000 gallons and measured sixteen by twenty-four feet. North of Pelton, except at Tuskan where a large spring was used to keep a concrete tank filled, the Oregon Trunk obtained water by pumping it from the river. South of Pelton, drilled wells provided the water. These wells were deep; for example, at Metolius, two wells passed through 300 feet of lava and then 300 feet of rock.

Oakbrook on the Oregon Trunk

Operations involved a terminal at Fallbridge and a terminal 115 miles upriver at Metolius (to be used by both the Oregon Trunk and the Des Chutes). Crossing the Columbia River on the bridge at Celilo, the tracks climb a grade of twenty-five feet per mile (about 0.6 percent), which persists as the line follows the Columbia River east for two miles until it reaches the Deschutes River. The 1.3 percent grade between South Junction and Madras was the steepest grade. To assist trains in making the steep grade, helper engines ran between Metolius and the turning wye at Jersey, which was between South Junction and Kaskela, and known earlier as U'Ren. In the 1950s, diesel engines eliminated the need for the helper engines and the wye.

The emergence of diesel locomotives is often called "dieselization" of the railroads. The purpose of the diesel engine is to produce electricity. Using this electricity, electrical traction motors placed over each two-wheel axle unit powered the locomotive wheels. There were good reasons for the demise of the steam locomotives. Diesel locomotives could generate more power. Adding more engines to create even more power was relatively simple, connecting several engines with jumper cables—a system easily controlled by a two-man crew no matter how many engines.

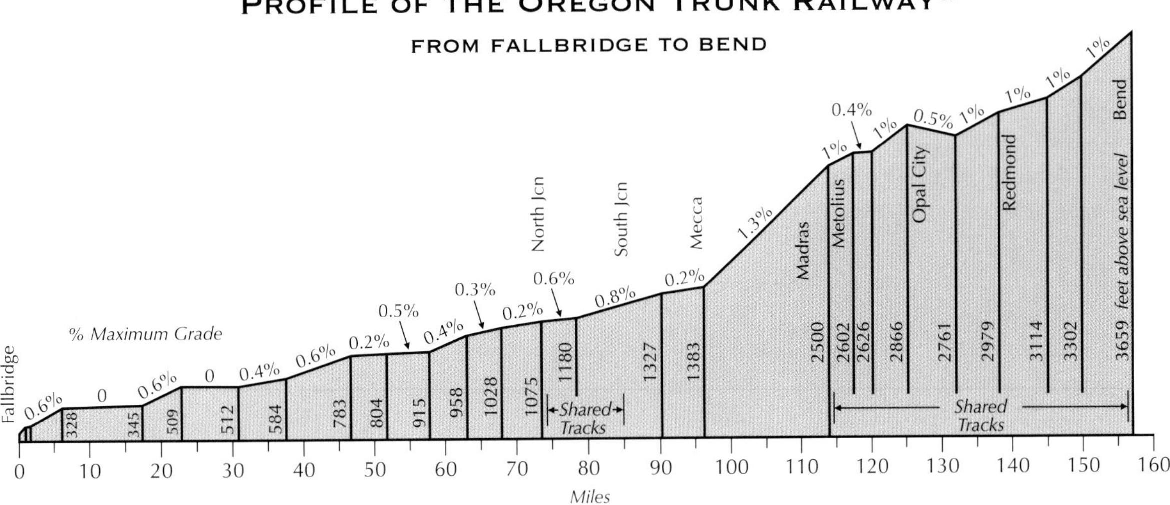

The support of fuel, water, and lubricant stations and personnel was not required, making operations more economical. For a long time, diesel fuel was relatively cheap. In 1932, the Burlington's *Zephyr* ran from Denver to Chicago, 1,015 miles in 13 hours 5 minutes, using $14.64 worth of fuel (418 gallons).[32]

The railroad yard at Fallbridge on the Washington side of the Columbia River, constructed in 1910 to 1912 for the joint use of the Oregon Trunk and the Spokane, Portland & Seattle, has six tracks, an engine house, and a turntable. Both lines used oil for fuel, drawing from a 30,000 barrel storage tank at Fallbridge. The Spokane, Portland & Seattle surveyed its line right through the houses of Indians living in the area; the Indian protests forced a relocation. Fallbridge (named as a combination of the Falls at Celilo and the projected bridge across the Columbia) was established in 1910.[33] A small town emerged to service the railroad men despite the fierce winds produced by the gorge that was just to the west. In 1926, the Hill lines St. Paul management changed the name of the station to Wishram, after the local Indian tribe (the accurate spelling of the tribal name was Wisham).[34] In 1926, the Great Northern Railway erected a stone monument in Wishram, which still stands, to honor Lewis and Clark and early settlers. The basalt rock for the monument was collected by a railroad crane at Dike on the Oregon Trunk Railway.[35]

Most of the buildings at Wishram are long gone. Trains heading east to Bend now leave the main line at Avery, but for many years, Wishram was the point at which cars were switched, crews changed, locomotives fueled. Some people still live in Wishram, and AMTRAK trains stop at the station.

The Oregon Trunk built depots at each station, complete with houses for agents and foremen and bunk houses for workers, all painted in the Hill line standard colors of yellow with green trim. Larger stations were built at Fallbridge, Madras, Metolius, and Culver. For ten years, Joseph C. McCarty, who came for the fishing, was the agent for the Oregon Trunk at North Junction.[36] At this site, he erected tents and cabins and maintained a general store—an early fishing resort.

After crossing the Crooked River, the tracks turn south to Terrebonne, a town first known as Hillman, after Hill and Harriman. But in September 1911, when a local real estate operator named Hillman acquired a nasty reputation, John Stevens suggested a name change to Terrebonne, "good earth" in French.[37]

The Des Chutes Railroad

J. P. O'Brien	President
George. W. Boschke	Chief Engineer
John D. Isaacs	Consulting Engineer
L. C. McCoy	District Engineer
Twohy Brothers Construction Company	

The Oregon Railroad & Navigation Company became the Oregon-Washington Railroad & Navigation Company when it was incorporated in Oregon on November 23, 1910, with all of its stock owned by the Union Pacific's Oregon Short Line Railroad.[38] The Des Chutes became a subsidiary of the Oregon-Washington Railroad & Navigation Company. The unavailability of original documents for the Des Chutes Railroad is partly explained by a report from Chief Engineer George W. Boschke to the auditing department of the Oregon-Washington Railroad & Navigation Company in 1914.[39] It states that all field engineers' correspondence and their files, all chief engineer's copies of contractor's reports, pile driving and bridge reports, progress reports, steam shovel reports, etc., were destroyed in a 1913 fire at the Columbia River dock of the Union Pacific. Other documents disappeared during several relocations of the Union Pacific Museum.

The Des Chutes Railroad started at Deschutes (now Ainsworth) on the Columbia River, three miles east of the mouth of the Deschutes River. Its tracks followed the east bank of the Deschutes River to North Junction. At North Junction, the Des Chutes and the Oregon Trunk shared 10.41 miles of joint track. At South Junction, the Des Chutes turned away from the river to follow Trout Creek up to Madras. At Metolius, the Des Chutes again connected with the Oregon Trunk track, which the two railroads shared for 42.7 miles to Bend.

As the Des Chutes Railroad turned east leaving the Deschutes River to follow Trout Creek, the line crossed a steel viaduct, and then followed a sharp horseshoe curve through a tunnel at mile point 92.5, climbing a 1.5 percent grade for sixteen miles. At the top of the grade, the Baldwin Land & Livestock Company was willing to sell its land to the Des Chutes, provided the railroad would build a station near its ranch, and this subsequently became the Gateway station.[40] Near Madras, the track crossed Willow Creek and the Oregon Trunk track on a steel bridge 250 feet high and 1,050 feet long.

The Des Chutes Railroad had five timber-lined tunnels that were 500 feet to 1,200 feet in length. One of the tunnels was at Beavertail. The horseshoe curve at Beavertail is larger than the one at Horseshoe Bend (Twin Crossings), located ten miles farther upstream, where the two railroads built their own tunnels 100 yards apart. The shortcut tunnel at Beavertail is not found on maps available today, but the old Des Chutes roadbed abuts rock fills that have obviously closed off the north and south portals of this tunnel. The excavation at the tunnel's north portal reveals the light-colored deposits from the explosion of Mount Mazama. The tunnel's location is depicted on an old map of the Deschutes River based on a survey performed in 1911 by the U.S. Geological Survey.[41]

The Des Chutes at Trout Creek

Beavertail — 1911

Beavertail — 2005

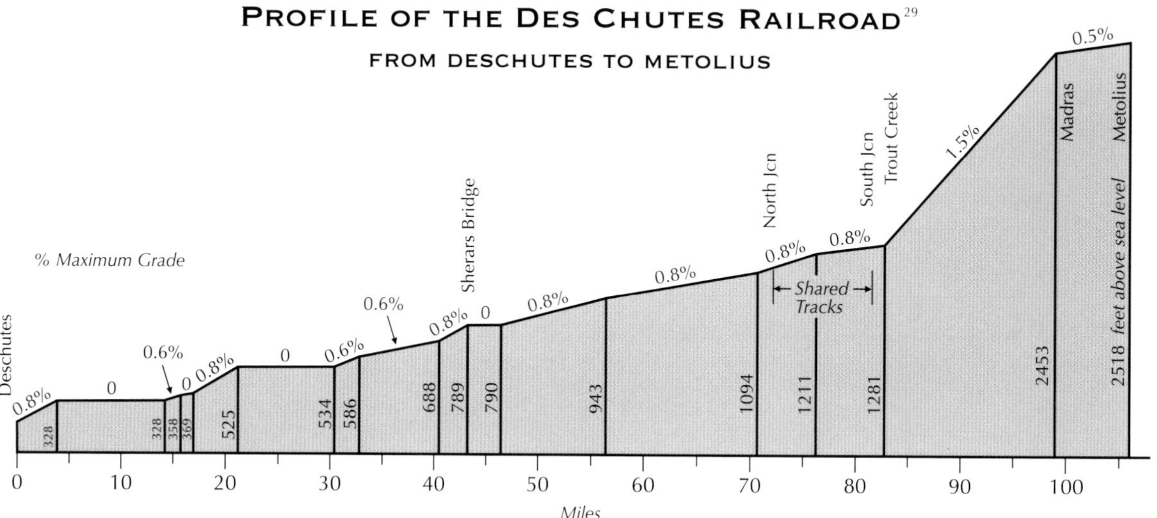

The Des Chutes built their roadbed fourteen feet wide on fills and sixteen feet wide on cuts. The Des Chutes track was laid with seventy-five-pound rail and ballasted with material secured from the adjacent right-of-way. Tie plates were used only on curves and bridges.[29] The Des Chutes placed steel water tanks of 65,000-gallon capacity at Madras and South Junction.

The gradient from the Columbia River to South Junction was less than 1 percent, but in this stretch, the Des Chutes had many curves, tunnels, and trestles. Above South Junction, the tracks following Trout Creek had to climb a 1.5 percent grade to Madras where the grade leveled out. The Des Chutes construction was lighter compared with the Oregon Trunk, probably because the Des Chutes had more steep grades and curves.[29] There were two curves with a 12° maximum, and a total of about 820° of curvature above 10°—because the railroad constructed the line to follow more closely the bottom of the canyon in order to avoid side-hill excavations.

The Prineville Railroad

Prineville is the oldest town in central Oregon, named after Francis "Barney" Prine, a merchant who primarily sold whiskey. The citizens of Prineville expected their city to be one of the stops on the Deschutes River railroad. However, Hill and Harriman both concluded that the potential of timber hauling from Bend exceeded revenues to be gained from wheat, cattle, and sheep around Prineville.[42] Furthermore, Prineville was out of the way for the ultimate goal, San Francisco. And so, Prineville was left a long nineteen miles away from the line. Because the negotiated settlement resolving the Deschutes competition included an agreement to split any traffic from Prineville, neither Hill nor Harriman wanted to build a feeder line to benefit the other man's railroad.

In 1911, James J. Hill stopped in Prineville on his way to the golden spike ceremony in Bend. Speaking after a banquet, he cautioned the people of Prineville regarding temporary and fleeting upsurges in business, seemingly placating the citizens for their out-of-the-way location.[43]

The citizens of Prineville had incorporated the Prineville and Eastern Railway in 1911, but not until 1916, when it was certain that the Deschutes line had bypassed them, did the city council announce plans to build a short line to join the Oregon Trunk near Redmond. The vote for a bond issue was passed 355 to 1 (the negative voter was branded as a cynic, who allegedly was the only citizen who failed to turn out for the parade and celebration).[44]

Sadly, no bids for the bonds were received, requiring another vote. This time 358 voted yes and 1 voted no (perhaps the same individual). Bonds were issued, and construction began in June 1917, but soon a second bond issue was deemed necessary to meet the cost of $227,000 (this time the vote was 202 to 14).[45]

Prineville — 1910

Money had to be raised yet again, but by March 1919, the railroad was in service. In the early years, the railroad had a locomotive that ran on gasoline and was known locally as the "Galloping Goose."

The nineteen-mile long Prineville Railway struggled until business boomed with timber cutting just before and after World War II. But since 1990, freight hauling has steadily declined, and its future is uncertain.[46]

Two Railroads, One Track

In accordance with the agreement signed on May 17, 1910, the Des Chutes Railroad asked the Oregon Trunk to share its track from Metolius to Bend. James J. Hill approved the request on January 31, 1911, and signed a contract on September 6, 1911, officially providing Bend, Oregon, with the service of two railroads.

The operating personnel of both lines made a joint service plan. Passenger trains coming from the north would be consolidated at Metolius and taken to Bend with one engine and crew. Heading south, the trains would split at Metolius to run over their own lines. Passenger trains ran daily; freight trains ran three times per week. This arrangement allowed the freight trains of each line to operate out of The Dalles and Fallbridge on opposite days.

The Oregon Trunk was soliciting business even before it was completed. Mr. Springer traveled the entire line, asking for business from merchants, especially in Prineville and Bend.[47] Wool that had been going to Shaniko for shipment on the Union Pacific lines was now carried by the Oregon Trunk.

OREGON TRUNK RY.

Read down — **Read up**

No. 6 Oregon Passenger Daily	No. 2 Inland Empire Express Daily	Miles	Spokane, Portland & Seattle Ry. Jan. 7, 1912	No. 7 Oregon Passenger Daily	No. 1 Inland Empire Express Daily
8 20	9 55	0.0	Lv .... **Portland†** .... Ar.	5 30	7 45
8 43	f10 12	7.0	St. Johns†	5 06	f 7 20
8 56	10 21	10.0	**Vancouver†**	4 55	7 10
9 27	......	24.4	Camas†	4 20	......
9 35	......	27.6	Washougal†	4 12	......
10 34	......	53.8	Stevenson†	3 13	f 5 46
11 17	......	72.6	Underwood	2 30	......
11 25	**12 04**	75.6	White Salmon†	2 22	5 05
11 48	**12 24**	85.3	**Lyle†**	2 00	4 47
12 08	**f12 39**	94.0	Granddalles†	1 41	f 4 31
12 40	**1 00**	106.1	Ar .... **Fallbridge†** .... Lv.	1 15	4 08

No. 102 Daily	Miles	Oregon Trunk Ry. Jan. 7, 1912	No. 101 Daily
1 10	106.1	Lv .... **Fallbridge†** .... Ar.	§¶**12 55**
1 27	111.3	Moody†	**12 38**
f 1 40	117.0	Kloan	**f12 26**
f 1 55	123.6	Lockit	**f12 12**
f 2 15	131.1	Dyke	f11 53
f 2 25	136.0	Sinamox†	f11 44
f 2 46	145.5	Oakbrook	f11 23
f 3 05	153.2	Sherar†	f11 05
f 3 12	156.4	Tuskan	f10 58
3 23	161.0	Maupin†	10 48
f 3 42	169.4	Nena	f10 29
f 3 51	173.1	Frieda	f10 20
f 4 05	179.2	Nathan	f10 07
4 10	181.0	North Junction†	10 02
f 4 19	185.8	Kaskela	f 9 52
f 4 28	189.6	Jersey	f 9 42
4 35	191.4	South Junction†	9 38
f 4 43	194.3	Coleman	f 9 32
5 00	201.4	Mecca†	9 15
f 5 13	206.3	Vanora	f 9 04
f 5 24	210.5	Pelton	f 8 54
5 40	216.7	Madras†	8 40
¶ **5 50**	220.8	Ar .... Metolius† .... Lv.	8 30
¶ **6 20**	220.8	Lv .... Metolius† .... Ar.	8 22
6 35	225.6	Culver†	8 13
f 6 53	232.5	Opal City	f 8 00
f 7 15	240.2	Terrebonne	f 7 37
7 30	245.6	Redmond†	7 21
f 7 55	254.7	Deschutes†	f 6 53
8 15	262.1	Ar .... Bend† .... Lv.	6 30

Light faced figures denote A. M. time. **Dark faced figures denote P. M. time.** f Stop on signal. †Telegraph. ¶Meals. §Connection between O. T. train No. 101 and S. P. & S. train No. 2 for Spokane and east. For S. P. & S. schedule see Page 2.

EQUIPMENT

Trains Nos. 6-102 and 101-7 carry first class coaches and smoking cars between Portland and Bend.

Trains Nos. 2 and 1 carry observation parlor cars, sleeping cars, dining cars, first class coaches and smoking cars between Portland and Fallbridge.

STAGES TO INTERIOR OREGON POINTS

Horse stages and autos leave points given below and charge the passenger fares shown below.

In most cases departures are on arrival of trains.

This information is from direct sources, but the Railway is not responsible for deviation therefrom.

TO / FROM	MAUPIN Horse	CULVER Horse	REDMOND Horse	REDMOND Auto	BEND Horse	BEND Auto
Lamonta		$1.25				
Prineville		2.50	$2.00	3.00		
Post		7.50	4.50			
Paulina		10.50	7.50			
Fife		10.50	9.50			
Riley		10.75	11.00			
La Pine					$3.00	5.00
Fremont					6.25	10.00
Crescent					5.00	10.00
Ft. Rock					6.50	12.00
Silver Lake					9.00	15.00
Burns		12.50	12.00			20.00
Paisley					15.00	25.00
Lakeview					19.00	
Victor	$ .50					
Wapinitia	1.00					

Bend's Wall Street — 1910

Wool receivers in Boston were contacted to tout the advantages of the Trunk. The transport of cattle to Portland was another early source of revenue.

But by the summer of 1912, it was apparent that the Oregon Trunk was struggling financially. The railroad employed 500 people; there were only 536 people living in Bend at the time.[48] The irrigation system at Redmond had not been completed, and no timber mills yet existed. Settlers did come to central Oregon, but many stayed only a short time and left; the Oregon Trunk commissioned a survey to learn why. Every morning in May 1912, an agent, twenty-five-year-old Stuart R. Strong from Portland who had just graduated from Yale, boarded the departing train from Bend to question those who were leaving. His reports convinced the railroad executives that progress would be slow. Some of those leaving Bend thought the climate was too dry and cold for farming, others complained of low wages and few jobs. In Strong's opinion, the area was better off without those who left, "a typical tramp ... a weak mouth and poor looking ... wouldn't talk."[7,49] Hill even sent Thomas Shaw, previously professor of animal husbandry at the University of Minnesota and now employed by the Great Northern, on a 1,000-mile automobile trip in central Oregon to prepare a report on agricultural possibilities.[49]

Passenger service on the Oregon Trunk persisted until 1971. Beginning in 1913, this service was available only at night. Trains left Bend and Portland in the evening and arrived at 8:00 A.M. The Union Pacific continued to operate passenger day trains until the mid-1930s. After World War II, passengers could travel only on so-called mixed trains, working freight trains with a mail car and one or two passenger cars.

Entrepreneurs from Minnesota, persuaded by Louis W. Hill, established the first lumber mills in Bend, on opposing sides of the Deschutes River. Thomas L. Shevlin, a star football player at Yale, had visited central Oregon in 1906 right after his graduation, and secured rights to pine lands. By 1915, his Shevlin and Hixon company owned more than 200,000 acres.[50] Shevlin, now president of his company, died of pneumonia in Minnesota in December 1915, three months before his plant opened.[51]

TIMELINE

July 27, 1909	Horseshoe Bend Confrontation.
August 15, 1909	Stevens Buys Oregon Trunk.
May 17, 1910	Des Chutes–Oregon Trunk Agreement.
November 1, 1911	First Train in Bend.
July 10, 1923	Oregon Trunk Track Abandoned.
March 28, 1935	Des Chutes Track Abandoned.
1981	The Oregon Trunk Merges into the Burlington Northern.
1987	Oregon-Washington Railroad & Navigation Merges into the Union Pacific.

Bend Depot — 1913

Lazard Freres, a national banking firm, owned almost a million acres of timber and range land in central Oregon. This land was originally a land grant to the Willamette Valley & Cascade Mountain Wagon Company to build a road to Idaho.[52] Louis W. Hill, along with a St. Paul capitalist, W.P. Davidson, purchased this land. This was the timber that Hill used to entice Brooks-Scanlon to Bend.

On May 10, 1915, the Shevlin-Hixon Lumber Company of Minnesota announced plans to build a large mill in Bend, and on August 18, 1911, Brooks-Scanlon Lumber Company, also of Minnesota, announced their plans for a mill. To serve these mills, the Oregon Trunk built spurs off of its main line. The mills opened in 1916, and by April 1923, thirty railroad cars of lumber were being shipped daily.[53] Shevlin-Hixon closed in December 1950, selling its land to Brooks-Scanlon. A shortage of timber eventually forced the closure of the Brooks-Scanlon mill in 1994.

AFTER WORLD WAR I, both the Des Chutes and the Oregon Trunk railroads were faced with expensive updating. How much of this duplication reflected the stubbornness of the two magnates, Hill and Harriman? Operating two lines along the Deschutes River was expensive, indeed, wasteful. The folly of the two railroads is palpable standing above

Horseshoe Bend/Twin Crossings and viewing the north and south portals of the abandoned second tunnel, the Des Chutes Railroad tunnel; the portals have been deliberately and forever sealed by the displacement of large volumes of rocks and dirt. The initial sealing of unused tunnels along the Deschutes River was the result of the U.S. Army practicing its demolition skills.[54]

The Oregon Trunk was the first to propose joint usage. On July 10, 1923, the Oregon Trunk abandoned the thirty-mile section between South Junction and Metolius, electing to use the Des Chutes tracks.[55] Even though the Des Chutes line between

South Junction and Metolius had a grade of 1.5 percent, it was about six miles shorter.[56] In addition, the thirty-mile segment of the Oregon Trunk to be discarded had several large wooden trestles that would support only one locomotive at a time, requiring special placements of helper engines. The Oregon Trunk removed its tracks between Metolius and South Junction in 1924 and abandoned three tunnels. The tunnel near Warm Springs was used for a while by a local rancher to store potatoes; the other two near Madras in the Willow Creek Canyon were used by the U.S. Army for demolition training during World War II.[57] The shared track out of South Junction climbed a 1.5 percent grade for sixteen miles, requiring helper engines. For this reason, the Oregon Trunk became the first portion of the Spokane, Portland & Seattle system to use only diesel engines.[58]

The initial agreement in 1910 gave the Oregon-Washington Railroad & Navigation Company (the new name for the Oregon Railroad & Navigation Company after November 23, 1910) the right to use Oregon Trunk track from the Columbia River to North Junction, but this was not immediately implemented. The impact of the Great Depression motivated the Oregon-Washington Railroad & Navigation Company to fully use the Oregon Trunk tracks. Because of declining business, the track charges by the Oregon Trunk would be less than the expense of maintaining the Des Chutes line. The Oregon-Washington Railroad & Navigation Company applied to the Interstate Commerce Commission for permission to abandon the Des Chutes Railroad from Ainsworth to North Junction (71.3 miles).[59] This change was authorized on March 28, 1935.[60] Only business at Maupin was affected, forcing goods to be trucked to the Oregon Trunk depot on the west bank. The Des Chutes Railroad relinquished its control of the segment between South Junction and Metolius, and the Oregon Trunk Line acquired total control from the Columbia River to Bend, an operational state that continues today with the Burlington Northern.

Five tunnels remain on the shared track from the Columbia River to Bend:

Tunnel No.		Railroad Mile Point
1	Moody	2.3
2	Horseshoe Bend	44.2
3	Dant	67.2
4	Whitehorse Rapids	76.0
5	Trout Creek Canyon	92.2

Tunnel No. 1 at Moody

Tunnel No. 2 at Horseshoe Bend

Tunnel No. 3 at Dant

Tunnel No. 4 at Whitehorse Rapids

Tunnel No. 5 in Trout Creek Canyon

Until the line along the Deschutes River was improved during and after World War II, curves and steep grades limited the top speed to thirty miles per hour. There were 276 curves (72.2 miles) and 84.7 miles of straight line.[61] Only 21.6 miles were totally level. Going south, there were nineteen ascending grades, covering 127.4 miles. The grade from the Columbia River to South Junction is 0.6 percent; climbing out of the canyon to Madras it is 1.5 percent. Between South Junction and Madras, trains moved at seven to ten miles per hour up the grade and twenty miles per hour downhill.

The slow climb out of the canyon provided an opportunity. An Oregon Trunk engineer, Orin Hall, had a highly deserved nickname, "Cocky." A brakeman climbed the cliff alongside the grade up Trout Creek and wrote in large letters on the cliff wall with white paint:

> EVERY DAY IN EVERY WAY
> I GET BETTER AND BETTER
> COCKY HALL[62]

Between Metolius and Bend, the grade is 1.0 percent in several locations. The 1.0 percent grade on the plateau to Bend restricted southbound trains to twenty-five miles per hour. This compared to a speed of forty miles per hour on the Spokane, Portland & Seattle mainline.[63]

Today, the abandoned railroad grade provides the following: (1) a seven-mile foot path on the east bank between Warm Springs and Trout Creek; (2) the gravel road eight miles upstream from Maupin to the locked gate of the Deschutes Club; and (3). fourteen miles of private road to North Junction.[64] Downstream from Maupin to Shears Falls, the paved road lies on the old Des Chutes Railroad grade, as well as the twenty-eight miles of road from Sherars Falls to Macks Canyon. The twenty-three miles of trail from Macks Canyon to the mouth of the river are mostly on abandoned railroad grade.[64]

In 1932, a group of forty men purchased a sheep ranch about twelve miles upstream from Maupin on the east bank and established the Deschutes Club, a private organization devoted to fishing (the membership fee was $50).[65] In the early years, to access the property, the fishermen traveled from the east plateau over an old, rough road that covered six miles to the edge of the canyon, followed by a steep descent to the clubhouse on a flat area across from the Frieda Oregon Trunk Station (later changed to Dant). When the Des Chutes Railroad abandoned its line, cattle and sheep ranchers on the east bank converted its roadbed to a road. The Deschutes Club acquired more land along

The Face, across the river from the Deschutes Club locked gate, a pattern produced when lava tubes drained, refilled, and cooled toward the center

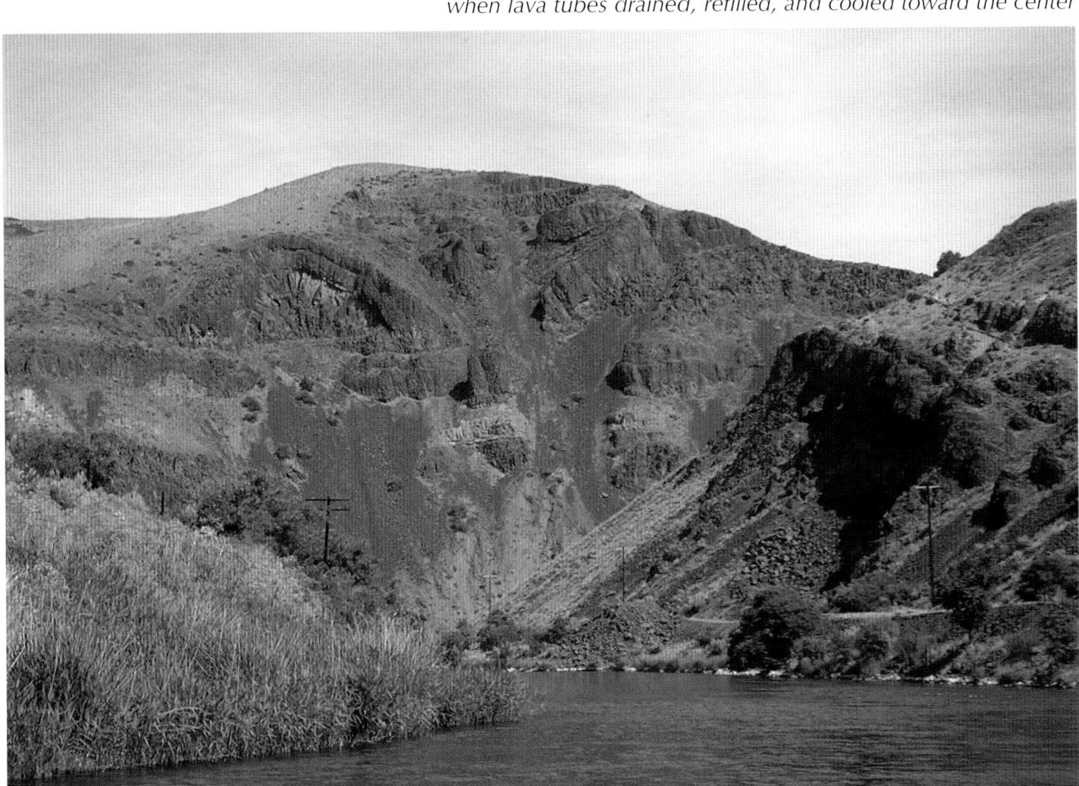

the road and joined the campaign to develop the road that eventually reached North Junction. Dant & Russell used the road to reach the perlite mine on the west side of the river. The mining company installed a large war-surplus lifeboat attached to a cable across the river and propelled it across the river by the action of its rudder against the current. The boat is still there, used by the private owners of the houses originally built by the mining company. The need for electric power to the mine brought an electric line to the east bank of the river, making electricity available for the ranchers and the Deschutes Club cabins.

A series of public efforts over the years tried to open the private road. The Deschutes Club successfully foiled each effort, but a policy was established by the Club, allowing fishermen on foot to pass the locked gate on the road. The Deschutes Club locked gate is about eight miles upstream from Maupin, just downstream from the Nena station on the Oregon Trunk.

HILL NEVER OPENLY indicated to John F. Stevens a desire or agenda to extend to California.[66] Although the Hill engineers completed a survey to Klamath Falls, construction was halted at Bend, until many years later. In 1928, the Great Northern applied for an extension of the Oregon Trunk, setting off another fight with the Union Pacific. Extensive negotiations yielded joint usage of Southern Pacific tracks to Klamath Falls, and a new Great Northern line was constructed, connecting with the Western Pacific Railroad at Bieber, California. This alternative north-south route connecting the Pacific Northwest with California and called the "Inside Gateway," began full operations on November 10, 1931.[67] Passenger service to California on this line was never established, as it mainly served the timber industry. But the Oregon Trunk does still end in Bend. The extension of the line beyond Bend was undertaken solely by the Great Northern.

During World War II, railroad business was booming; the Oregon Trunk increased its volume by 200 railroad cars per day going in each direction.[68] During World War II, the Spokane, Portland & Seattle and the Oregon Trunk reballasted all of their tracks with crushed stone.[69] The Oregon Trunk installed an automatic block signal system between 1949 and 1951.

Rock slides were always a problem on the Oregon Trunk until the railroad erected slide fences connected to the automatic block signaling system. Sliding rock breaking one of the horizontal wires in the slide fences would immediately trigger the block signaling system. But even then, some parts of the track were still not protected from rock slides. The well-known derailment that gave Box Car Rapids its name occurred in 1954, when a train hit a rock slide, causing the engine unit to slide into the Deschutes River, drowning the engineer and fireman.

The charter for the Oregon Trunk had a lifespan of fifty years. On November 2, 1959, the charter was amended to allow the Trunk to exist in perpetuity. On March 3, 1970, the Great Northern, Northern Pacific, and Chicago, Burlington & Quincy merged as the Burlington Northern, Inc. The Spokane,

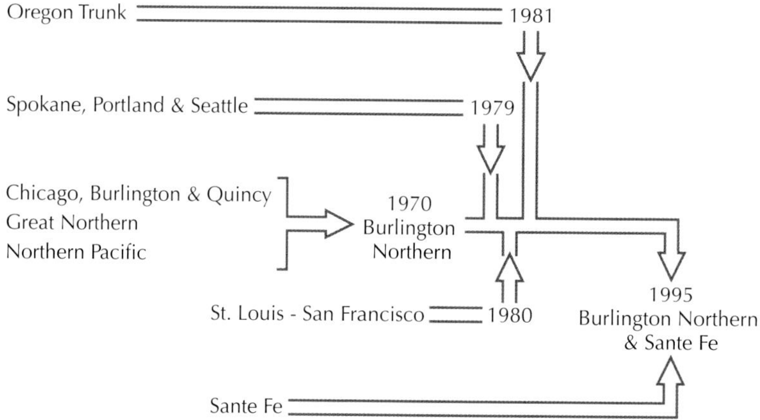

BNSF train at Cedar Island, river mile 31

Portland & Seattle was leased to the new company and functioned totally as part of the Burlington Northern. The Oregon Electric and Oregon Trunk did not officially merge into the Burlington Northern, but like the Spokane, Portland & Seattle, these lines were operated by the Burlington Northern.[70] In 1979, the Spokane, Portland & Seattle finally merged into the Burlington Northern, and in 1981 the Oregon Electric and the Oregon Trunk also made the merger. In 1985, the new name became the Burlington Northern Railroad Company.[71] When the Santa Fe was added in 1995, the company became the Burlington Northern & Santa Fe Corporation.

In 1936, the Union Pacific re-organized its subsidiaries, which had been permanently leased to them, and the Des Chutes Railroad became part of the Oregon-Washington Railroad & Navigation Company. Finally, on December 30, 1987, the Oregon-Washington Railroad & Navigation Company and the Oregon Short Line merged into the Union Pacific.[40]

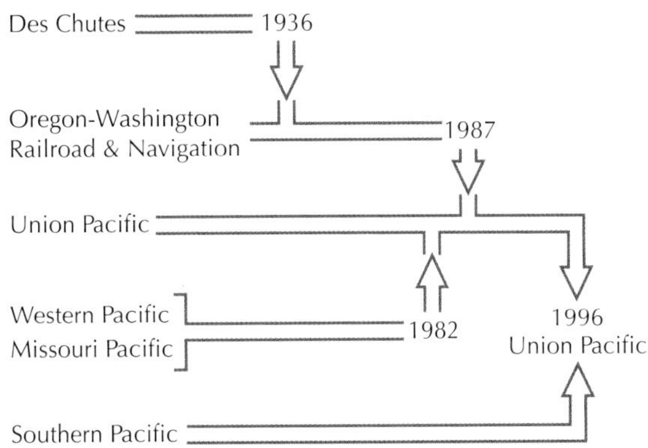

Today, ten to twelve freight trains run daily between Bend and Wishram, three of which are Union Pacific trains; the rest belong to the Burlington Northern & Sante Fe.[72] It takes about eight to ten hours to travel this distance, slowing down for curves, grades, and bridges. The traffic is eventually destined for California in the south and the distribution yards in Pasco and Vancouver, Washington, in the north.

THE HILL LINE was the first to Bend, the winner of its court battles with the Harriman lawyers, and the one who made the key purchases of the Oregon Trunk and the Central Oregon Railroad. It is hard to disagree with observers who concluded that "...It becomes more evident every day that the Hill people are somewhat shrewder than their opponents."[73] Nevertheless, the fact that there were two opposing railroads building tracks, tunnels, and bridges that would eventually be discarded questions the wisdom and shrewdness of the opposing magnates. On the other hand, their competition was a driving force, bringing railroad service to central Oregon with a speed that must be admired.

The Deschutes River is unique and so is the railroad that runs along its banks. It is, in its construction, a symbol of human drama and the energy and passion of thousands of individuals, from high and mighty business entrepreneurs to hard-working common laborers.

Epilogue

A Typical Trip with the *Oregon Trunk Flyer*

There is something mystical about a railroad. From the early beginning of the construction to the complex operations of the finished line, it is a rich expression of human abilities. A passing train or a lonely whistle heard on a quiet night provokes a powerful sense of nostalgia. The railroad along the Deschutes River is no exception. With its feats of construction, picturesque scenery, and historical record, it is a match for any railroad in the world.

Kenny Prager worked for the Spokane, Portland & Seattle Railway for forty-four years. He enjoyed his work in steam and diesel locomotives and had many stories. After he passed away in 1998, Prager's wife, Laurel, preserved his stories in a small book for his family.[1] Prager most loved the run from Wishram to Bend on the Oregon Trunk, but at the same time he and most engineers regarded this route as the most dangerous because of its curves and rock slides. The following description of a typical trip up the Deschutes River with a mixed freight and passenger train, train 102, the *Oregon Trunk Flyer,* is based on one of Prager's chapters.[2]

THE FIREMAN is the first to arrive at the steam engine in the Wishram roundhouse around 11:45 P.M. By the time he checks the water, fuel oil, firebox, and cab supplies, he is joined by the engineer, called a "hoghead." While the engineer walks around with a long, spouted oil can, the firemen cleans the cab, first with kerosene and then a deck hose. All engineers and firemen enjoy the sounds of a working engine as the air pumps, the blower, and the oil atomizer talk to them. An engine coming alive was part of the love these men had for their work. When the brakeman arrives, the men take the engine, a Pacific 4-6-2, to the train. The brakeman lines the switches; the fireman fills the water tender. The fireman always runs the water over the tank so that the engineer knows with certainty that a full load of water is on board. No hoghead wanted to stop before Tuskan for water. Some even ask if the fireman has tamped the water down!

The mail car, baggage car, and passenger cars from Portland are already at the depot along with freight boxcars. The boxcars number from as few as two to as many as twenty. This mixed train bound for Bend carries the post office mail car, the Railway Express car, baggage, freight, and last the three passenger cars. The engine coupled to the train pulls up to the Wishram depot to load more passengers. On many nights, and especially Friday nights, a load of fishermen are waiting, to be let off along the way. In those days, the train would stop at whatever special fishing hole was requested. The train departed Wishram at 12:30 A.M.

After crossing the Celilo bridge over the Columbia River, the train climbs the 0.6 percent grade on the other side, passing through Tunnel No. 1 at mile point 2.3. The falls at Celilo are easily recognized by their roar. In autumn, climbing the grade upstream of the falls, the smell of drying salmon and rotting salmon waste in the Indian village on the left is distinctly unpleasant. Working up the grade, the effort produces a strong draft allowing the fireman to add five or six scoopfuls of sand to the firebox to scour the carbon out of the flues.

The train makes many stops. Besides delivering fishermen to their favorite holes, the train stops at most of the railroad stations to deliver supplies, groceries, or something ordered from a catalog. The train delivers mail to the small post offices, so remote they depend on kerosene lamps for lights. The passenger cars are at the end of the train. With no radios in those days, when a passenger or even some freight is to be unloaded, a light hanging on the side of the passenger car is turned on, signaling the engineer to stop at the next station. The fishermen wanting to get off somewhere other than a station tell the conductor who sends a message up to the engineer, indicating a stop at a specific milepost or landmark.

The fireman is constantly looking out for rocks, and at the same time adjusting the fire and water to meet the demands of speeding up and slowing down. Nevertheless, the fireman has time to enjoy the sights of the river provided by the many curves, especially on a moonlit night.

The first open telegraph office is at Dike, a site with no roads or electricity, but maintained by a family living in the station house. A yellow lamp would indicate if there were orders from the dispatcher to be picked up on the fly (radio communication was not installed until 1983[3]). If the train does not have to stop, the telegraph operator holds up a bamboo hoop containing the orders and at the same time shines a light on the hoop. As the engine passes, the fireman moves to the gangway to catch the hoop. The orders would tell the crew of trains coming in the opposite direction and at which set of passing tracks the meeting would take place. The meeting place was not always the same, determined by the speed and progress of each train. On this night, the *Oregon Trunk Flyer* is ordered to a siding at Oakbrook to allow a northbound freight train to pass.

The sound of the engine is loud in the canyon, echoing off the cliff walls. Approaching the meeting place, the engineer lets loose with two long and one short blasts on the whistle at the post that marks one mile to the switch, letting the crew know they are approaching a meeting point. The brakeman is far back in the coaches, so at the switch, the fireman drops to the ground, unlocks the switch with a key, throws the switch, and signals to the engineer to pull ahead. The train stops clear of the main line and waits for the brakeman in the back of the train to restore the switch back to the main. Seeing the oncoming train, the engineer extinguishes his headlight, a signal to the oncoming train that the line is clear. The passing train says hello by dimming its headlight, and blows its whistle. One engineer was called "Whistling Walter," because he enjoyed blowing his whistle constantly up and down the Oregon Trunk line. The engineer and fireman call out the passing engine's number to confirm that it is the train in the orders they caught in the basket. While the train is passing, the brakeman walks over the tops of the cars to the cab of the engine. He hands the engineer a list of stops for the fishermen. The brakeman will stay in the cab until the train reaches Maupin where he will work the switches to pick up empty cars and spot a car to be loaded with lumber.

The crossing at Horseshoe Bend through Tunnel No. 2 at mile point 44.3 provides a pleasant sight of the Deschutes River, not once, but twice on the twin bridges. Just past Sherars Bridge, the train stops at Tuskan for water. This water tank catches water flowing from springs in the canyon walls. The fireman climbs on the tender to spot the stop for the water spout. But most engineers knew a landmark to provide a perfect stop. While taking water, the engineer walks around with his oil can to check the running gear. Later, engines had grease fittings, but it was still said that an old hoghead couldn't walk around an engine without an oil can in his hand.

As the train rounds the curve into Maupin, mile point 54.7, the engineer yells "yellow board," meaning he sees the signal light that there are orders to be picked up. Mail and passengers are unloaded at the Maupin depot. The orders indicate that oncoming freight trains have to wait on passing tracks as the mixed freight and passenger train has priority.

At Nena, a red fuse burning on the track warns of a flagman waving a stop sign ahead. The flagman (the brakeman on the other train) says that his freight train is on the main line because they have too many cars for the side track. So even though train 102 has priority, it must pass through the siding. The fireman gets off to work the switch at the end of the siding, and yells a few choice words at the crew in the freight caboose as it goes by. The *Oregon Trunk Flyer* passes through Tunnel No. 3 at Dant, mile point 67.2.

Crossing the river at North Junction, the train stops to let a fisherman off, passes through Tunnel No. 4 at mile point 76, then stops again after Whitehorse Rapids to deliver supplies from Portland for the farm at Axford. Passing the Jersey Wye, the engineer and fireman see a sleeping crew in the helper engine, waiting for the heavy freight train that follows this train. The train stops at the water tank before the South Junction depot to load up before the uphill climb of the 1.5 percent grade to Madras. The mail is delivered at South Junction and the train sets off up the grade. There are ten freight cars left, along with the three passenger cars, and this is not an undue load. As the engine exerts itself up the hill, the fireman sands her out again. The speed up the grade is about fifteen miles per hour. At mile point 92.2 the train passes through Tunnel No. 5.

Coming to Gateway, the crew hears exploding torpedoes on the track, giving warning that another red fuse lies ahead. Stopping at Gateway depot, the flagman of the freight train boards, having dropped off the slow freight ahead that is struggling because one of its two engines isn't working normally. The train crosses the trestles, and the crew keeps their eyes forward, looking for the freight train caboose. Coming onto straight track at Paxton, the caboose is easily seen lit up with fuses. The train couples into the freight train's caboose and becomes a helper train, pushing at twelve miles per hour.

At Madras, the *Oregon Trunk Flyer* passes the freight train. The eastern sky is getting light, and as the train passes over the steel bridge, Madras looks like a toy village below. Madras is just waking up, and the train crew once again enjoys a rising sun after already experiencing the beauty of the Deschutes Canyon in the moonlight.

At Metolius, the crew receives more orders. Running thirty minutes late, they are instructed to leave the remaining freight cars behind to gain speed and deliver the mail and the three cars of passengers on time. The engineer is soon exceeding the speed limit from Metolius to Bend. Just before Opal City, the engineer and fireman are treated to the spectacular colors of the rising sun hitting Mount Jefferson.

The train slows down for the Crooked River Bridge. Even though the crew has crossed the bridge many times, the fireman is a little frightened every time he looks down to the river. A quick stop lets a passenger off at Terrabone, and the next stop meets the City of Prineville Railroad at Prineville Junction, mile point 132.3. One Prineville engine and coach accept the mail and some passengers for delivery to Prineville, nineteen miles away. The Prineville engine reminds the Oregon Trunk crew of an "old tea kettle of an engine."

At Redmond, the crew unloads the mail and some freight, taking just ten minutes to do so. The engineer steps down to look his engine over, then passes time in the depot. The fireman takes a short nap.

The engine takes the last 16.5-mile stretch to Bend going flat out and passing the Union Pacific train waiting on a siding at Deschutes. The *Oregon Trunk Flyer* arrives in Bend, mile point 151.5, at 8:10 A.M., only ten minutes late! The brakeman cuts the cars off the engine, and the locomotive moves to the wye to turn around for the trip back that night. The engineer parks the locomotive in the roundhouse to wait out the day. The crew stays at the Marley Hotel, either catching their sleep or walking around town seeking some action, of which there is little.

THE RAILROAD along the Deschutes River has passed from the era of the steam locomotive that served the "neighborhood" to a commercial route with modern communications and powerful electro-diesel engines. But at least one thing remains the same. There isn't a fisherman on the Deschutes River who doesn't stop to enjoy watching a passing train. The stories in this book will hopefully add to their enjoyment.

Appendix One

Railroad and River Mile Points

	Oregon Trunk Railroad Mile Points	River Miles from the Columbia River
Union Pacific connection	1.5	
Tunnel No. 1	2.3	
Moody	5.7	1
Free Bridge/Kloan	11.6	7
Harris Canyon		12
Lockit	18.0	13.3
Dike	26.4	21.7
Macks Canyon		24
Sinamox	30.6	25.9
Beavertail		31.5
Oakbrook		36
Wreck Rapids		40
Horseshoe Bend	44.2	41
Sherars Bridge	47.7	44
White River		46.3
Tuskan	50.8	48
Maupin	54.7	52
Boxcar Rapids		54
Locked Gate		59.2
Nena	63.8	61
Tunnel No. 3	67.2	
Dant	67.5	64
North Junction	75.4	73
Tunnel No. 4	76.0	
Whitehorse Rapids		75–77
Kaskela	80.3	79
Jersey	84.0	82
South Junction	85.8	84
Trout Creek	88.3	88
Tunnel No. 5	92.2	
Gateway	93.0	
Mecca Flat	95.6	96
Warm Springs		98
Willow Creek	111.0	
Madras	113	
Metolius	115.2	
Culver	114.9	
Opal City	122	
Crooked River	126	
Terrabone	129.5	
Prineville Junction	132.3	
Redmond	135	
Deschutes	144.2	
Bend	151.5	

Appendix Two

Origin of Station Names on the Oregon Trunk[1]

Fallbridge	Named for Celilo Falls and the bridge across the Columbia River. Changed to Wishram February 1, 1926.
Celilo	Perhaps derived from the Si-le-lah Indian tribe.
Moody	Named for Malcolm A. Moody of The Dalles, who owned a power site near the Deschutes River and was elected to the U.S. House of Representatives.
Kloan	Chinook for "three;" third station; near the Free Bridge.
Lockit	Chinook for "four."
Dike	Unknown.
Sinamox	Chinook for "seven."
Oakbrook	Named for the large oak trees along the creek.
Sherar or Sherars Bridge	After an Irishman from Vermont, Joseph Sherar, who came to Oregon from California.
Tuskan	Indians called this area Tush-kan-ee.
Maupin	After Howard Maupin, who came to Oregon in 1863 from Kentucky. Maupin was acclaimed for his killing of Paulina, a renegade and thief Indian.
Nena	Nee-nee, Indian for tall white cottonwoods.
Frieda	Became Dant in 1950 after Thomas Dant of Dant and Russell.
Dixon	After T. F. Dixon, vice-president of Spokane, Portland & Seattle.
North Junction changed to Davidson	After A. J. Davidson, general manager of Spokane, Portland & Seattle, although Davidson's ranch was at this site in 1910.
U'Ren changed to Jersey in 1911	Eliminated in 1950 when wye and helper engines were retired.
Mecca	On abandoned tracks, site where an old wagon road to Madras crossed the Deschutes. Named for relief workers felt when they came out of the canyon.
Madras	Thought to have been named randomly after a bolt of cloth in a store.
Metolius	After the river the Indians called Mpto-ly-as, which perhaps means white fish, referring to bright, silvery salmon.
Opal City	After Opal Springs, with its opal-like pebbles, located in the Crooked River Canyon.
Hillman	A hybrid of HIll and Harriman. Later changed to Terrebonne.
Redmond	After Frank T. Redmond.

Reference

1. *The Dope Bucket. Gold Spike Issue. The Oregon Trunk 1911–1961*, Vol. 23, No. 3, Spokane Portland and Seattle Railway, Spokane, 1961.

Chapter References

CHAPTER ONE

1. **Alt D, Hyndman DW**, *Northwest Exposure. A Geologic Story of the Northwest,* Mountain Press Publishing Company, Missoula, Montana, 1995, reprinted 2001, p.48.
2. **Bishop EM**, *In Search of Ancient Oregon. A Geological and Natural History,* Timber Press, Portland, Oregon, 2003, p.132.
3. Ibid., p.141.
4. **Orr EL, Orr WN**, *Geology of Oregon,* Fifth Edition, Kendall/Hunt Publishing Company, Dubuque, Iowa, 2000, pp.121–139.
5. **Smith G**, Geology along U.S. highways 197 and 97 between The Dalles and Sunriver, Oregon, *Oregon Geology* 60:3-19, 1998.
6. **Bishop EM**, *In Search of Ancient Oregon. A Geological and Natural History,* Timber Press, Portland, Oregon, 2003, p.250.
7. **Allen JE, Burns M, Sargent SC**, *Cataclysms on the Columbia. A Layman's Guide to the Features Produced by the Catastrophic Bretz Floods in the Pacific Northwest,* Timber Press, Portland, Oregon, 1986, reprinted 2002.
8. Ibid., p.97.
9. Ibid., p.78.
10. Ibid., p.64.
11. **Pardee JT**, Unusual currents in glacial Lake Missoula, Montana, *Geol Soc America Bull* 53:1569-1600, 1942.
12. **Allen JE, Burns M, Sargent SC**, *Cataclysms on the Columbia. A Layman's Guide to the Features Produced by the Catastrophic Bretz Floods in the Pacific Northwest,* Timber Press, Portland, Oregon, 1986, reprinted 2002, p.84.

CHAPTER TWO

1. **Abbot HL**, Report upon Explorations for a Railroad Route from the Sacramento Valley to the Columbia River. *Reports of Explorations and Surveys to Ascertain the Most Practicable and Economical Route for a Railroad from the Mississippi River to the Pacific Ocean, Made under the Direction of the Secretary of War, in 1853-4,* Vol. VI, Government Printing Office, Washington, DC, 1857, p.29.
2. Ibid., p.45.
3. Ibid., p.84.
4. Ibid., p.45.
5. **McArthur LA, McArthur LL**, *Oregon Geographic Names, 7th Edition,* Oregon Historical Society Press, Portland, 2003, p.282.
6. Ibid., p.281.

7. **O'Connor JE**, **Grant GE**, eds., *A Peculiar River. Geology, Geomorphology, and Hydrology of the Deschutes River, Oregon. Water Science and Application 7,* American Geophysical Union, Washington, DC, 2003.

8. **Russell IC**, *Preliminary Report on the Geology and Water Resources of Central Oregon, U. S. Geological Survey Bulletin No. 252,* Government Printing Office, Washington, DC, 1905.

9. **O'Connor JE**, **Grant GE**, **Haluska TL**, Overview of geology, hydrology, geomorphology, and sediment budget of the Deschutes River basin, Oregon, In: O'Connor JE, Grant GE, eds., *A Peculiar River. Geology, Geomorphology, and Hydrology of the Deschutes River, Oregon. Water Science and Application 7,* American Geophysical Union, Washington, DC, 2003, p.7.

10. Ibid., p.11.

11. **Beebee RA**, **O'Connor JE**, **Grant GE**, Geology and Geomorphology of the Lower Deschutes River Canyon, Oregon, *Field Guide to Geologic Processes in Cascadia: Oregon Department of Geology and Mineral Industries,* Special Paper 36:91-108, 2002.

12. **O'Connor JE**, **Grant GE**, **Haluska TL**, Overview of geology, hydrology, geomorphology, and sediment budget of the Deschutes River basin, Oregon, In: O'Connor JE, Grant GE, eds., *A Peculiar River. Geology, Geomorphology, and Hydrology of the Deschutes River, Oregon. Water Science and Application 7,* American Geophysical Union, Washington, DC, 2003, p.11.

13. Ibid., p.15.

14. Ibid., p.19.

15. **Russell IC**, *Preliminary Report on the Geology and Water Resources of Central Oregon, U. S. Geological Survey Bulletin No. 252,* Government Printing Office, Washington, DC, 1905, p.23.

16. **Gannett MW**, **Liete Jr. KE**, **Morgan DS**, **Collins CA**, Ground-water Hydrology of the Upper Deschutes Basin, Oregon, *U.S. Geol. Surv. Water Resour. Inv. Rep.00-4162,* 2001.

17. **Gannett MW**, **Manga M**, **Lite Jr. KE**, Groundwater hydrology of the upper Deschutes basin and its influence on streamflow, In: O'Connor JE, Grant GE, eds., *A Peculiar River. Geology, Geomorphology, and Hydrology of the Deschutes River, Oregon. Water Science and Application 7,* American Geophysical Union, Washington, DC, 2003, p.38.

18. **James ER**, **Manga M**, **Rose TP**, **Hudson GB**, The use of temperature and the isotopes of O, H, C and noble gases to determine the pattern and spatial extent of groundwater flow, *J Hydrol* 237:100-112, 2000.

19. **Gannett MW**, **Liete Jr. KE**, **Morgan DS**, **Collins CA**, Ground-water Hydrology of the Upper Deschutes Basin, Oregon, *U.S. Geol. Surv. Water Resour. Inv. Rep.00-4162,* 2001.

20. **Gannett MW**, **Manga M**, **Lite Jr. KE**, Groundwater hydrology of the upper Deschutes basin and its influence on streamflow, In: O'Connor JE, Grant GE, eds., *A Peculiar River. Geology, Geomorphology, and Hydrology of the Deschutes River, Oregon. Water Science and Application 7,* American Geophysical Union, Washington, DC, 2003, p.37.

21. **Gannett MW**, **Liete Jr. KE**, **Morgan DS**, **Collins**, **CA** Ground-water Hydrology of the Upper Deschutes Basin, Oregon, *U.S. Geol. Surv. Water Resour. Inv. Rep.00-4162,* 2001.

22. **O'Connor JE**, **Curran JH**, **Beebee RA**, **Grant GE**, **Sarna-Wojcicki A**, Quaternary geology and geomorphology of the lower Deschutes River canyon, Oregon, In: O'Connor JE, Grant GE, eds., *A Peculiar River. Geology, Geomorphology, and Hydrology of the Deschutes River, Oregon. Water Science and Application 7,* American Geophysical Union, Washington, DC, 2003, pp.77,78.

23. Ibid.

24. **O'Connor JE**, **Curran JH**, **Beebee RA**, **Grant GE**, **Sarna-Wojcicki A**, Quaternary geology and geomorphology of the lower Deschutes River canyon, Oregon, In: O'Connor JE, Grant GE, eds., *A Peculiar River. Geology, Geomorphology, and Hydrology of the Deschutes River, Oregon. Water Science and Application 7,* American Geophysical Union, Washington, DC, 2003, p.83.

25. Ibid., p.84.

26. **Allen JE**, *Perlite deposits near the Deschutes River, southern Wasco County, Oregon. GMI Short Paper No. 16,* State of Oregon, Department of Geology and Mineral Industries, Portland, Oregon, 1946.

27. Ibid.

28. Ibid.

29. **Snow B**, *The History of the Deschutes Club,* Touchstone Press, Portland, Oregon, 1966.

30. **Curran JH**, **O'Connor JE**, Formation and evolution of valley-bottom and channel features, lower Deschutes River, Oregon, In: O'Connor JE, Grant GE, eds., *A Peculiar River. Geology, Geomorphology, and Hydrology of the Deschutes River, Oregon. Water Science and Application 7,* American Geophysical Union, Washington, DC, 2003, pp.95–119.

31. **Beebee RA**, **O'Connor JE**, The Outhouse Flood: a large Holocene flood on the lower Deschutes River, Oregon, In: O'Connor JE, Grant GE, eds., *A Peculiar River. Geology, Geomorphology, and Hydrology of the Deschutes River, Oregon. Water Science and Application 7,* American Geophysical Uniion, Washington, DC, 2003, p.148.

32. **O'Connor JE**, **Curran JH**, **Beebee RA**, **Grant GE**, **Sarna-Wojcicki A**, Quaternary geology and geomorphology of the lower Deschutes River canyon, Oregon, In: O'Connor JE, Grant GE, eds., *A Peculiar River. Geology, Geomorphology, and Hydrology of the Deschutes River, Oregon. Water Science and Application 7,* American Geophysical Union, Washington, DC, 2003, p.90.

33. Ibid., p.91.

34. **Curran JH**, **O'Connor JE**, Formation and evolution of valley-bottom and channel features, lower Deschutes River, Oregon, In: O'Connor JE, Grant GE, eds., *A Peculiar River. Geology, Geomorphology, and Hydrology of the Deschutes River, Oregon. Water Science and Application 7,* American Geophysical Union, Washington, DC, 2003, p.110.

35. Ibid.

36. **Zimmerman CE**, **Ratliff DE**, Controls on the distribution and life history of fish populations in the Deschutes River: geology, hydrology, and dams, In: O'Connor JE, Grant GE, eds., *A Peculiar River. Geology, Geomorphology, and Hydrology of the Deschutes River, Oregon. Water Science and Application 7,* American Geophysical Union, Washington, DC, 2003, p.61.

37. Ibid., p.63.

38. Ibid.

CHAPTER THREE

1. **Kirkman MM**, *Building and Repairing Railways,* World Railway Publishing Company, New York, 1901, p.22.

2. Ibid., p.23.
3. Ibid., p.4.
4. **Clarke TC, Bogart J, Forney MN, Alexander EP, Prout HG, Porter H, et al**, *The American Railway. Its Construction, Development, Management, and Appliances,* Charles Scribner's Sons, New York, 1892, p.7.
5. Ibid., p.9.
6. **Middleton WD**, *Landmarks on the Iron Road. Two Centuries of North American Railroad Engineering,* Indiana University Press, Bloomington, 1999, p.73.
7. **Armstrong JH**, *The Railroad. What It Is, What It Does. The Introduction to Railroading, 4th Ed.,* Simmons-Boardman Books, Inc., Omaha, Nebraska, 1998, p.26.
8. Ibid., p.30.
9. **The Construction of the Oregon Trunk and the Des Chutes Railways in Central Oregon**, *Railway Age Gazette,*1912:680.
10. **Armstrong JH**, *The Railroad. What It Is, What It Does. The Introduction to Railroading, 4th Ed.,* Simmons-Boardman Books, Inc., Omaha, Nebraska, 1998, p.36.
11. Ibid., p.40.
12. Ibid., p.49.
13. Ibid., pp.55–56.
14. Ibid., p.59.
15. Ibid., p.61.
16. Ibid., pp.105–111.
17. Ibid., p.68.
18. **Daniels R**, *Trains Across the Continent. North American Railroad History,* Indiana University Press, Bloomington, Second Edition, 2000, p.69.
19. Ibid., pp.46–47.
20. **Middleton WD**, *Landmarks on the Iron Road. Two Centuries of North American Railroad Engineering,* Indiana University Press, Bloomington, 1999, pp.141–143.
21. Ibid., p.143.
22. **Kirkman MM**, *Building and Repairing Railways,* World Railway Publishing Company, New York, 1901, p.56.
23. **Competitive Railway Building in the Des Chutes River Canyon**, *Railway Age Gazette,*1910:767.
24. **Kirkman MM**, *Building and Repairing Railways,* World Railway Publishing Company, New York, 1901, p.95.
25. Ibid., pp.140–143.
26. **Gaertner JT**, *North Bank Road. The Spokane, Portland & Seattle Railway,* Washington State University Press, Pullman, Washington, 1990, pp.97–120.

27. *The Madras Pioneer*, November 15, 1909.

28. **Kirkman MM**, *Building and Repairing Railways,* World Railway Publishing Company, New York, 1901, p.143.

29. Ibid., pp.163–174.

30. **Grande WR**, *The Northwest's Own Railway. Spokane, Portland & Seattle Railway and its Subsidiaries,* Grande Press, Portland, 1992, p.35.

CHAPTER FOUR

1. **Goetzmann WH**, *Army Exploration in the American West 1803-1863,* Texas State Historical Association, Austin, 1991.

2. Ibid., pp.262–304.

3. Ibid., p.275.

4. **Sawyer RW**, Abbot railroad surveys, 1855. Part I, *Ore Hist Quarterly* 33:1–24, 1932, p.3.

5. *Reports of Explorations and Surveys, to Ascertain the Most Practicable and Economical Route for a Railroad from the Mississippi River to the Pacific Ocean, Made under the Direction of the Secretary of War, in 1853-4. Volumes I-XII,* Government Printing Office, Washington, DC, 1855-1861.

6. **Sawyer RW**, Abbot railroad surveys, 1855. Part I, *Ore Hist Quarterly* 33:1–24, 1932, pp.3,4.

7. **Goetzmann WH**, *Army Exploration in the American West 1803-1863,* Texas State Historical Association, Austin, 1991, p.294.

8. **Sawyer RW**, Abbot railroad surveys, 1855. Part I, *Ore Hist Quarterly* 33:1–24, 1932, pp.11,12.

9. Ibid., p.20.

10. **Sawyer RW**, Abbot railroad surveys, Part II, *Ore Hist Quarterly* 33:115–135, 1932, p.117.

11. **Goetzmann WH**, *Army Exploration in the American West 1803-1863,* Texas State Historical Association, Austin, 1991, p.195.

12. **Anderson GM, Martin DT**, The public domain and nineteenth century transfer policy, *Cato Journal* 6:905–923, 1987, p.911.

13. Ibid., p.908.

14. Ibid., p.913.

15. **Henry RS**, The railroad land grant legend in American history texts, *Mississippi Valley Hist Rev* 32:171–194, 1945.

16. **National Railroad Museum**, Nation building: 1860–1900, *http://www.nationalrrmuseum.org/collections-018-historical-outline,* 2005.

17. **Ambrose SE**, *Nothing Like It in the World. The Men Who Built the Transcontinental Railroad 1863–1869,* Touchstone, New York, 2000.

18. Ibid., p.18.

19. Ibid., p.80.

20. **The Pacific Railway Act**, *12 Stat. 489, Ch. 120*, July 1, 1862.

21. **Haney LH**, *A Congressional History of Railways in the United States,* Augustus M. Kelley, Publishers, New York, First Edition 1908 & 1910, Reprinted 1968.

22. **Brown D**, *Hear That Lonesome Whistle Blow. The Epic Story of the Trnascontinental Railroads,* Henry Holt and Company, New York, 1977, Owl Books Edition 2001, p.40.

23. **Ambrose SE**, *Nothing Like It in the World. The Men Who Built the Transcontinental Railroad 1863–1869,* Touchstone, New York, 2000, p.78.

24. **Haney LH**, *A Congressional History of Railways in the United States,* Augustus M. Kelley, Publishers, New York, First Edition 1908 & 1910, Reprinted 1968.

25. **Second Pacific Railway Act**, *13 Stat. 356, Ch. 216*, July 2, 1864.

26. **Daniels R**, *Trains Across the Continent. North American Railroad History,* Indiana University Press, Bloomington, Second Edition, 2000, p.5.

27. **Draffan G**, Chronology of the Northern Pacific & Related Land Grant Railroads, *http://www.endgame.org/rrcc-history.html,* 2005.

28. **Henry RS**, The railroad land grant legend in American history texts, *Mississippi Valley Hist Rev* 32:171–194, 1945.

29. **Ambrose SE**, *Nothing Like It in the World. The Men Who Built the Transcontinental Railroad 1863–1869,* Touchstone, New York, 2000, p.86.

30. **Klein M**, *Union Pacific. Birth of a Railroad 1862–1893,* Doubleday & Company, Inc., New York, 1987, p.52.

31. **Brown D**, *Hear That Lonesome Whistle Blow. The Epic Story of the Trnascontinental Railroads,* Henry Holt and Company, New York, 1977, Owl Books Edition 2001, p.76.

32. **Ambrose SE**, *Nothing Like It in the World. The Men Who Built the Transcontinental Railroad 1863–1869,* Touchstone, New York, 2000, p.93.

33. Ibid., p.375.

34. Ibid., p.140.

35. Ibid., p.152.

36. Ibid., p.231.

37. Ibid., p.161.

38. Ibid., pp.139–140.

39. Ibid., p.204.

40. Ibid., p.180.

41. **Brown D**, *Hear That Lonesome Whistle Blow. The Epic Story of the Transcontinental Railroads,* Henry Holt and Company, New York, 1977, Owl Books Edition 2001, p.65.

42. **Ambrose SE**, *Nothing Like It in the World. The Men Who Built the Transcontinental Railroad 1863–1869,* Touchstone, New York, 2000, p.181.

43. Ibid., p.212.

44. Ibid., p.317.

45. **Utley RM**, The dash to Promontory, *Utah Hist Quart* 29:99–117, 1961.

46. **Klein M**, *Union Pacific. Birth of a Railroad 1862–1893,* Doubleday & Company, Inc., New York, 1987, pp.207–208.

47. Ibid., pp.223–227.

48. **Daniels R**, *Trains Across the Continent. North American Railroad History,* Indiana University Press, Bloomington, Second Edition, 2000, p.85.

CHAPTER FIVE

1. **Martin A**, *James J. Hill and the Opening of the Northwest,* Oxford University Press, New York, 1976, p.531.

2. Ibid., p.108.

3. Ibid., p.529.

4. Ibid., p.16.

5. Ibid., p.28.

6. **Stevens JF**, *An Engineer's Recollections,* McGraw-Hill Publishing Company, Inc., Reprinted from Engineering News-Record, 1935, p.42.

7. **Galvani WH**, Recollections of J.F. Stevens and Senator Mitchell, *Ore Hist Quarterly* 44:312-326, 1943, p.314.

8. **Stevens JF**, *An Engineer's Recollections,* McGraw-Hill Publishing Company, Inc., Reprinted from Engineering News-Record, 1935, p.26.

9. Ibid., p.9.

10. Ibid., p.12.

11. Ibid., p.16.

12. Ibid., p.21.

13. **Murray G**, *Marias Pass. Its Part in the History and Development of the Northwest, Studies in Northwest History No. 12,* State University of Montana, Missoula, 1930.

14. **Martin A**, *James J. Hill and the Opening of the Northwest,* Oxford University Press, New York, 1976, p.382.

15. **Stevens JF**, *An Engineer's Recollections,* McGraw-Hill Publishing Company, Inc., Reprinted from Engineering News-Record, 1935, p.22.

16. **Brimlow GF**, Marias Pass explorer John F. Stevens, *Montana Magazine of History* III:39-44, 1953.

17. **Clark E**, John F. Stevens. Pathfinder for Western Railroads, *The American West* May, 1971:28-33,62-63.

18. **Stevens JF**, *An Engineer's Recollections,* McGraw-Hill Publishing Company, Inc., Reprinted from Engineering News-Record, 1935, p.25.

19. Ibid., p.26.

20. **Flynn EF**, Stevens monument dedicated by historical expedition, *Engineering News-Record* 95:428-430, 1925.

21. **Stevens JF**, *An Engineer's Recollections,* McGraw-Hill Publishing Company, Inc., Reprinted from Engineering News-Record, 1935, p.30.

22. **Hildy RW**, John F. Stevens, Great Northern engineer, *Minnesota History* 41:345-361, 1969.

23. **Rae JB**, The Great Northern's Land Grant, *J Economic History* 12:140-145, 1952.

24. **Klein M**, *The Life & Legend of E. H. Harriman,* The University of North Carolina Press, Chapel Hill, 2000, pp.48–49.

25. Ibid., p.113.

26. Ibid., p.117.

27. Ibid., p.119.

28. Ibid., p.144.

29. Ibid., pp.181–200.

CHAPTER SIX

1. **Asay J**, *Union Pacific Northwest. The Oregon-Washington Railroad & Navigation Company,* Pacific Fast Mail, Edmonds, Washington, 1991, p.8.

2. **Grande WR**, *The Northwest's Own Railway. Spokane, Portland & Seattle Railway and its Subsidiaries,* Grande Press, Portland, 1992, p.105.

3. **Asay J**, *Union Pacific Northwest. The Oregon-Washington Railroad & Navigation Company,* Pacific Fast Mail, Edmonds, Washington, 1991, p.23.

4. **Gaston J**, The genesis of the Oregon railway system, *Ore Hist Quarterly* 7:105–132, 1906.

5. **Poppleton IL**, Oregon's first monopoly–the O.S.N.Co., *Ore Hist Quarterly* 9:276-304, 1908.

6. **Klein M**, *Union Pacific. Birth of a Railroad 1862–1893,* Doubleday & Company, Inc., New York, 1987, pp.567–583.

7. **Asay J**, *Union Pacific Northwest. The Oregon-Washington Railroad & Navigation Company,* Pacific Fast Mail, Edmonds, Washington, 1991, p.51.

8. Ibid., p.73.

9. Ibid., p.75.

10. Ibid., p.80.

11. **Holbrook SH**, *The Age of the Moguls,* Doubleday & Company, Inc., Garden City, N. Y., 1953.

12. **Martin A**, *James J. Hill and the Opening of the Northwest,* Oxford University Press, New York, 1976, p.446.

13. Ibid., p.425.

14. Ibid., pp.436,439.

15. Ibid., p.482.

16. Ibid., p.483.

17. **Klein M**, *Union Pacific. Birth of a Railroad 1862–1893,* Doubleday & Company, Inc., New York, 1987, p.264.

18. **Overton RC**, *Burlington Route. A History of the Burlington Lines,* Alfred A. Knopf, New York, 1965, p.44.

19. Ibid., p.72.

20. **Hedges JB**, Promotion of immigration to the Pacific Northwest by the railroads, *Mississippi Valley Hist Rev* 15:183-203, 1928.

21. **Greever WS**, A comparison of railroad land grant policies, *Agricultural History* 25:83-90, 1951.

22. **Klein M**, *Union Pacific. Birth of a Railroad 1862–1893,* Doubleday & Company, Inc., New York, 1987, p.249.

23. Ibid., p.257.

24. **Martin A**, *James J. Hill and the Opening of the Northwest,* Oxford University Press, New York, 1976, p.506.

25. **Wood C**, **Wood D**, *Spokane Portland and Seattle Ry. The Northwest's Own Railway,* Superior Publishing Company, Seattle, 1974.

26. **Gilman LC**, The Spokane, Portland and Seattle Railroad Company, *Washington Hist Quarterly* 14:14-20, 1923.

27. **Gaertner JT**, *North Bank Road. The Spokane, Portland & Seattle Railway,* Washington State University Press, Pullman, Washington, 1990, p.16.

28. **Gilman LC**, The Spokane, Portland and Seattle Railroad Company, *Washington Hist Quarterly* 14:14-20, 1923.

29. **Martin A**, *James J. Hill and the Opening of the Northwest,* Oxford University Press, New York, 1976, pp.563,565.

30. **Gaertner JT**, *North Bank Road. The Spokane, Portland & Seattle Railway,* Washington State University Press, Pullman, Washington, 1990, p.ix.

31. **White BM**, Working for the railroad: life in the general offices of the Great Northern and Northern Pacific, *Minnesota History* 46:24–30, 1978.

32. **Wood C**, **Wood D**, *Spokane Portland and Seattle Ry. The Northwest's Own Railway,* Superior Publishing Company, Seattle, 1974, pp.70–79.

33. **Gaertner JT**, *North Bank Road. The Spokane, Portland & Seattle Railway,* Washington State University Press, Pullman, Washington, 1990, pp.150–173.

34. Ibid., pp.175–200.

35. **Wood C, Wood D**, *Spokane Portland and Seattle Ry. The Northwest's Own Railway,* Superior Publishing Company, Seattle, 1974, pp.80–84.

36. **Klein M**, *Union Pacific. Birth of a Railroad 1862–1893,* Doubleday & Company, Inc., New York, 1987, p.408.

37. Ibid., p.434.

38. Ibid., p.435.

39. Ibid., p.69.

40. Ibid., p.70.

41. *The Oregonian*, September 11, 1909.

42. **Martin A**, *James J. Hill and the Opening of the Northwest,* Oxford University Press, New York, 1976, p.614.

CHAPTER SEVEN

1. *The Bend Bulletin*, August 25, 1909.

2. **Stevens JF**, *An Engineer's Recollections,* McGraw-Hill Publishing Company, Inc., Reprinted from Engineering News-Record, 1935, p.60.

3. **Krantz SO**, Railroad war in the mountains, *Technical World Magazine* 18:27-34, 1912.

4. **Overholser WD**, *Oregon Trunk,* Thomas T. Beeler, Publisher, Hampton Falls, New Hampshire, 1978.

5. *The Oregonian*, August 17, 1907.

6. **Competitive Railway Building in the Des Chutes River Canyon**, *Railway Age Gazette,* 1910:767–771.

7. **Stevens JF**, *An Engineer's Recollections,* McGraw-Hill Publishing Company, Inc., Reprinted from Engineering News-Record, 1935, p.60.

8. **Editorial**, *The Oregonian*, September 17, 1903.

9. **Editorial**, *The Oregonian*, April 12, 1904.

10. **Editorial**, *The Oregonian*, May 13, 1905.

11. Ibid.

12. **Editorial**, *The Oregonian*, June 14, 1905.

13. **Editorial**, *The Oregonian*, July 16, 1904.

14. *The Oregonian*, August 9, 1905.

15. **Editorial**, *The Oregonian*, August 10, 1905.

16. **Editorial**, *The Oregonian*, August 11, 1905.

17. **Editorial**, *The Oregonian*, October 2, 1905.

18. **Gaertner JT**, *North Bank Road. The Spokane, Portland & Seattle Railway,* Washington State University Press, Pullman, Washington, 1990, pp.97–110.

19. **Competitive Railway Building in Central Oregon**, *Railway Age Gazette,* 1909:905–906.

20. **Asay J**, *Union Pacific Northwest. The Oregon-Washington Railroad & Navigation Company,* Pacific Fast Mail, Edmonds, Washington, 1991.

21. **Gaertner JT**, *North Bank Road. The Spokane, Portland & Seattle Railway,* Washington State University Press, Pullman, Washington, 1990, pp.97–110.

22. **Frank B. Gill Collection**, Oregon Historical Society, Box 5, Folder 12.

23. **Great Northern Railway Company Records**, Minnesota Historical Society, Saint Paul, Minnesota, Folder 2, Legal Papers 1906–1909, Articles of Incorporation, Des Chutes Railroad Company.

24. *The Bend Bulletin*, February 24, 1909.

25. **Gaertner JT**, *North Bank Road. The Spokane, Portland & Seattle Railway,* Washington State University Press, Pullman, Washington, 1990, pp.97–110.

26. Ibid., p.98.

27. **Austin E**, **Dill T**, *S.P.&S. The Spokane Portland & Seattle Railway,* Pacific Fast Mail, Edmonds, Washington, 1996, pp.195–228.

28. **Great Northern Railway Company Records**, Minnesota Historical Society, Saint Paul, Minnesota, Box No. 132.G.2.3. (B), Folder 1.

29. **Oregon Historical Society**, Collection 21, Great Northern Railway Company Correspondence and Clippings Regarding the Oregon Trunk Railway, 1911–1913, Letter, April 17, 1906.

30. **Oregon Historical Society**, Collection 21, Great Northern Railway Company Correspondence and Clippings Regarding the Oregon Trunk Railway, 1911–1913, Telegram, May 12, 1906.

31. **Wood C**, **Wood D**, *Spokane Portland and Seattle Ry. The Northwest's Own Railway,* Superior Publishing Company, Seattle, 1974, p.89.

32. **Great Northern Railway Company Records**, Minnesota Historical Society, Saint Paul, Minnesota, Folder 5, Amberg File.

33. *The Bend Bulletin,* February 24, 1909.

34. **The Construction of the Oregon Trunk and the Des Chutes Railways in Central Oregon**, *Railway Age Gazette,* 1912:680–685.

35. *The Dope Bucket. Gold Spike Issue. The Oregon Trunk 1911–1961,* Vol. 23, No.3, Spokane Portland and Seattle Railway, Spokane, 1961.

36. *The Bend Bulletin,* February 24, 1909.

37. **Gaertner JT**, *North Bank Road. The Spokane, Portland & Seattle Railway,* Washington State University Press, Pullman, Washington, 1990, pp.97–110, p.98.

38. Ibid., p.100.

39. *The Bend Bulletin,* February 24, 1909.

40. **Great Northern Railway Company Records**, Minnesota Historical Society, Saint Paul, Minnesota, Folder 2, Legal Papers 1906–1909.

41. *The Bend Bulletin*, March 3, 1909.

42. **Gaertner JT**, *North Bank Road. The Spokane, Portland & Seattle Railway*, Washington State University Press, Pullman, Washington, 1990, pp.97–110, p.100.

43. *The Dope Bucket. Gold Spike Issue. The Oregon Trunk 1911–1961,* Vol. 23, No.3,, Spokane Portland and Seattle Railway, Spokane, 1961.

44. *Spokane Chronicle*, July 31, 1909.

45. **Oregon Historical Society**, Collection 21, Great Northern Railway Company Correspondence and Clippings Regarding the Oregon Trunk Railway, 1911–1913, Letter, September 30, 1908.

46. *Spokane Chronicle*, July 31, 1909.

47. *The Dalles Weekly Chronicle*, July 30, 1909.

48. *The Dope Bucket. Gold Spike Issue. The Oregon Trunk 1911–1961,* Vol. 23, No.3, Spokane Portland and Seattle Railway, Spokane, 1961.

49. *The Oregonian*, September 4, 1908.

50. **Gaertner JT**, *North Bank Road. The Spokane, Portland & Seattle Railway*, Washington State University Press, Pullman, Washington, 1990, pp.97–110, p.100.

51. *The Bend Bulletin*, July 7, 1909.

52. **Asay J**, *Union Pacific Northwest. The Oregon-Washington Railroad & Navigation Company*, Pacific Fast Mail, Edmonds, Washington, 1991.

53. *The Bend Bulletin*, July 14, 1909.

54. **Great Northern Railway Company Records**, Minnesota Historical Society, Saint Paul, Minnesota, Folder 2, Legal Papers 1906–1909.

55. **Hildy RW**, John F. Stevens, Great Northern engineer, *Minnesota History* 41:345–361, 1969.

56. **Stevens JF**, *An Engineer's Recollections,* McGraw-Hill Publishing Company, Inc., Reprinted from Engineering News-Record, 1935.

57. Ibid., p.60.

58. *The Oregonian*, August 16, 1909.

59. Ibid.

60. *The Bend Bulletin,* July 14, 1909.

61. **James J. Hill Letterpress Books**, *James J. Hill Library, Saint Paul, Minnesota,* Volume 20, March 14, 1908–May 26, 1911, James J. Hill to E. T. Nichols, March 10, 1910, p.484.

62. **James J. Hill Papers**, *James J. Hill Library, Saint Paul, Minnesota*, John F. Stevens to James J. Hill, Telegram, July 4, 1909.

63. Ibid., Letter July 4, 1909.

64. **Stevens JF**, *An Engineer's Recollections,* McGraw-Hill Publishing Company, Inc., Reprinted from Engineering News-Record, 1935, p.60.

65. **Oregon Historical Society**, Collection 21, Great Northern Railway Company Correspondence and Clippings Regarding the Oregon Trunk Railway, 1911–1913, Letter, September 30, 1908.

66. **Great Northern Railway Company Records**, Minnesota Historical Society, Saint Paul, Minnesota, Folder 2, Legal Papers 1906–1909.

67. **Stevens JF**, *An Engineer's Recollections,* McGraw-Hill Publishing Company, Inc., Reprinted from Engineering News-Record, 1935, p.60.

68. Ibid., p.84.

69. Ibid.

70. *The Oregonian,* August 16, 1909.

71. Ibid.

72. **Great Northern Railway Company Records**, Minnesota Historical Society, Saint Paul, Minnesota, Folder 7, Correspondence and Legal Papers, 1906–1908.

73. Ibid., Box 133.E.2.2 (F), Folder 15344.

74. **Stevens JF**, *An Engineer's Recollections,* McGraw-Hill Publishing Company, Inc., Reprinted from Engineering News-Record, 1935, p.62.

75. **James J. Hill Letterpress Books**, *James J. Hill Library, Saint Paul, Minnesota,* Volume 20, March 14, 1908–May 26, 1911, James J. Hill to John F. Stevens, August 14, 1909, p.306.

76. *The Bend Bulletin*, October 9, 1909.

77. *The Madras Pioneer*, October 14, 1909.

78. **Great Northern Railway Company Records**, Minnesota Historical Society, Saint Paul, Minnesota, Box 133.E.2.2. (F), Folder 15344.

79. **Gaertner JT**, *North Bank Road. The Spokane, Portland & Seattle Railway,* Washington State University Press, Pullman, Washington, 1990, pp.97–110, p.103.

80. *The Oregonian*, September 21, 1909.

81. *The Dope Bucket. Gold Spike Issue. The Oregon Trunk 1911–1961,* Vol. 23, No.3, Spokane Portland and Seattle Railway, Spokane, 1961.

82. *The Oregonian*, November 4, 1909.

83. **Great Northern Railway Company Records**, Minnesota Historical Society, Saint Paul, Minnesota, Box No. 132.G.2.3. (B), Folder 1.

84. **Great Northern Railway Company Records**, Minnesota Historical Society, Saint Paul, Minnesota, Box 132.F.8.10 (F), Letter to the General Land Office from Oregon Trunk lawyers, March 28, 1913.

85. *The Bend Bulletin*, November 13, 1908.

86. **Competitive Railroad Building in Central Oregon**, *Railway Age Gazette,* 1909: 905–906.

87. **Gaertner JT**, *North Bank Road. The Spokane, Portland & Seattle Railway,* Washington State University Press, Pullman, Washington, 1990, pp.97–110, p.100.

88. *The Oregonian*, February 17, 1909.

89. **Oregon Historical Society**, Collection 21, Great Northern Railway Company Correspondence and Clippings Regarding the Oregon Trunk Railway, 1911–1913, Letters, September 13, 1909, October 1, 1909.

90. *The Dalles Weekly Chronicle*, July 16, 1909.

91. *The Bend Bulletin*, July 28, 1909.

92. Ibid., p.4.

CHAPTER EIGHT

1. *The Dope Bucket. Gold Spike Issue. The Oregon Trunk 1911–1961,* Vol. 23, No.3, Spokane Portland and Seattle Railway, Spokane, 1961.

2. *The Bend Bulletin*, August 4, 1909.

3. *Sherman County Observer*, July 30, 1909.

4. **Quinn JM**, **Quinn JK**, **King JG**, *Handbook to the Deschutes River Canyon, 3rd Edition,* Educational Adventures, Inc., Bend, Oregon, 1979.

5. Ibid., pp.8–11.

6. **Due JF**, **Grench G**, *Rails to the Mid-Columbia Wheatlands: The Columbia Southern and Great Southern Railroads and the Development of Sherman and Wasco Counties, Oregon,* University Press of America, Washington, DC, 1979, p.230.

7. *The Dalles Weekly Chronicle,* July 30, 1909.

8. **Donovan F**, Canyon war, *Railroad Magazine,* 1956:22-26.

9. *The Dalles Weekly Chronicle,* August 6, 1909.

10. *The Grass Valley Journal,* July 30, 1909.

11. **Quinn JM**, **Quinn JK**, **King JG**, *Handbook to the Deschutes River Canyon, 3rd Edition,* Educational Adventures, Inc., Bend, Oregon, 1979, pp.8–11.

12. Ibid.

13. **Callvert RG**, *The Oregonian,* August 4, 1909.

14. *The Oregonian,* August 16, 1909.

15. *The Oregonian,* August 10, 1909.

16. *The Grass Valley Journal,* August 6, 1909.

17. *The Oregonian,* August 12, 1909.

18. *The Bend Bulletin,* August 11, 1909.

19. *The Grass Valley Journal,* August 13, 1909.

20. *The Madras Pioneer,* September 23, 1909.

21. **James J. Hill Letterpress Books**, *James J. Hill Library, Saint Paul, Minnesota,* Volumes 20, March 14, 1908–May 26, 1911, James J. Hill to John F. Stevens, August 23, 1909, p.321.

22. **Quinn JM**, **Quinn JK**, **King JG**, *Handbook to the Deschutes River Canyon, 3rd Edition,* Educational Adventures, Inc., Bend, Oregon, 1979, p.82.

23. *The Bend Bulletin,* August 18, 1909.

24. *The Madras Pioneer,* August 12, 1909.

25. *The Oregonian,* August 18, 1909.

26. *The Oregonian,* August 21, 1909.

27. *The Oregonian,* August 25, 1909.

28. *The Oregonian,* August 31, 1909.

29. *The Oregonian,* September 10, 1909.

30. **Stevens JF**, *An Engineer's Recollections,* McGraw-Hill Publishing Company, Inc., Reprinted from Engineering News-Record, 1935.

31. **Putnam GP**, *The Oregonian,* September 3, 1909.

32. *The Bend Bulletin,* October 19, 1910.

33. **The Construction of the Oregon Trunk and the Des Chutes Railways in Central Oregon**, *Railway Age Gazette,* 1912:680–685.

34. *The Oregon Journal,* May 1, 1910.

35. **Quinn JM**, **Quinn JK**, **King JG**, *Handbook to the Deschutes River Canyon, 3rd Edition,* Educational Adventures, Inc., Bend, Oregon, 1979, pp.8–11.

36. **Due JF**, **Grench G**, *Rails to the Mid-Columbia Wheatlands: The Columbia Southern and Great Southern Railroads and the Development of Sherman and Wasco Counties, Oregon,* University Press of America, Washington, DC, 1979, p.203.

37. Ibid., p.204.

38. **Quinn JM**, **Quinn JK**, **King JG**, *Handbook to the Deschutes River Canyon, 3rd Edition,* Educational Adventures, Inc., Bend, Oregon, 1979, p.80.

39. **Wood C**, **Wood D**, *Spokane Portland and Seattle Ry. The Northwest's Own Railway,* Superior Publishing Company, Seattle, 1974, p.86.

40. **Quinn JM**, **Quinn JK**, **King JG**, *Handbook to the Deschutes River Canyon, 3rd Edition,* Educational Adventures, Inc., Bend, Oregon, 1979, p.80.

41. **von Borstel M**, The Sherar Family, *Sherman County: For The Record,* Sherman County Historical Society, 3:10–23, 1985.

42. **Brogan PF**, *East of the Cascades, Fourth Edition, 1977,* Binford & Mort, Portland, Oregon, 1964, pp.48–59.

43. *The Madras Pioneer,* November 4, 1909.

44. **Culp ED**, *Stations West,* Bonanza Books, New York, 1978, p.103.

45. Ibid., p.100.

46. **Due JF**, **Grench G**, *Rails to the Mid-Columbia Wheatlands: The Columbia Southern and Great Southern Railroads and the Development of Sherman and Wasco Counties, Oregon,* University Press of America, Washington, DC, 1979, pp.31–32.

47. Ibid., p.50.

48. **McArthur LA**, **McArthur LL**, *Oregon Geographic Names, 7th Edition,* Oregon Historical Society Press, Portland, 2003.

49. **Due JF**, **Grench G**, *Rails to the Mid-Columbia Wheatlands: The Columbia Southern and Great Southern Railroads and the Development of Sherman and Wasco Counties, Oregon,* University Press of America, Washington, DC, 1979, p.51.

50. Ibid., p.66.

51. Ibid., pp.72–73.

52. Ibid., pp.100–101.

53. Ibid., pp.151–153.

54. Ibid., p.168.

55. Ibid., p.199.

56. Ibid., p.216.

57. Ibid., p.238.

58 Ibid., pp.262–263.

59. *The Madras Pioneer,* November 25, 1909.

60. **Due JF**, **Grench G**, *Rails to the Mid-Columbia Wheatlands: The Columbia Southern and Great Southern Railroads and the Development of Sherman and Wasco Counties, Oregon,* University Press of America, Washington, DC, 1979, p.106.

61. **Krantz SO**, Railroad war in the mountains, *Technical World Magazine* 18:27–34, 1912.

62. *The Madras Pioneer,* September 23, 1909.

63. **Krantz SO**, Railroad war in the mountains, *Technical World Magazine* 18:27–34, 1912.

64. Ibid.

65. **Morrell JF**, **French G**, Bubble skinner, *Ore Hist Quarterly* 69:293–305, 1968.

66. Ibid., p.294.

67. Ibid., p.297.

68. Ibid., p.298.

69. Ibid.

70. **Due JF, Grench G**, *Rails to the Mid-Columbia Wheatlands: The Columbia Southern and Great Southern Railroads and the Development of Sherman and Wasco Counties, Oregon,* University Press of America, Washington, DC, 1979, p.12.

71. **Austin E, Dill T**, *S.P.&S. The Spokane Portland & Seattle Railway,* Pacific Fast Mail, Edmonds, Washington, 1996, pp.195–228.

72. **Great Northern Railway Company Records**, *Minnesota Historical Society, Saint Paul, Minnesota,* Box No. 132.G.2.3. (B), Folder 5, Balance Sheets, 1910.

73. **The Construction of the Oregon Trunk and the Des Chutes Railways in Central Oregon**, *Railway Age Gazette,* 1912:680–685.

74. **Galveston History Foundation**, Galveston—A Brief History, *www.galvestonhistory.org/history.htm,* 2005.

75. *The Dope Bucket. Gold Spike Issue. The Oregon Trunk 1911–1961,* Vol. 23, No.3, Spokane Portland and Seattle Railway, Spokane, 1961, p.14.

76. *The Oregonian*, November 4, 1909.

77. **US Code Collection, Rights of several roads through canyons**, *Legal Information Institute, Cornell University,* Title 43, Chapter 22, Section 942-2:http://straylight.law.cornell.edu/uscode/html/uscode43/usc_sec_43_00000942----0000000942-.htlm, 2005.

78. *The Oregonian,* May 9 and 11, 1910.

79. *The Oregon Journal,* May 24, 1910.

80. *The Oregonian,* May 26, 1910.

81. *The Oregonian,* May 21, 1910.

82. *The Oregon Journal,* May 22, 1910.

83. *The Oregonian,* May 19, 1910.

84. **James J. Hill Letterpress Books**, *James J. Hill Library, Saint Paul, Minnesota,* Volume 20, March 14, 1908–May 26, 1911, James J. Hill to John F. Stevens, February 20, 1910, p.370.

85. Ibid., p.374.

86. Ibid., p.490.

87. Ibid., p.36.

88. **Great Northern Railway Company Records**, *Minnesota Historical Society, Saint Paul, Minnesota,* Box 132. G.2.3. (B) Folder 6, Oregon Trunk Railway, Box 133.1.20.5.(B), Folder 8532.

89. *The Oregonian*, May 18, 1910.

90. *The Madras Pioneer,* May 5, 1910.

91. **Gaertner JT**, *North Bank Road. The Spokane, Portland & Seattle Railway,* Washington State University Press, Pullman, Washington, 1990, pp.97–119.

CHAPTER NINE

1. **Krantz SO**, Railroad war in the mountains, *Technical World Magazine* 18:27–34, 1912.

2. **Twohy JR**, *Ten Spikes to the Rail,* Goat Rock Publications, Jenner, California, 1983, p.66

3. *The Madras Pioneer,* August 19, 1909.

4. *The Dalles Weekly Chronicle,* October 22, 1909.

5. **White WT**, Race, ethnicity, and gender in the railroad work force: the case of the far northwest, 1883–1918, *Western Hist Quart* 16:265–283, 1985.

6. Ibid., p.277.

7. *The Bend Bulletin,* March 9, 1910.

8. *The Dope Bucket. Gold Spike Issue. The Oregon Trunk 1911–1961,* Vol. 23, No.3, Spokane Portland and Seattle Railway, Spokane, 1961.

9. **Wood C**, **Wood D**, *Spokane Portland and Seattle Ry. The Northwest's Own Railway,* Superior Publishing Company, Seattle, 1974, p.93.

10. **McArthur LA**, **McArthur LL**, *Oregon Geographic Names, 7th Edition,* Oregon Historical Society Press, Portland, 2003.

11. **Wasco County Historical Society**, **Clackamas County Historical Society**, *Barlow Road,* J. Y. Hollingsworth Co., Portland, Oregon, 1976.

12. **Due JF**, **Grench G**, *Rails to the Mid-Columbia Wheatlands: The Columbia Southern and Great Southern Railroads and the Development of Sherman and Wasco Counties, Oregon,* University Press of America, Washington, DC, 1979, pp.2–4.

13. Ibid., p.15.

14. **McKeown MF**, Historic Umatilla House at The Dalles, *Ore Hist Quarterly* 3:37–41, 1930.

15. **Due JF**, **Grench G**, *Rails to the Mid-Columbia Wheatlands: The Columbia Southern and Great Southern Railroads and the Development of Sherman and Wasco Counties, Oregon,* University Press of America, Washington, DC, 1979, pp.23,24.

16. Ibid., p.77.

17. Ibid., p.88.

18. **Taylor GH**, **Hatton RR**, *The Oregon Weather Book. A State of Extremes,* Oregon State University Press, Corvallis, 1999, p.15.

19. **Lueneburger K**, The Western Rattlesnake *(Crotalus viridis), http://www.uoregon.edu/~titus/herp/viridishistory.htm,* 2005.

20. **Quinn JM**, **Quinn JK**, **King JG**, *Handbook to the Deschutes River Canyon, 3rd Edition,* Educational Adventures, Inc., Bend, Oregon, 1979.

21. **Hughes D**, *Deschutes,* Frank Amato Publications, Portland, Oregon, 1990, pp.26–33.

22. **Taylor GH**, **Hatton RR**, *The Oregon Weather Book. A State of Extremes,* Oregon State University Press, Corvallis, 1999, p.10.

23. Ibid., p.15.

24. *The Dalles Weekly Chronicle,* November 26, 1909.

25. **Edward R. Armstrong's Diary: Camp Raven**, **Deschutes River Railroad**, *Sherman County: For The Record,* Sherman County Historical Society, 17:3–56, 1999.

26. *The Oregonian,* August 16, 1909.

27. *The Madras Pioneer,* September 23, 1909.

28. **Freeman OS**, **Jay C. Freeman**, Horse and Buggy Sheriff, *Sherman County: For The Record,* Sherman County Historical Society, 4:3–13, 1986, p.7.

29. **Quinn JM**, **Quinn JK**, **King JG**, *Handbook to the Deschutes River Canyon, 3rd Edition,* Educational Adventures, Inc., Bend, Oregon, 1979, p.29.

30. *The Madras Pioneer,* September 8, 1909.

31. *The Dalles Weekly Chronicle,* September 10, 1909.

32. *The Bend Bulletin,* December 1, 1909.

33. *The Madras Pioneer,* December 9, 1909.

34. **Oregon Historical Society**, Collection 21, Great Northern Railway Company Correspondence and Clippings Regarding the Oregon Trunk Railway, 1911–1913.

35. *The Madras Pioneer,* June 15, 1911.

36. *The Madras Pioneer,* December 16, 1909.

37. *The Madras Pioneer,* March 24, 1910.

38. **Due JF**, **Grench G**, *Rails to the Mid-Columbia Wheatlands: The Columbia Southern and Great Southern Railroads and the Development of Sherman and Wasco Counties, Oregon,* University Press of America, Washington, DC, 1979, p.226.

39. **Coe UC**, *Frontier Doctor. Observations on Central Oregon and the Changing West, originally published 1940,* Oregon State University Press, Corvallis, Oregon, 2003.

40. Ibid., p.248.

41. **Hughes D**, *Deschutes,* Frank Amato Publications, Portland, Oregon, 1990, pp.26–33.

42. *The Madras Pioneer,* November 15, 1909.

43. *The Dalles Weekly Chronicle,* October 29, 1909.

44. **Morrell JF**, **French G**, Bubble skinner, *Ore Hist Quarterly* 69:293–305, 1968, p.299.

45. *The Madras Pioneer,* January 6, 1910.

CHAPTER TEN

1. **Middleton WD**, *Landmarks on the Iron Road. Two Centuries of North American Railroad Engineering,* Indiana University Press, Bloomington, 1999, p.2.

2. Ibid., p.4.

3. **Ploss KM**, The Polish Bridge Builder, *www.polishamericancenter.org/KayaArticle_Mod.htm,* 2005.

4. **Bridge Construction on the Oregon Trunk Railway**, *Railway Age Gazette,*1912:756–759.

5. Ibid.

6. *The Madras Pioneer,* August 24, 1911.

7. *The Dope Bucket. Gold Spike Issue. The Oregon Trunk 1911–1961,* Vol. 23, No.3, Spokane Portland and Seattle Railway, Spokane, 1961.

8. **Gaertner JT**, *North Bank Road. The Spokane, Portland & Seattle Railway,* Washington State University Press, Pullman, Washington, 1990.

9. *The Bend Bulletin,* May 17, 1911.

10. *The Madras Pioneer,* June 15, 1911.

11. **Coe UC**, *Frontier Doctor. Observations on Central Oregon and the Changing West, originally published 1940,* Oregon State University Press, Corvallis, Oregon, 2003, pp.251–252.

12. *The Oregonian,* September 24, 1910.

13. **James J. Hill Letterpress Books**, *James J. Hill Library, Saint Paul, Minnesota,* Volume 21, March 14, 1908–May 26, 1911.

14. *The Madras Pioneer,* November 15, 1909.

15. **The Northwest's Own Railway**, *Spokane, Portland and Seattle Historical Society,* Fall, 1987, p.5.

16. **McArthur LA**, **McArthur LL**, *Oregon Geographic Names, 7th Edition,* Oregon Historical Society Press, Portland, 2003.

17. **Prager K**, *That Reminds Me of Another Story. Stories of the SP&S Railway,* Laurel Prager, Hillsboro, Oregon, 1999, pp.64–65.

CHAPTER ELEVEN

1. *The Bend Bulletin,* October 4, 1911.

2. *The Bend Bulletin,* September 13, 1911.

3. *The Bend Bulletin,* October 7, 1911.

4. *The Bend Bulletin,* September 22, 1911.

5. **Schwantes CA**, Problems of empire building: The Oregon Trunk Railway survey of disappointed home-seekers, *Ore Hist Quarterly* 83:371–390, 1982, p.372.

6. *The Bend Bulletin,* October 11, 1911.

7. **Schwantes CA**, Problems of empire building: The Oregon Trunk Railway survey of disappointed home-seekers, *Ore Hist Quarterly* 83:371–390, 1982, p.373.

8. *The Dope Bucket. Gold Spike Issue. The Oregon Trunk 1911–1961,* Vol. 23, No.3, Spokane Portland and Seattle Railway, Spokane, 1961.

9. *The Bend Bulletin,* April 27, 1999.

10. *The Madras Pioneer,* February 16, 1911.

11. *The Bend Bulletin,* February 22, 1911.

12. *The Bend Bulletin,* May 17, 1911.

13. *The Madras Pioneer,* February 23, 1911.

14. *The Bend Bulletin,* March 8, 1911.

15. *The Madras Pioneer,* March 2, 1911.

16. **Stevens JF**, *An Engineer's Recollections,* McGraw-Hill Publishing Company, Inc., Reprinted from Engineering News-Record, 1935.

17. **Great Northern Railway Company Records**, *Minnesota Historical Society, Saint Paul, Minnesota*, Box 133. E.2.2. (F), Folder 15344.

18. **Gaertner JT**, *North Bank Road. The Spokane, Portland & Seattle Railway,* Washington State University Press, Pullman, Washington, 1990.

19. **Due JF**, **Grench G**, *Rails to the Mid-Columbia Wheatlands: The Columbia Southern and Great Southern Railroads and the Development of Sherman and Wasco Counties, Oregon,* University Press of America, Washington, DC, 1979, p.105.

20. **Quinn JM**, **Quinn JK**, **King JG**, *Handbook to the Deschutes River Canyon, 3rd Edition,* Educational Adventures, Inc., Bend, Oregon, 1979, p.87.

21. *The Oregon Journal,* February 22, 1911.

22. *The Bend Bulletin,* November 1, 1911.

23. **Great Northern Railway Company Records**, *Minnesota Historical Society, Saint Paul, Minnesota*, Box 133. F.17.10 (F), Annual Report Oregon Trunk Railway to Railroad Commission of the State of Oregon, Year Ending June 30, 1912.

24. Ibid., Box 132.F.8.10 (F), Letter to the General Land Office from Oregon Trunk Lawyers.

25. Ibid., Box 133.F.17.13 (B), Annual Report Oregon Trunk Railway to the Interstate Commerce Commission, Year Ending June 30, 1912.

26. **Austin E**, **Dill T**, *S.P.&S. The Spokane Portland & Seattle Railway,* Pacific Fast Mail, Edmonds, Washington, 1996, pp.195–228.

27. **Wood C**, **Wood D**, *Spokane Portland and Seattle Ry. The Northwest's Own Railway,* Superior Publishing Company, Seattle, 1974, p.87.

28. **Asay J**, *Union Pacific Northwest. The Oregon-Washington Railroad & Navigation Company,* Pacific Fast Mail, Edmonds, Washington, 1991, p.87.

29. **The Construction of the Oregon Trunk and the Des Chutes Railways in Central Oregon**, *Railway Age Gazette,*1912:680-685.

30. *The Madras Pioneer,* October 21, 1909.

31. *The Madras Pioneer,* August 4, 1910.

32. **Stover JF**, *The Routledge Historical Atlas of the American Railroads,* Routledge, New York, 1999, pp.58, 59.

33. **Grande WR**, *The Northwest's Own Railway. Spokane, Portland & Seattle Railway and its Subsidiaries,* Grande Press, Portland, 1992, p.138.

34. Ibid., pp.133,143.

35. Ibid., p.144.

36. *The Oregonian,* August 2, 1930.

37. **McArthur LA**, **McArthur LL**, *Oregon Geographic Names, 7th Edition,* Oregon Historical Society Press, Portland, 2003.

38. **Wood C**, **Wood D**, *Spokane Portland and Seattle Ry. The Northwest's Own Railway,* Superior Publishing Company, Seattle, 1974, p.145.

39. **Frank B. Gill Collection**, Oregon Historical Society, Box 6, Folder 17.

40. **Asay J**, *Union Pacific Northwest. The Oregon-Washington Railroad & Navigation Company,* Pacific Fast Mail, Edmonds, Washington, 1991.

41. **Henshaw FF**, **Lewis JH**, **McCaustland EJ**, *Deschutes River, Oregon, and Its Utilization, Department of the Interior, United States Geological Survey, Water-Supply Paper 344,* Government Printing Office, Washington, DC, 1914.

42. **Mills RV**, Prineville's municipal railroad in central Oregon, *Ore Hist Quarterly* 42:256–262, 1941.

43. Ibid., p.257.

44. Ibid., p.258.

45. Ibid., p.260.

46. *The Bend Bulletin*, May 18, 2003.

47. **Oregon Historical Society**, Collection 21, Great Northern Railway Company Correspondence and Clippings Regarding the Oregon Trunk Railway, 1911–1913, Jackson to Costello, February 28, 1911.

48. **Great Northern Railway Company Records**, *Minnesota Historical Society, Saint Paul, Minnesota,* Box 133. F.17.10 (F), Annual Report Oregon Trunk Railway to Railroad Commission of the State of Oregon, Year Ending June 30, 1912.

49. *The Oregonian,* October 24, 1910.

50. **Brogan PF**, *East of the Cascades, Fourth Edition, 1977,* Binford & Mort, Portland, Oregon, 1964, p.253.

51. **Wood C**, **Wood D**, *Spokane Portland and Seattle Ry. The Northwest's Own Railway,* Superior Publishing Company, Seattle, 1974, p.97.

52. Ibid.

53. **Gaertner JT**, *North Bank Road. The Spokane, Portland & Seattle Railway,* Washington State University Press, Pullman, Washington, 1990, p.111.

54. **Prager K**, Recorded observations, 1989, *Audiotape,* with the permission of Laurel Prager, 2005.

55. **Great Northern Railway Company Records**, *Minnesota Historical Society, Saint Paul, Minnesota,* Box 133.1.20.5. (B), Folder 8532.

56. **Asay J**, *Union Pacific Northwest. The Oregon-Washington Railroad & Navigation Company,* Pacific Fast Mail, Edmonds, Washington, 1991, p.190.

57. **Austin E**, **Dill T**, *S.P.&S. The Spokane Portland & Seattle Railway,* Pacific Fast Mail, Edmonds, Washington, 1996, pp.195–228.

58. Ibid., p.210.

59. **Asay J**, *Union Pacific Northwest. The Oregon-Washington Railroad & Navigation Company,* Pacific Fast Mail, Edmonds, Washington, 1991, p.193.

60. **Austin E**, **Dill T**, *S.P.&S. The Spokane Portland & Seattle Railway,* Pacific Fast Mail, Edmonds, Washington, 1996, pp.195–228.

61. **Great Northern Railway Company Records**, *Minnesota Historical Society, Saint Paul, Minnesota,* Box 133. F.17.10 (F), Annual Report Oregon Trunk Railway to Railroad Commission of the State of Oregon, Year Ending June 30, 1912.

62. **Prager K**, *That Reminds Me of Another Story. Stories of the SP&S Railway,* Laurel Prager, Hillsboro, Oregon, 1999, p.4.

63. **Gaertner JT**, *North Bank Road. The Spokane, Portland & Seattle Railway,* Washington State University Press, Pullman, Washington, 1990, p.114.

64. **Hughes D**, *Deschutes,* Frank Amato Publications, Portland, Oregon, 1990, pp.26–33.

65. **Snow B**, *The History of the Deschutes Club,* Touchstone Press, Portland, Oregon, 1966.

66. **Stevens JF**, *An Engineer's Recollections,* McGraw-Hill Publishing Company, Inc., Reprinted from Engineering News-Record, 1935.

67. **Austin E**, **Dill T**, *S.P.&S. The Spokane Portland & Seattle Railway,* Pacific Fast Mail, Edmonds, Washington, 1996, pp.195–228.

68. **Gaertner JT**, *North Bank Road. The Spokane, Portland & Seattle Railway,* Washington State University Press, Pullman, Washington, 1990, p.115.

69. **Grande WR**, *The Northwest's Own Railway. Spokane, Portland & Seattle Railway and its Subsidiaries,* Grande Press, Portland, 1992, p.35.

70. Ibid., pp.46–48.

71. Ibid., p.50.

72. **Melonas G**, Burlington Northern & Sante Fe, Personal communication, May 19, 2005.

73. *The Bend Bulletin,* August 25, 1909.

EPILOGUE

1. **Prager K**, *That Reminds Me of Another Story. Stories of the SP&S Railway,* Laurel Prager, Hillsboro, Oregon, 1999.

2. Ibid., pp.76–86.

3. **Kamholz G**, Personal communication, June 18, 2005.

Illustration Acknowledgments

Aerial photographs, taken on August 31, 2005, are by Craig P. Markham, Dundee, Oregon. Photographs not acknowledged below are by the author. Maps and diagrams are by Becky Slemmons, Portland, Oregon.

CHAPTER THREE

Harris track-laying machine	Des Chutes Historical Center, Bend, Oregon, No. 9547
Harris track-laying machine	Crook County Historical Society, Prineville, Oregon
McCoy track-laying machine	Des Chutes Historical Center, Bend, Oregon, No. 262

CHAPTER FIVE

James J. Hill	Minnesota Historical Society, St. Paul, Minnesota, por/8540/p3, Negative No. 83724
Edward H. Harriman	Union Pacific Museum Collection, Council Bluffs, Iowa, Image No. 45-138

CHAPTER SEVEN

Edward H. Harriman	Union Pacific Museum Collection, Council Bluffs, Iowa, Image No. 5-139
"Peg" Anspach, Oregon Trunk surveyor	Oregon Historical Society, Portland, Oregon, No. 88913
Oregon Trunk surveyors,	Oregon Historical Society, Portland, Oregon, No. 105479
John F. Stevens — 1910	Library of Congress, Washington, D.C., US 262-124261

CHAPTER EIGHT

Harry E. Carleton — 1921	Courtesy of Harry Carleton's granddaughter, Susan Brown, Wasco, Oregon

Illustration	Source
G.P. Putnam in Deschutes Canyon — 1909	Des Chutes Historical Center, Bend, Oregon, No. 2390
Johnson Porter	Oregon Historical Society, Portland, Oregon, No. 105476
Tony Scapelli	Oregon Historical Society, Portland, Oregon, No. 105483
Construction camp at Beavertail, river mile 31.5	Courtesy of Harry Carleton's granddaughter, Susan Brown, Wasco, Oregon
Oregon Trunk north portal, Horseshoe Bend	Courtesy of Harry Carleton's granddaughter, Susan Brown, Wasco, Oregon
Mustachioed Harry Carleton at north portal, Horseshoe Bend	Oregon Historical Society, Portland, Oregon, No. 88912
Harry Carleton at Horseshoe Bend	Courtesy of Harry Carleton's granddaughter, Susan Brown, Wasco, Oregon
Oregon Trunk north crossing, Horseshoe Bend	Oregon Historical Society, Portland, Oregon, No. 102632
Construction stations, south side of Horseshoe Bend	Oregon Historical Society, Portland, Oregon, No. 95531
South crossing, Horseshoe Bend, Des Chutes Tunnel in background	Des Chutes Historical Center, Bend, Oregon, No. 1963
Twin Crossings, Horseshoe Bend	Oregon Historical Society, Portland, Oregon, No. 3628
Oregon Trunk steam shovel at mouth of Deschutes River, ORNC track and bridge	Oregon Historical Society, Portland, Oregon, No. 105482
Coyote blast	Oregon Historical Society, Portland, Oregon, No. 95529
After a coyote blast	Oregon Historical Society, Portland, Oregon, No. 95330
River Mile 57–58, upstream of Maupin, Oregon Trunk on right	Oregon Historical Society, Portland, Oregon, No. 51388
River Mile 66, Oregon Trunk fill	Oregon Historical Society, Portland, Oregon, No. 51399

Mucking a cut	Oregon Historical Society, Portland, Oregon, No. 105467
Large fill on the Oregon Trunk	Oregon Historical Society, Portland, Oregon, No. 95281
Grading upstream of Sherar's Bridge	Oregon Historical Society, Portland, Oregon, No. 65920
Ballast gang, Oregon Trunk	Oregon Historical Society, Portland, Oregon, No. 83641
Free Bridge, looking upstream	Oregon Historical Society Portland, Oregon, No. 105505
Sherar's Bridge & Hotel on west bank	Oregon Historical Society, Portland, Oregon, No. CN 020278
Sherar's Bridge & Hotel	Des Chutes Historical Center, Bend, Oregon, No. 1280
Joseph Sherar and his Chinese cook	Sherman County Historical Society, Moro, Oregon
Dufur — 1910	Oregon Historical Society, Portland, Oregon, No. Gi 356
Hauling trestle timbers	Oregon Historical Society, Portland, Oregon, No. 105480
Supply wagon	Oregon Historical Society, Portland, Oregon, No. 105475
Porter Brothers	Oregon Historical Society, Portland, Oregon, No. 27388
Norma	Oregon Historical Society, Portland, Oregon, No. 72728
Unloading *Norma*	Oregon Historical Society, Portland, Oregon, No. CN 020283
Loading ramp for *Norma*	Courtesy of John Blau, Vancouver, Washington, Engineer on the BNSF
Willow Creek Canyon near Madras	Oregon Historical Society, Portland, Oregon, No. 002508

Louis Hill, William Hanley, E.C. Leedy	Oregon Historical Society, Portland, Oregon, No. 61662

CHAPTER NINE

Porter Brothers headquarters at The Dalles	Oregon Historical Society, Portland, Oregon, No. 105472
Shaniko — 1910	Oregon Historical Society, Portland, Oregon, No. 6143
Harris track-laying machine work gang	Des Chutes Historical Center, Bend, Oregon, No. 4184
Harris track-laying machine work gang	Des Chutes Historical Center, Bend, Oregon, No. 4186
Oregon Trunk work gang	Oregon Historical Society, Portland, Oregon, No. 95684
Working by hand on the Oregon Trunk	Oregon Historical Society, Portland, Oregon, No. 105470
Oregon Trunk construction camp at Sinamox	Oregon Historical Society, Portland, Oregon, No. 105468
Coyote blast	Oregon Historical Society, Portland, Oregon, No. 105503
Oregon Trunk in Willow Creek Canyon	Oregon Historical Society, Portland, Oregon, No. 49314
Oregon Trunk approach to the Warm Springs Tunnel	Oregon Historical Society, Portland, Oregon, No. 105508
Mostly moonshine	Oregon Historical Society, Portland, Oregon, No. 020279
Italian musician	Oregon Historical Society, Portland, Oregon, No. 105481
Workers hiking a roadbed	Oregon Historical Society, Portland, Oregon, No. 102116

CHAPTER TEN

Des Chutes Railroad Trout Creek Viaduct	Des Chutes Historical Center, Bend, Oregon, No. 1846

Illustration	Source
Des Chutes Railroad Willow Creek Bridge	Crook County Historical Society, Prineville, Oregon
Oregon Trunk Trestle near South Junction	Des Chutes Historical Center, Bend, Oregon, No. 1577
Oregon Trunk Trestle in Willow Creek Canyon	Oregon Historical Society, Portland, Oregon, No. 95262
Oregon Trunk Trestle in Willow Creek Canyon	Oregon Historical Society, Portland, Oregon, No. CN 020275
Crooked River Bridge	Des Chutes Historical Center, Bend, Oregon, No. 18942
Crooked River Bridge donkey engine	Des Chutes Historical Center, Bend, Oregon, No. 18941
Crooked River Bridge, final span	Des Chutes Historical Center, Bend, Oregon, No. 12577
Going to work	Oregon Historical Society, Portland, Oregon, No. 83642
Walking the plank	Oregon Historical Society, Portland, Oregon, No. 25883
First train over the Crooked River Bridge	Oregon Historical Society, Portland, Oregon, No. 9966
Columbia River Bridge, swing span over Government Canal	Oregon Historical Society, Portland, Oregon, No. 001585
Indian Village on north bank, Celilo Village across the river on left	Columbia Discovery Center, The Dalles, Oregon
Columbia River Bridge, low water	Oregon Historical Society, Portland, Oregon, No. 78633
Columbia River Bridge, north bank wye	Oregon Historical Society, Portland, Oregon, No. 72726

CHAPTER ELEVEN

Illustration	Source
Bend Railroad Day Parade	Des Chutes Historical Center, Bend, Oregon, No. 15183
William Hanley laying 1911 cornerstone	Des Chutes Historical Center, Bend, Oregon, No. 18938

James J. Hill and golden spike	Minnesota Historical Society, St. Paul, Minnesota, Por 8540/p13, Negative No. 83936
James J. Hill in Bend	Minnesota Historical Society, St. Paul, Minnesota, Por 8540/p13, Negative No. 83936
James J. Hill in Bend	Minnesota Historical Society, St. Paul, Minnesota, Por 8540/r4, Negative No. 83728
Madras — 1910, "redlight" tent city in foreground	Oregon Historical Society, Portland, Oregon, No. 105477
Madras welcome arch	Oregon Historical Society, Portland, Oregon, No. 66759
Redmond Railroad Day, alfalfa welcome arch	Des Chutes Historical Center, Bend, Oregon, No. 9023
Redmond Spike Ceremony, Laura Jones in center	Des Chutes Historical Center, Bend, Oregon, No. 4272
Oregon Trunk Harris track-laying machine entering Bend	Des Chutes Historical Center, Bend, Oregon, No. 11356
Tunnel at Whitehorse Rapids	Oregon Historical Society, Portland, Oregon, No. 105507
Oakbrook on the Oregon Trunk	Oregon Historical Society, Portland, Oregon, No. 78639
The Des Chutes at Trout Creek	Oregon Historical Society, Portland, Oregon, No. 105502
Beavertail — 1911	Oregon Historical Society, Portland, Oregon, No. 105506
Prineville — 1910	Oregon Historical Society, Portland, Oregon, No. GI 3434
Bend's Wall Street — 1910	Oregon Historical Society, Portland, Oregon, No. 105484
Bend Depot — 1913	Library of Congress, Washington, D.C., No. 11309
Oregon Trunk advertisement	Oregon Historical Society, Portland, Oregon, No. 53762

Bibliography

Most of the primary source material for the Union Pacific's Des Chutes Railroad has been lost. Some original documents from the office of Frank B. Gill, an auditor for the Oregon–Washington Railroad & Navigation Company, are in the possession of the Oregon Historical Society. Among them is a 1914 letter from Chief Engineer George W. Boschke, which states that documents such as engineers' correspondence and files, contractor reports, and progress reports were destroyed in 1913 in a fire at the Columbia River dock of the Union Pacific. Any remaining documents were lost in the process of several relocations of the Union Pacific Museum.

BOOKS

Allen JE, **Burns M**, **Sargent SC**, *Cataclysms on the Columbia. A Layman's Guide to the Features Produced by the Catastrophic Bretz Floods in the Pacific Northwest,* Timber Press, Portland, Oregon, 1986, reprinted 2002.

Alt D, **Hyndman DW**, *Northwest Exposure, A Geologic Story of the Northwest,* Mountain Press Publishing Company, Missoula, Montana, 1995, reprinted 2001.

Ambrose SE, *Nothing Like It in the World. The Men Who Built the Transcontinental Railroad 1863–1869,* Touchstone, New York, 2000.

Armstrong JH, *The Railroad. What It Is, What It Does. The Introduction to Railroading, 4th Ed.,* Simmons–Boardman Books, Inc., Omaha, Nebraska, 1998.

Asay J, *Union Pacific Northwest. The Oregon-Washington Railroad & Navigation Company,* Pacific Fast Mail, Edmonds, Washington, 1991.

Austin E, **Dill T**, *S.P.&S. The Spokane Portland & Seattle Railway,* Pacific Fast Mail, Edmonds, Washington, 1996.

Bartlett RA, *Great Surveys of the American West,* University of Oklahoma Press, Norman, 1962.

Bishop EM, *In Search of Ancient Oregon. A Geological and Natural History,* Timber Press, Portland, Oregon, 2003.

Brogan PF, *East of the Cascades,* Fourth Edition, 1977, Binford & Mort, Portland, Oregon, 1964.

Brown D, *Hear That Lonesome Whistle Blow. The Epic Story of the Transcontinental Railroads,* Henry Holt and Company, New York, 1977, Owl Books Edition 2001.

Clarke TC, **Bogart J**, **Forney MN**, **Alexander EP**, **Prout HG**, **Porter H**, **et al**, *The American Railway. Its Construction, Development, Management, and Appliances,* Charles Scribner's Sons, New York, 1892.

Coe UC *Frontier Doctor. Observations on Central Oregon and the Changing West,* originally published 1940, Oregon State University Press, Corvallis, Oregon, 2003.

Culp ED, *Stations West,* Bonanza Books, New York, 1978.

Daniels R, *Trains Across the Continent. North American Railroad History,* Indiana University Press, Bloomington, Second Edition, 2000.

Due JF, Grench G, *Rails to the Mid–Columbia Wheatlands: The Columbia Southern and Great Southern Railroads and the Development of Sherman and Wasco Counties, Oregon,* University Press of America, Washington, DC, 1979.

Gaertner JT, *North Bank Road. The Spokane, Portland & Seattle Railway,* Washington State University Press, Pullman, Washington, 1990.

Goetzmann WH, *Army Exploration in the American West 1803–1863,* Texas State Historical Association, Austin, 1991.

Goetzmann WH, *Exploration and Empire. The Explorer and the Scientist in the Winning of the American West,* Texas State Historical Association, Austin, 2000.

Grande WR, *The Northwest's Own Railway. Spokane, Portland & Seattle Railway and its Subsidiaries,* Grande Press, Portland, 1992.

Haney LH, *A Congressional History of Railways in the United States,* Augustus M. Kelley, Publishers, New York, First Edition 1908 & 1910, Reprinted 1968.

Holbrook SH, *The Age of the Moguls,* Doubleday & Company, Inc., Garden City, New York, 1953.

Hubbard FH, *Railroad Avenue. Great Stories and Legends of American Railroading,* McGraw–Hill Book Company, Inc., New York, 1945.

Hughes D, *Deschutes,* Frank Amato Publications, Portland, Oregon, 1990.

Jones E, *Principles of Railway Transportation,* The Macmillan Company, New York, 1929.

Kirkman MM, *Building and Repairing Railways,* World Railway Publishing Company, New York, 1901.

Klein M, *Union Pacific. Birth of a Railroad 1862–1893,* Doubleday & Company, Inc., New York, 1987.

Klein M, *Union Pacific. The Rebirth 1894–1969,* Doubleday, New York, 1989.

Klein M, *The Life & Legend of E. H. Harriman,* The University of North Carolina Press, Chapel Hill, 2000.

Lewty PJ, *Across the Columbia Plain. Railroad Expansion in the Interior Northwest, 1885–1893,* Washington State University Press, Pullman, Washington, 1995.

Martin A, *James J. Hill and the Opening of the Northwest,* Oxford University Press, New York, 1976.

McArthur LA, McArthur LL, *Oregon Geographic Names, 7th Edition,* Oregon Historical Society Press, Portland, 2003.

Middleton WD, *Landmarks on the Iron Road. Two Centuries of North American Railroad Engineering,* Indiana University Press, Bloomington, 1999.

Murray G, *Marias Pass. Its Part in the History and Development of the Northwest, Studies in Northwest History No. 12,* State University of Montana, Missoula, 1930.

O'Connor JE, **Grant GE**, **eds**, *A Peculiar River. Geology, Geomorphology, and Hydrology of the Deschutes River, Oregon. Water Science and Application 7,* American Geophysical Union, Washington, DC, 2003.

Orr EL, **Orr WN**, *Geology of Oregon,* Fifth Edition, Kendall/Hunt Publishing Company, Dubuque, Iowa, 2000.

Overholser WD, *Oregon Trunk,* Thomas T. Beeler, Publisher, Hampton Falls, New Hampshire, 1978.

Overton RC, *Burlington Route. A History of the Burlington Lines,* Alfred A. Knopf, New York, 1965.

Prager K, *That Reminds Me of Another Story. Stories of the SP&S Railway,* Laurel Prager, Hillsboro, Oregon, 1999.

Quinn JM, **Quinn JK**, **King JG**, *Handbook to the Deschutes River Canyon, 3rd Edition,* Educational Adventures, Inc., Bend, Oregon, 1979.

Renz LT, *The History of the Northern Pacific Railroad,* Ye Galleon Press, Fairfield, Washington, 1980.

Schwantes CA, *Railroad Signatures across the Pacific Northwest,* University of Washington Press, Seattle, 1999.

Snow B, *The History of the Deschutes Club,* Touchstone Press, Portland, Oregon, 1966.

Stevens JF, *An Engineer's Recollections,* McGraw–Hill Publishing Company, Inc., Reprinted from Engineering News–Record, 1935.

Stover JF, *The Routledge Historical Atlas of the American Railroads,* Routledge, New York, 1999.

Taylor GH, **Hatton RR**, *The Oregon Weather Book. A State of Extremes,* Oregon State University Press, Corvallis, 1999.

Twohy JR, *Ten Spikes to the Rail,* Goat Rock Publications, Jenner, California, 1983.

Wasco County Historical Society, **Clackamas County Historical Society**, *Barlow Road,* J. Y. Hollingsworth Co., Portland, Oregon, 1976.

Welsh J, **Boyd J**, **Howes Jr. WF**, *The American Railroad,* MBI Publishing Company, Osceola, Wisconsin, 1999.

Wood C, **Wood D**, *Spokane Portland and Seattle Ry. The Northwest's Own Railway,* Superior Publishing Company, Seattle, 1974.

BOOK CHAPTERS

Beebee RA, **O'Connor JE**, The Outhouse Flood: a large Holocene flood on the lower Deschutes River, Oregon, In: O'Connor JE, Grant GE, eds. *A Peculiar River. Geology, Geomorphology, and Hydrology of the Deschutes River, Oregon. Water Science and Application 7,* American Geophysical Union, Washington, DC, 2003, pp.147–166.

Brogan PF, Railroads into the Pines, In: Phillips LK, ed. *East of the Cascades,* Binford & Mort, Publishers, Portland, Oregon, 1977.

Curran JH, **O'Connor JE**, Formation and evolution of valley–bottom and channel features, lower Deschutes River, Oregon, In: O'Connor JE, Grant GE, eds. *A Peculiar River. Geology, Geomorphology, and Hydrology of the Deschutes River, Oregon. Water Science and Application 7,* American Geophysical Union, Washington, DC, 2003, pp.95–119.

Gannett MW, **Manga M**, **Lite Jr. KE**, Groundwater hydrology of the upper Deschutes basin and its influence on streamflow, In: O'Connor JE, Grant GE, eds. *A Peculiar River. Geology, Geomorphology, and Hydrology of the Deschutes River, Oregon. Water Science and Application 7,* American Geophysical Union, Washington, DC, 2003, pp.31–49.

Nolan TB, **Rabbitt MC**, The USGS at 100 and the advancement of geology in the public service, In: Leviton AE, Rodda PU, Yochelson EL, Aldrich ML, eds. *Frontiers of Geological Exploration of Western North America,* Pacific Division of the American Association for the Advancement of Science, San Francisco, 1982, pp.11–17.

O'Connor JE, **Curran JH**, **Beebee RA**, **Grant GE**, **Sarna–Wojcicki A**, Quaternary geology and geomorphology of the lower Deschutes River canyon, Oregon, In: O'Connor JE, Grant GE, eds. *A Peculiar River. Geology, Geomorphology, and Hydrology of the Deschutes River, Oregon. Water Science and Application 7,* American Geophysical Union, Washington, DC, 2003, pp.73–94.

O'Connor JE, **Grant GE**, **Haluska TL**, Overview of geology, hydrology, geomorphology, and sediment budget of the Deschutes River basin, Oregon, In: O'Connor JE, Grant GE, eds. *A Peculiar River. Geology, Geomorphology, and Hydrology of the Deschutes River, Oregon. Water Science and Application 7,* American Geophysical Union, Washington, DC, 2003, pp.7–29.

Zimmerman CE, **Ratliff DE**, Controls on the distribution and life history of fish populations in the Deschutes River: geology, hydrology, and dams, In: O'Connor JE, Grant GE, eds. *A Peculiar River. Geology, Geomorphology, and Hydrology of the Deschutes River, Oregon. Water Science and Application 7,* American Geophysical Union, Washington, DC, 2003, pp.51–70.

JOURNAL ARTICLES

Anderson GM, **Martin DT**, The public domain and nineteenth century transfer policy, *CATO JOURNAL* 6:905–923, 1987.

Beebee RA, **O'Connor JE**, **Grant GE**, Geology and Geomorphology of the Lower Deschutes River Canyon, Oregon, *Field Guide to Geologic Processes in Cascadia: Oregon Department of Geology and Mineral Industries* Special Paper 36:91–108, 2002.

Clarke SA, The Oregon Central Railroad, *Ore Hist Quarterly* 7:133–144, 1906.

Cotroneo RR, Western land marketing by the Northern Pacific, *Pacific Historical Rev* 37:299–320, 1968.

Fairweather HW, The Northern Pacific Railroad and some of its history, *Washington Hist Quarterly* 10:95–101, 1919.

Flinn AD, Stevens finds Marias Pass, *Stone & Webster J* 41:61–65, 1927.

Flynn EF, Stevens monument dedicated by historical expedition, *Engineering News–Record* 95:428–430, 1925.

Freeman OS, Jay C. Freeman, Horse and Buggy Sheriff, *Sherman County: For The Record,* Sherman County Historical Society, 4:3–13, 1986.

Galvani WH, Recollections of J.F. Stevens and Senator Mitchell, *Ore Hist Quarterly* 44:312–326, 1943.

Gaston J, The genesis of the Oregon railway system, *Ore Hist Quarterly* 7:105–132, 1906.

Gilman LC, The Spokane, Portland and Seattle Railroad Company, *Washington Hist Quarterly* 14:14–20, 1923.

Greever WS, A comparison of railroad land grant policies, *Agricultural History* 25:83–90, 1951.

Hedges JB, The colonization work of the Northern Pacific Railroad, *Mississippi Valley Hist Rev* 13:311–342, 1926.

Hedges JB, Promotion of immigration to the Pacific Northwest by the railroads, *Mississippi Valley Hist Rev* 15:183–203, 1928.

Henry RS, The railroad land grant legend in American history texts, *Mississippi Valley Hist Rev* 32:171–194, 1945.

Hildy RW, John F. Stevens, Great Northern engineer, *Minnesota History* 41:345–361, 1969.

James ER, **Manga M**, **Rose TP**, **Hudson GB**, The use of temperature and the isotopes of O, H, C and noble gases to determine the pattern and spatial extent of groundwater flow, *J Hydrol* 237:100–112, 2000.

Kemble JH, The transpacific railroad, 1869–1915, *Pacific Historical Rev* 18:331–343, 1949.

McKeown MF, Historic Umatilla House at The Dalles, *Ore Hist Quarterly* 3:37–41, 1930.

Mills RV, Prineville's municipal railroad in central Oregon, *Ore Hist Quarterly* 42:256–262, 1941.

Mills RV, A history of transportation in the Pacific Northwest, *Ore Hist Quarterly* 47:281–312, 1946.

Morrell JF, **French G**, Bubble skinner, *Ore Hist Quarterly* 69:293–305, 1968.

Pardee JT, Unusual currents in glacial Lake Missoula, Montana, *Geol Soc America Bull* 53:1569–1600, 1942.

Poppleton IL, Oregon's first monopoly—the O.S.N.Co., *Ore Hist Quarterly* 9:276–304, 1908.

Rae JB, The Great Northern's Land Grant, *J Economic History* 12:140–145, 1952.

Sawyer RW, Abbot railroad surveys, 1855. Part I, *Ore Hist Quarterly* 33:1–24, 1932.

Sawyer RW, Abbot railroad surveys, Part II, *Ore Hist Quarterly* 33:115–135, 1932.

Schwantes CA, Problems of empire building: The Oregon Trunk Railway survey of disappointed homeseekers, *Ore Hist Quarterly* 83:371–390, 1982.

Smith G, Geology along U.S. highways 197 and 97 between The Dalles and Sunriver, Oregon, *Oregon Geology* 60:3–19, 1998.

Utley RM, The dash to Promontory, *Utah Hist Quarterly* 29:99–117, 1961.

von Borstel D, Sherar's Grade History, *Sherman County: For The Record,* Sherman County Historical Society, 3:3–10, 1985.

von Borstel M, The Sherar Family, *Sherman County: For The Record,* Sherman County Historical Society, 3:10–23, 1985.

White BM, Working for the railroad: life in the general offices of the Great Northern and Northern Pacific, *Minnesota History* 46:24–30, 1978.

White WT, Race, ethnicity, and gender in the railroad work force: the case of the far northwest, 1883–1918, *Western Hist Quarterly* 16:265–283, 1985.

Edward R. Armstrong's Diary: Camp Raven, Deschutes River Railroad, *Sherman County: For The Record,* Sherman County Historical Society, 17:3–56, 1999.

MAGAZINE ARTICLES

Brimlow GF, Marias Pass explorer John F. Stevens, *Montana Magazine of History* III:39–44, 1953.

Carter CG, Hill Against Harriman, *The Western Railroader,* 1956:3–8.

Clark E, John F. Stevens. Pathfinder for Western Railroads, *The American West,* May, 1971:28–33,62–63.

Cushing GH, Hill against Harriman, *The American Magazine* 68:419–429, 1909.

Donovan F, Canyon war, *Railroad Magazine,* 1956:22–26.

Edwards HR, Jim Hill's Great Adventure, *Railroad Stories; The Railroad Man's Magazine,* 1937:34–53.

Krantz SO, Railroad war in the mountains, *Technical World Magazine* 18:27–34, 1912.

Moody J, Turner GK, The masters of capital in America, *McClure's Magazine,* 1910:123–140.

Competitive Railway Building in the Des Chutes River Canyon, *Railway Age Gazette,* 1910:767–771.

The Construction of the Oregon Trunk and the Des Chutes Railways in Central Oregon, *Railway Age Gazette,* 1912:680–685.

Bridge Construction on the Oregon Trunk Railway, *Railway Age Gazette,* 1912:756–759.

Competitive Railway Building in Central Oregon, *Railway Age Gazette,* 1909:905–906.

The Dope Bucket. Gold Spike Issue. The Oregon Trunk 1911–1961, Spokane, Portland and Seattle Railway, Spokane, 1961.

The Northwest's Own Railway, Spokane, Portland and Seattle Railway Historical Society, Tacoma, Washington, Fall, 1987.

COLLECTIONS

Collection 21, **Great Northern Railway Company Correspondence and Clippings Regarding the Oregon Trunk Railway**, **1911–1913**, Oregon Historical Society.

Frank B. Gill Collection, Oregon Historical Society, Boxes 5 and 6.

Gill FB, *Railroad Building in the Northwest. Its Crude Beginnings, Halting Progress and Vicissitudes of Fortune Throughout Half a Century of Heroic Pioneering,* Oregon Historical Society, Call No. 385 G475r, From a series of articles in 20 issues of the Pacific Semaphore, July 30, 1914 to June 5, 1915.

Great Northern Railway Company Records, Minnesota Historical Society, Saint Paul, Minnesota.

James J. Hill Letterpress Books, James J. Hill Library, Saint Paul, Minnesota.

James J. Hill Papers, James J. Hill Library, Saint Paul, Minnesota.

William Hurst Collection, Oregon Historical Society, ORG Lot 525.

GOVERNMENT DOCUMENTS

Abbot HL, Report upon Explorations for a Railroad Route from the Sacramento Valley to the Columbia River. *Reports of Explorations and Surveys to Ascertain the Most Practicable and Economical Route for a Railroad from the Mississippi River to the Pacific Ocean, Made under the Direction of the Secretary of War, in 1853–4,* Vol. VI,Government Printing Office, Washington, DC, 1857.

Allen JE, *Perlite deposits near the Deschutes River, southern Wasco County, Oregon. GMI Short Paper No. 16,* State of Oregon, Department of Geolory and Mineral Industries, Portland, Oregon, 1946.

Gannett MW, **Liete Jr. KE**, **Morgan DS**, **Collins CA**, *Ground-water Hydrology of the Upper Deschutes Basin, Oregon,* U.S. Geol. Surv. Water Resour. Inv. Rep. 00–4162, 2001.

Henshaw FF, Lewis JH, McCaustland EJ, *Deschutes River, Oregon, and Its Utilization, Department of the Interior, United States Geological Survey, Water-Supply Paper 344,* Government Printing Office, Washington, DC, 1914.

Russell IC, *Preliminary Report on the Geology and Water Resources of Central Oregon, U. S. Geological Survey Bulletin No. 252,* Government Printing Office, Washington, DC, 1905.

NEWSPAPERS

The Bend Bulletin

The Dalles Optimist

The Dalles Weekly Chronicle

The Dufur Dispatch

The Grass Valley Journal

The Madras Pioneer

The Oregonian (Portland)

The Oregon Journal (Portland)

The Prineville Review

Sherman County Observer (Moro)

MISCELLANEOUS

Ploss KM, The Polish Bridge Builder, *www.polishamericancenter.org/KayaArticle_Mod.htm,* 2005.

Prager K, Recorded observations, 1989, *Audiotape* with the permission of Laurel Prager, 2005.

Index

E

F

G

H

I

O

P

R

S

About the Type

The body text of this book was set in Adobe Garamond, a font based on the matrices originally created by the Frenchman, Claude Garamond, in 1541. Garamond was a type founder, publisher, punch cutter, and type designer. When he first entered the printing trade, printers were required to develop nearly all skills required in the book-making process, from type design to binding. Garamond was the first in Paris to specialize in type design, punch cutting, and type founding. He offered his services as an independent craftsman to many of the well-known publishers of his time. The typefaces Garamond created in the years 1530 to 1545 are considered the monumental letterforms of the sixteenth century. Garamond typeface experienced a rebirth in the twentieth century, the result of a search for clean, easy-to-read fonts. The specific version of Garamond used in this book, Adobe Garamond, was created in 1989 by Robert Slimbach.

The chapter and graphic titles have been set in Copperplate, a gothic font of all capital letters. This font was designed by an American, Frederic W. Goudy, in the early 1900s, close to the time of the events described in this book. Copperplate in varying weights was subsequently created by Clarence C. Marder. The font's name refers to the fact that the tiny hairline serifs echo those made with the flick of the burin on edges of letters engraved on copperplate.

The charts, graphs, maps, and image captions are set in Optima, a font originally designed by Herman Zapf in 1958. Despite the clarity of its modern look, its design influences can be traced to the stone inlay alphabets of Roman antiquity.

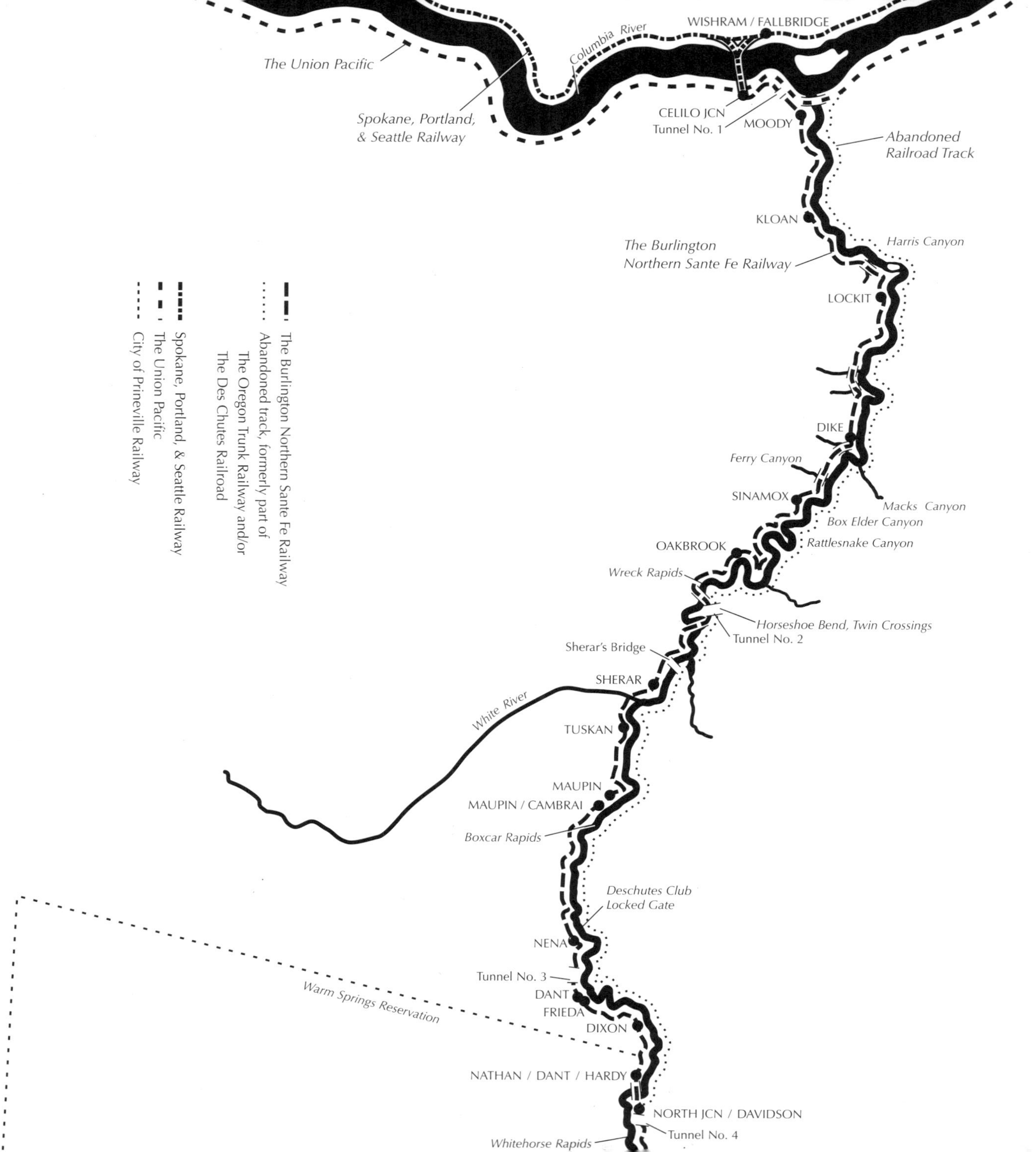

WISHRAM / FALLBRIDGE
Columbia River
The Union Pacific
Spokane, Portland, & Seattle Railway
CELILO JCN
Tunnel No. 1
MOODY
Abandoned Railroad Track
KLOAN
The Burlington Northern Sante Fe Railway
Harris Canyon
LOCKIT
DIKE
Ferry Canyon
SINAMOX
Macks Canyon
Box Elder Canyon
Rattlesnake Canyon
OAKBROOK
Wreck Rapids
Horseshoe Bend, Twin Crossings
Tunnel No. 2
Sherar's Bridge
SHERAR
White River
TUSKAN
MAUPIN
MAUPIN / CAMBRAI
Boxcar Rapids
Deschutes Club Locked Gate
NENA
Tunnel No. 3
DANT
FRIEDA
DIXON
Warm Springs Reservation
NATHAN / DANT / HARDY
NORTH JCN / DAVIDSON
Tunnel No. 4
Whitehorse Rapids
The Burlington Northern Sante Fe Railway
Abandoned track, formerly part of The Oregon Trunk Railway and/or The Des Chutes Railroad
Spokane, Portland, & Seattle Railway
The Union Pacific
City of Prineville Railway

E
N ← S
W